The Southwell–Sibthorpe Commonplace Book

Folger MS. V.b.198

MEDIEVAL & RENAISSANCE
TEXTS & STUDIES

VOLUME 147

RENAISSANCE ENGLISH TEXT SOCIETY

SEVENTH SERIES
VOLUME XX (FOR 1995)

The Southwell-Sibthorpe Commonplace Book

Folger MS. V.b.198

edited by

Jean Klene, C.S.C.

MEDIEVAL & RENAISSANCE TEXTS & STUDIES
Tempe, Arizona
1997

The manuscript plates are reproduced by permission of the
Folger Shakespeare Library, Washington, D.C.

© Copyright 1997

Arizona Board of Regents for Arizona State University

Library of Congress Cataloging-in-Publication Data

Southwell, Anne, Lady, 1573–1636.
　The Southwell-Sibthorpe commonplace book : Folger Ms V.b.198 / edited by
Jean Klene.
　　p. cm. — (Medieval & Renaissance texts & studies ; v. 147) (The Renaissance
English Text Society ; 7th ser., vol. 40)
　A miscellany of writing chiefly by Lady Anne Southwell, with some by Henry
Sibthorpe, and others.
　Includes bibliographical references and index.
　ISBN 0-86698-187-X (hardcover : alk. paper)
　1. Southwell, Anne, Lady, 1573–1636 — Notebooks, sketchbooks, etc. 2. Women
poets, English — Early modern, 1500–1700 — Biography — Sources. 3. Women and
literature — England — History — 17th century — Sources.　4. Southwell, Anne,
Lady, 1573–1636 — Marriage. 5. Renaissance — England — Sources. 6. Women —
England — Poetry. 7. Commonplace-books. I. Sibthorpe, Henry. II. Klene, Jean.
III. Folger Shakespeare Library. Manuscript. V.b. 198. IV. Title. V. Series. VI.
Series: Renaissance English Text Society (Series) ; vol. 40.
PR2349.S49A6　1995
828'.309—dc20　　　　　　　　　　　　　　　　　　　　　　　　　　　95-21783
　　　　　　　　　　　　　　　　　　　　　　　　　　　　　　　　　　　　CIP

This book was edited and produced
by MRTS at SUNY Binghamton.
This book is made to last.
It is set in Caslon,
smythe-sewn and printed on acid-free paper
to library specifications.

Printed in the United States of America

Table of Contents

Acknowledgements — vi

Bibliography of Frequently Cited References — viii

Introduction — xi

Texts — 1

Appendix I: Southwell as a Compiler and Composer — 117

Appendix II: British Library Lansdowne MS. 740 — 124

Manuscript Plates — 164

Textual Notes — 177

Commentary Notes — 187

First-Line Index of Poems — 208

Acknowledgements

Editing a long dead and little noted woman has been an exhilarating journey for me. I did not make it alone: I owe much to the generosity and support I received from others along the way.

I am very grateful to my editors, officers of the Renaissance Text Society, President Arthur F. Kinney, Carolyn Kent, and the late Josephine Roberts. Their initial skepticism challenged me to greater efforts at proof of the lady's authorship and talents. Other officers who also contibuted information and encouragement include Steven W. May, Elizabeth Hageman, and Janel Mueller. I am also deeply indebted to Mario A. Di Cesare for many aspects of the book's completion, and to Catherine Di Cesare and other members of the MRTS staff for their care in printing the edition.

The work took me to many libraries, including the Folger Shakespeare Library, whose manuscript is my main source, the Bodleian, the Dublin Public Library, the Boston Public Library, and library of the Totnes Museum near Cornworthy, where Lady Anne grew up, that of the Dukes of Devonshire at Chatsworth, many other small libraries and record offices in England, and of course the libraries of my home campus, Saint Mary's and its neighbor, Notre Dame. Librarians, staff, and visiting scholars at all these institutions were uniformly helpful. Particular thanks are due to Laetitia Yeandle, Curator of Manuscripts at the Folger, who generously gave my transcription, introduction and paleographical notes a careful reading. Without her encouragement and advice, this edition would probably not exist. Gratitude also goes to Robert Hohl at Saint Mary's, who discharged with scholarly aplomb the various bibliographical tasks that came up when I was working at home.

I have profited by conversation or correspondence with many scholars, including Margaret Arnold, Pamela Benson, Esther Cope, Donald W. Foster, Mary Ellen Lamb, Elizabeth McCutcheon, Thomas P. Roche, Robert E. Rodes, Jr., Sara Jayne Steen, Ernest Sullivan II, Carolyn R.

Swift, John Velz, and R. L. Widmann. It was an especial pleasure to consult with Lady Anne's descendents, the seventh Viscount Southwell, and the late Commander Gordon Southwell, as well as with Commander Southwell's wife Belinda.

I greatly enjoyed also the experience of exploring some of Lady Anne's home territory. Mr. Charles Bellingham, churchwarden of Saint Peter's Church in Cornworthy, Devonshire, showed me the tomb of Lady Anne's parents, and took me to the top of the bell tower to look over the landholdings of her neighbor, Sir Walter Ralegh, and the Cornworthy area. In London, the local historian, T. Harper Smith, guided me in exploring the parish of Saint Mary's, Acton, where Lady Anne spent her last years. Thanks to him, I was able to visualize a good deal of what life must have been like there in Jacobean times.

Here at Saint Mary's, I have had the support of sisters of my community of Holy Cross, many of whom read galleys for me, and of faculty colleagues, especially Jeanne Rodes. My warm thanks to all.

Saint Mary's College
Notre Dame, Indiana
Feast of St. Teresa of Avila, 1996

Bibliography of Frequently Cited References
with their short titles or abbreviations

Arnold — *Queen Elizabeth's Wardrobe Unlock'd: The Inventories of the Wardrobe of Robes prepared in July 1600*, ed. with commentary by Janet Arnold. Leeds, England: Maney, 1988.

Burke — John Burke. *A Genealogical and Heraldic History of the Commoners of Great Britain and Ireland.* London: Henry Colburn, 1838.

Chamberlain — *The Letters of John Chamberlain*, Memoirs XII, ed. Norman E. McClure, 2 vols. Philadelphia: The Philosophic Society, 1939.

Crum — *The Poems of Henry King*, ed. Margaret Crum. Oxford: Clarendon Press, 1965.

DAPW — James O. Halliwell-Phillips. *Dictionary of Archaic and Provincial Words.* London: Routledge & Sons, 1924.

DNB — Leslie Stephen [and Sidney Lee] eds., *Dictionary of National Biography.* 63 vols. London: Smith, Elder, and Co., 1885–1901.

Doughtie — *Lyrics from English Airs 1596–1622*, ed. Edward Doughtie. Cambridge: Harvard Univ. Press, 1970.

Elyot — Sir Thomas Elyot. *The Dictionary of syr Thomas Eliot knyght.* Londini in aedibus Thomae Bertheleti typis impress. cum priuilegio ad imprimendum solum. London [1538].

GEC — G.E. C[okayne]. *The Complete Peerage of England, Scotland, Ireland, Great Britain and the United Kingdom.* 13 vols. London: The St. Catherine Press, Ltd., 1910–1959.

Heninger — S.K. Heninger, Jr. *Touches of Sweet Harmony: Pythagorean Cosmology and Renaissance Poetics.* San Marino, California: The Huntington Library, 1974.

Hill — *New Ways of Looking at Old Texts: Papers of the Renaissance English Text Society, 1985–1991*, ed. W. Speed Hill. Binghamton, New York: Medieval & Renaissance Texts & Studies in conjunction with Renaissance English Text Society, 1993.

HMC, Sal.   *The Historical Manuscripts Commission Calendar of the Manuscripts of the Most Honorable The Marquess of Salisbury, preserved at Hatfield House,* 21 vols. London: His Majesty's Stationery Office, 1883– .

KJ   *The Holy Bible and International Bible Encyclopedia and Concordance: Authorized or King James Version.* New York: Garden City Publishing Co., Inc., 1940.

OED   *The Oxford English Dictionary,* 2nd ed., prepared by J. A. Simpson & E. S. C. Weiner. New York: Oxford Univ. Press & Oxford: Clarendon Press, 1989.

Plato   *The Works of Plato,* trans. by B. Jowett, four volumes complete in one. New York: Tudor Publishing Co. [1936].

R & B   Hyder E. Rollins and Herschel Baker, eds. *The Renaissance in England: Non-dramatic Prose and Verse of the Sixteenth Century.* Lexington, Mass.: D. C. Heath and Co., 1954.

Ringler   William A. Ringler, Jr., ed. *The Poems of Sir Philip Sidney.* Oxford: At the Clarendon Press, 1962.

STC   A. W. Pollard and G. R. Redgrave. *A Short-Title Catalogue of Books Printed in England, Scotland, and Ireland... 1475–1640,* 2nd ed., rev & enl. 3 vols. London: The Bibliographical Society, 1976–1991.

Skeat   *A Glossary of Tudor and Stuart Words, Especially from the Dramatists,* collected by Walter W. Skeat, ed. A. L. Mayhew. Oxford: At the Clarendon Press, 1914.

Steer   Sir Francis W. Steer. *Woodrising Church, Norfolk: Notes on the Southwell and other families connected with the parish,* with a foreword by the earl of Verulam. The Diocese of Norwich, 1959.

West.   Henry S. Gehman, ed. *The New Westminster Dictionary of the Bible.* Philadelphia: Westminster Press, 1970.

Introduction

This edition of Folger MS. V.b.198 is titled *The Southwell-Sibthorpe Commonplace Book* with the name "Southwell" first because the manuscript is predominantly made up of "The workes of the Lady Ann Sothwell" (fol. 1ʳ), née Harris, who was born in 1573,[1] married Thomas Southwell in 1593 and, after his death in 1626, Captain Henry Sibthorpe. She died in 1636. The name "Sibthorpe" is joined to that of "Southwell" because he not only gave Lady Anne the folios at the time of their wedding and composed at least two entries (probably fol. 27 and certainly most of fols. 73 and 74), but also critiqued the poetry of the woman he praised effusively. The last phrase of the title, "commonplace book," indicates that the collection of poems, letters, aphorisms, inventories, a mini-bestiary, scriptural commentary, and receipts resembles similar collections of the early seventeenth century, called commonplace books, which gentlemen frequently kept.[2] Because Folger MS. V.b.198

---

[1] According to Sibthorpe's statement on fol. 74.

[2] See Edwin Wolf, *The Textual Importance of Manuscript Commonplace Books of 1620–1660*, An Address before the Bibliographical Society of the University of Virginia (Charlottesville, Va.: Bibliographical Society of the Univ. of Virginia, 1949), 1. On the importance to a humanist education of keeping a notebook, see R. R. Bolgar, *The Classical Heritage and its Beneficiaries* (Cambridge: Cambridge Univ. Press, 1954), 265–75; Sister Joan Marie Lechner, *Renaissance Concepts of the Commonplaces* (New York: Pageant Press, 1962); Ann Blair, "Humanist Methods in Natural Philosophy: The Commonplace Book," *Journal of the History of Ideas* 53:4 (Oct.–Dec. 1992): 541–60; Mary Thomas Crane, *Framing Authority: Sayings, Self, and Society in Sixteenth Century England* (Prince-

xii INTRODUCTION

contains memorabilia significant for both Lady Anne Southwell and Captain Henry Sibthorpe and illustrates interaction between husband and wife in the making of the volume, the result offers a unique example of the genre.

I. Lady Anne Southwell's Life and Writing

Her Life

The commonplace book and public records offer ample detail about the woman who composed most of the poems. She was born in 1573 to Elizabeth (Pomeroy) and Thomas Harris of Cornworthy. The first of four children, Anne had two brothers and one sister: Edward, who studied law, was knighted, and later became Chief Justice of the King's Bench in Munster; Christopher, who was also knighted and died at Ostend; and Honor, who married Sir Hugh Harris of Scotland.[3] The Harris home had been a Devon priory situated in Cornworthy on the west side of the River Dart, halfway between the two towns of Totnes and Dartmouth.[4] One wall of the priory still stands on a hill opposite St. Peter's Church. In the chancel is the tomb of Sir Thomas Harris with his effigy in a lawyer's attire and that of his wife in Elizabethan costume. Because Anne's father was a sergeant-at-law of the Middle Temple Inn and Member of Parliament, the family probably lived in London at times.[5]

Lands owned by Sir Walter Ralegh are only a few miles from Cornworthy, where the Harris family lived. Given Ralegh's official capacities in the southwest and his reputation for persuading the gentry, he must have been an occasional visitor, at least at Dartmouth if not at Cornworthy.

---

ton: Princeton Univ. Press, 1993); and Peter Beal, "Notions in Garrison: The Seventeenth-Century Commonplace Book," Hill, 131–48.

[3] Burke, 4:430–31. I am grateful to the Reverend Paul Trenchard, vicar of St. Peter's Church in Cornworthy, who sent a transcription containing the same family information engraved on the tomb of Sir Thomas Harris. For the fall of Ostend, see *A Jacobean Journal Being a record of those things most talked of during the years 1603–1606*, ed. G. B. Harrison (London: G. Routledge and Sons, Ltd., 1941), 159–60.

[4] John Prince, *Danmonii orientales illustres: or, The Worthies of Devon* (London: Rees & Curtis, 1810), 469–71.

[5] Thomas Harris was M. P. for Callington in 1584, Portsmouth in 1586 and 1589, Bossiney in 1593 and 1597, and Truro in 1601, according to P. W. Hasler, ed., *The History of Parliament: The House of Commons, 1558–1603*, 3 vols. (London: Published for the History of Parliament Trust by Her Majesty's Stationery Office, 1981), 2:260–63.

INTRODUCTION   xiii

Many of Ralegh's maritime ventures probably began at Dartmouth. Occasionally he must have conferred with Thomas Harris, a fellow member of the Middle Temple Inn, and especially when both served in the House of Commons for towns in Devon. Historians suggest that the two worked together for their constituents, as in opposing a 1593 request by Burleigh for three rather than two subsidies to fund Queen Elizabeth's campaigns against Spain. It is no surprise that Lady Southwell included in her commonplace book a poem attributed to Ralegh, "The Lie," for the satire was in circulation by 1595. Like others in the manuscript culture of the Renaissance, she apparently added a few lines of her own to a poem she had copied into her commonplace book. Ralegh was imprisoned for many years, and finally executed in 1618; the treatment he endured, coupled with the deprivation experienced by his loyal wife, may have contributed to the tone of disillusionment about the court which appears in much of Lady Anne's writing.[6]

On 24 June 1594, she married "Thomas Suthwell," of Spixworth, Norfolk, at the Church of St. Clement Danes in London.[7] The groom was apparently the man of her father's choice, judging from what she says in the meditation on adultery, that is, that maidens are bound unto their father's will and therefore should pray for his "care and skill / to choose for them a wise and honest mate" (fol. 51ᵛ). Thomas's mother had been Alice Cornwallis, daughter of Sir Thomas Cornwallis of Brome in Suffolk. Through her, Anne may have met Sir William Cornwallis and other London writers.[8] Thomas's father Richard belonged to a prominent Norfolk family with

---

[6] For Ralegh's biographical data, including appointments as steward of the Duchy of Cornwall and Lord Warden of the Stanneries in 1585, see Steven W. May, *Sir Walter Ralegh* (Boston: Twayne Publishers, 1989), xiii, and a discussion of "The Lie" and its author, 61–62; for Ralegh's collaboration with Harris, J. E. Neale, *Elizabeth I and Her Parliaments* (New York: St. Martin's Press, 1958), 300 and 344; and J. H. Adamson and H. F. Folland, *The Shepherd of the Ocean: An Account of Sir Walter Ralegh And His Times* (London: The Bodley Head, 1969), 286. For lines of "The Lie" which Lady Anne added, see the commentary for fol. 2ʳ below.

[7] I am indebted to Miss M. J. Swarbrick, chief archivist, City of Westminster, for a copy of the church records. Joseph Hunter says that Herrick wrote an epithalamium for their wedding (British Library Additional MS. 24487, *Chorus Vatum Anglicanorum Collections concerning the Poets and Verse-Writers of the English Nation*, [London, 1838], 1:280ᵛ). If so, it must have been for a later anniversary, for Herrick was but four years old when they married.

[8] See the "Pedigree of Cornwallis From the Records of the College of Arms, Wills, Registers and other authorities," citing Alice Cornwallis, wife of Richard Southwell, and

xiv INTRODUCTION

more than one courtly connection. Although at least seven in the sixteenth century had the name "Thomas Southwell," only two of them in the early seventeenth century had a title. Sir Francis Steer's history of the Southwells, citing Blomefield's *History of Norfolk*, shows that Thomas Southwell of Spixworth, Anne's husband, was the one knighted in 1603. The more notorious Thomas Southwell of Woodrising, born around 1596, was knighted in 1615.[9]

The uncle of Anne's husband was Robert Southwell, the Jesuit poet and martyr for the Roman cause. Thomas, however, reinforced proclamations offering a reward for the heads of Catholic "traitors," according to the copy of a 1620 letter in British Library Harleian MS. 697 (fol. 104[r]) which he co-signed. Anne was also a staunch Protestant and mocked "Popelings" more than once. Nevertheless, Father Robert Southwell's book of poems, *Saint Peters Plaint* (fol. 66[r], no. 97), and another book about his religious superior and companions, *Garnet, a Iesuite, & his Confederat's* (fol. 65[v], no. 41), are listed as part of the Southwell-Sibthorpe library.

Thomas and Anne may have lived at first in London or on one of the Southwell estates, and he or both may have gone to Ireland within a few years. Youghal records show that in 1597 a Thomas Southwell had acquired property from Ralegh and that he was in Ireland on business for Elizabeth I in 1598.[10]

---

her place in the Cornwallis family in *The Private Correspondence of Jane Lady Cornwallis; 1613–44, from the Originals in the Possession of the Family* (London, 1842), xxxv. Anne's mother-in-law may have introduced her to the young writer Sir William Cornwallis during the early years of their marriage, or she may have met him when, in 1605, Thomas Southwell sought the money owed him by Sir Charles Cornwallis, Ambassador to Spain, from the elder Sir William Cornwallis, who was serving as "surety" for Sir Charles's debts (*HMC, Sal.*, part 17, ed. M. S. Giuseppi [1938], 314, 322–23, and 641). For Cornwallis's friendship with Sir Thomas Overbury and John Donne, see *Essayes, By Sir William Cornwallis, the Younger*, ed. Don Cameron Allen (Baltimore: The Johns Hopkins Press, 1946), xii–xvi.

[9] The other Thomas Southwell alive in 1603 was unmarried and unknighted; he died in 1609. For the family tree, see the pedigree in the folded overleaf in Steer, and for other dates, p. 20 (citing Blomefield, *History of Norfolk*, 10:277). I am indebted to the late commander Gordon E. H. Southwell for access to Steer.

[10] The unmarried Thomas Southwell could be the one of these records. He is included in Steer's pedigree and that given by Redcliffe Salaman, who says that he is "of Moulton, Norfolk (b. 1550, d. 1609)," in *The History and Social Influence of the Potato* (Cambridge: Cambridge Univ. Press, 1949), 144–45. Because records show that Anne's husband, "Sir Thomas Southwell" (the only Thomas Southwell who was a knight between 1603 and 1615) settled at Poulnelong in the seventeenth century, it is likely

INTRODUCTION   XV

At the time of the coronation of James I, Anne and her husband were in London, for Thomas was one of many knighted on 23 July 1603 and Anne was either one of the ladies "of all degrees" sent to Berwick or one who went on her own to welcome Queen Anne. According to enigmatic letters written to Cecil, Mrs. Southwell was peremptorily ordered to leave Berwick and return to London. Captain Skinner, who reports his delivery of the summons and Mrs. Southwell's response to it, gives no explanation for the command. Whatever the reason, she refused to obey the command and "betook herself to her bed" instead. According to Skinner, she complained that the king would have to send horses and money, lest she "be murthered." Furthermore, she insisted that she did not believe the King knew "anything of her; with many other violent exclamations."[11]

According to the expense account submitted by Thomas Meade, Mrs. Southwell finally made the trip. Shortly afterwards, her husband petitioned Cecil to clear her name, although his letter includes no statement of accusations against her. He blamed whatever misunderstanding had taken place on "malicious slanderers" and argued, "Not alone our estates, but reputations are endangered. It was the Queen's letters, that moved my wife's journey; if we had pretended without such a cause, there had been the less regard due to us." Agnes Strickland tells us, however, that most of the other ladies were also rejected. Barbara Lewalski adds that Queen Anne "warmed only to those who had rushed on their own to Scotland to meet her, especially the Countess of Bedford and her mother, Lady Harrington, Lady Dorothy Hastings, and Lady Elizabeth Hatton." The queen refused to dismiss the

---

though not certain that Anne's husband is the one who received lands from Ralegh in 1598. Salaman says that the brothers Anthony and Thomas Southwell "settled in County Cork ... presumably ... before 1609." He quotes Miss Aher of Youghal that this Thomas Southwell is the one mentioned in the conveyance of Ralegh's lands to Richard Boyle, who later became the earl of Cork. The document reads: "To Thomas Southwell, all his seignories, lands and tenements in Cork and Waterford Counties and elsewhere in Ireland, with other lands and things Dated 27th May, 40th Elizabeth, i.e., in 1598" (Salaman, 155, n. 1, citing Samuel Hayman, *Annals of Youghal* [1852], 18). John Winton also says that Thomas Southwell was a friend of Ralegh's (*Sir Walter Ralegh* [London: Michall Joseph, 1975], 228), but does not mention the number of men with the same name.

[11] William A. Shaw, *Knights of England* (London: Sherratt and Hughes, 1906), 2:124. For the Berwick expedition, see Agnes Strickland, *The Lives of the Queens of England from the Norman Conquest*, a new edition with corrections and additions (New York: Thomas R. Knox & Co., 1885), 3:647–49. For the letters about Mrs. Southwell, *HMC, Sal.*, part 15, ed. M. S. Giuseppi (1930), 74, 90–91, 124, and 388.

xvi INTRODUCTION

Danish and Scottish ladies who had attended her for thirteen years and appoint strangers.[12] Lady Anne's reputation may never have been cleared or else a new problem arose, for she later tells us that she has "litle reason to flatter ... that happy land" where she was born because it had laid on her "an envious stepdames hand" (appendix II, stanza 69, fol. 151ᵛ).

The new king sent Sir Thomas into Ireland "to promote the plantation of Munster," and the Southwells settled at Castle Poulnelong (or "Shippool") in County Cork, seven miles from Kinsale, up the Bandon river. The two letters of 1623, part of the Lismore papers now at Chatsworth, were sent from Poulnelong.[13]

Although the Folger manuscript says little about household matters or children, *The Peerage of Ireland* says that the couple had two daughters: Elizabeth and Frances.[14] Evil children and servants are emphasized by the only drawings of pointing fingers in the volume (fol. 10ʳ), strange as such an emphasis on the evilness of children seems. Although Lady Anne admits briefly that "if they bee good," servants can be one's "humble friends," she speaks in two poems of greedy attendants, happy to choke their masters (fol. 10ʳ, 20–23 & fol. 31ᵛ, 47–57). The lines suggest a situation which must have been true to the way many an Irish servant felt about an English planter. At best, life must have been difficult.

Considering the anger in her satiric poems, we have to wonder about the relationship between Sir Thomas and his wife. The lines often suggest that her first husband was unfaithful. He may even have been more interested in another man than in his wife. The meditation against adultery, the most extended poem on the conduct of a husband, begins with four stanzas con-

---

[12] *HMC, Sal.,* 15:388. Ethel Carleton Williams, *Anne of Denmark Wife of James VI of Scotland: James I of England* (London: Longman Group Ltd., 1970), 76; and Barbara Lewalski, *Writing Women in Jacobean England* (Cambridge: Harvard Univ. Press, 1993), 22; see also Leeds Barroll, "The Court of the first Stuart queen," in Linda Levy Peck, ed., *The Mental World of the Jacobean Court* (New York: Cambridge Univ. Press, 1991), 200–204. For particulars of the queen's progress, see the Shrewsbury Papers, vol. xvi, fol. 103, Lambeth MS. 709, recommended in *Lives of the Princesses of England from the Norman Conquest,* by Mary Anne Everett Green (London: Published for Henry Colburn by his successors, Hurst & Blackett, 1854), 5:150, n. 4.

[13] Vol. XIV, fols. 160 and 174.

[14] John Lodge, *The Peerage of Ireland: or, A Genealogical History of the Present Nobility of that Kingdom,* rev. M. Archdall, 4 vols. (London: William Johnston, 1754), 4:228, n. e; see also Steer, overleaf of the family tree. The death certificate of Sir Thomas, however, records only one daughter, Elizabeth (British Library Additional MS. 4820, fol. 98ᵛ).

INTRODUCTION   xvii

demning a "double damning vyle Hermophrodite" (fol. 47ᵛ, 1–24), for he "infect[s] socyetye" (line 6). If Bruce Mazlish, commenting on Caroline Bingham's "Seventeenth-Century Attitudes Toward Deviant Sex," is correct in saying that sodomy was discussed in images of infection, then Lady Anne may be suggesting such a connection when she complains that she has received "infection" from him and "is dying" (fol. 11ʳ).[15] She seems to vent her wrath against the practice in more than one poem. As Donne, Marston, Jonson, and others were virulently satirizing the conduct of a sodomite as a "young man-about-town, with his mistress on one arm and his 'catamite' on the other,"[16] so she may also have been exercising her satiric powers on this practice.

In a few instances, Lady Anne also harshly criticizes women. Five stanzas in the meditation against adultery condemn a "weak feamale" who might think that her sins should be ignored "for sexes sake." Complaints about unfaithful men, however, are more frequent and sometimes more virulent. Perhaps part of the revulsion and hostility that Lady Anne expresses against a "double damning vyle Hermophradite" (fol. 47ᵛ) can be found in the Renaissance identification of Popery and ecclesiastical abuses with homosexuality.[17] She also must have deplored the conduct of her husband's profligate cousin, Sir Thomas Southwell of Woodrising, and that of the convicted sodomite, Mervyn Touchet (executed 1631).[18] But regardless of how many she knew who were involved in sodomy, the anger expressed against a "man that's vassaliz'd to pleasure," who can only starve on the specious pleasures of "Sodom Apples" ("Blessed Life," fol. 8ᵛ), suggests personal anguish. As a partner, Sir Thomas was probably akin to the "husband that is nought" with which the meditation on adultery concludes (fol. 51ᵛ), whatever weaknesses and infidelities the "nought" may encompass.

---

[15] Bruce Mazlish, "Comment," *The Journal of Interdisciplinary History* 1, no. 2 (Spring 1971): 468–72, on Caroline Bingham, "Seventeenth-Century Attitudes Toward Deviant Sex," in the same, 447–67.

[16] Allan Bray, *Homosexuality in Renaissance England* (London: Gay Men's Press, 1982, repr. 1988), 34.

[17] Bray, 20 and 58; see also Bruce Smith, *Homosexual Desire in Shakespeare's England: A Cultural Poetics* (Chicago: Univ. of Chicago Press, 1991), 43.

[18] For Sir Thomas Southwell of Woodrising, knighted in 1615, see Steer, the overleaf of the family tree and p. 20; Bingham, "Seventeenth-Century Attitudes"; and for Mervyn Touchet's crime, see the commentary for fol. 7ʳ, and for his trial, *Cobbett's Complete Collection of State Trials and Proceedings for High Treason and other Crimes and Misdemeanors from the Earliest Period to the Present Time*, 3:1627–40 (London: Printed by T. C. Hansard, Published by R. Bagshaw, 1809), 401–16.

Far from becoming introverted in an alien land, Lady Anne broadened her world through books and by contact with other people; she wrote to and about men and women in England, Ireland, and other countries. Her poetry illustrates that she was thinking not only on important topics, old and new, but also about human needs, her own and others'. Sometimes she is granting favors and at other times begging for them. A verse epistle honored Doctor Bernard Adams, bishop of Limerick (fols. 18ʳ–19ʳ) and a pretended elegy teased her good friend Cicely MacWilliams, Lady Ridgeway ("sometime maid of honour to Queen Elizabeth"), who died in 1627.[19] Other elegies praised, albeit in rather perfunctory ways, Gustavus Adolphus, king of Sweden (fol. 22ʳ), and Frances Howard, countess of Somerset (fol. 23ʳ). The most surprising thing about the latter elegy is that Lady Anne makes no reference in it to the news which was intriguing most Londoners at the time, that is, the case of a woman who had gained an annulment from her first marriage to Robert Devereux, earl of Essex, her remarriage to Robert Carr, earl of Somerset, and her conviction for the murder of Sir Thomas Overbury, who had opposed the divorce (see the commentary for fol. 23). Lady Anne also wrote a short poem to the Duchess of Lennox (fol. 22ʳ), primarily to ask about the "princes" Elizabeth, who became the queen of Bohemia.

Copies of two letters by Lady Anne are included in *The Southwell-Sibthorpe Commonplace Book*. One letter was sent to her friend Cicely MacWilliams to argue for the superiority of poetry over prose (fol. 3), and the other was sent to Henry Carey, viscount Falkland, to console him in his demotion and recall to England (fol. 4ʳ). Unfortunately, she makes no mention of his wife Elizabeth Carey, perhaps because of the latter's conversion to Catholicism.

That Lady Anne understood music theory and enjoyed music is evident in her poems and in the inventory, indicating that her virginals were sent from Clerkenwell to Acton (fol. 61ʳ). Besides using phrases like the "Dorian strayne" and "double diapason" appropriately, she shows a complex knowledge in the letter to Dr. Bernard Adams, bishop of Limerick (fols. 18ʳ–19ʳ), when she says things like, "A songe of eight tymes three parts I would singe." The speaker "would singe" a song of twenty-four measures, the first and last identical parts framing the middle, resulting in "true harmony." She also praises Dr. Adams for having "bestowed much money in repairing Saint Mary's

---

[19] GEC, 8:106.

INTRODUCTION   xix

Cathedral of Limerick and in the adorning it with organs and several ornaments."[20] That she considered beauty of many kinds appropriate to meaning-
ful worship is evidenced by her use of lines from the Book of Revelation to
pray, "our golden candelsticke take not awaye / for our neglec*t* or coldnis in
devosion" (fol. 45ʳ).

Shortly after Sir Thomas's death in June of 1626[21] she married Captain
Henry Sibthorpe. He must have been a relative, probably the son, of the
John Sibthorpe who signed nine receipts in 1587 and 1588 (fols. 5 and 6).
On fol. 74 Henry Sibthorpe says that he and Lady Anne had been married
ten years before her death in 1636, and fol. 1 begins with the title, "The
workes of the Lady Ann Sothwell / Decemb: 2° 1626°." Henry must have
given the folios to her at the time of their marriage or shortly afterwards.

Until the clear identification on fols. 73 and 74, Sibthorpe rarely asserts
himself, but in an examination of the volume we see his contributions and
the evolving story of a Renaissance relationship. In the title of the booklist
on fols. 64ᵛ–66ʳ, "A List of my Bookes," the pronoun "my" has to refer to
him, for some of the books were not published until after Lady Anne's
death. The calligraphy of the booklist, more bold and flamboyant than any
other by him in the volume, seems to proclaim his pride in having a good
library. In the love poem on fol. 27, Sibthorpe's name does not appear, but
his hopes for their future surely do. He must have sent the poem long
before their wedding, for he mentions the "patience" the two need to
practice until "fate shall all the putt-betweenes remoue." Lady Anne probably kept the poem hidden until sometime after their marriage when the
well-creased page was tipped into the book. Judging from marginalia like
"wyf / lyfe to ofte" (fol. 49ʳ) in his hand, he also saw himself as critic and
mentor. Her changes of the rhyme to which he objected illustrate some of
the collaboration which makes the volume unique. The collection concludes
with signed testimonials to the woman Sibthorpe saw as the "Honour and
ornamᵗ of her sexe" (fol. 74ʳ) and a "Darlinge of the Nine" (fol. 73ʳ).

Very little information about her second husband has emerged, and most
of it points to his military and civil functions. In 1618 John Chamberlain
asked Sir Dudley Carleton, on behalf of John West, Henry Sibthorpe's
uncle, to help the nephew. Although West had hoped for service of another
kind for Henry, the uncle was nevertheless grateful when Sibthorpe was

---

[20] Anthony A Wood, *Athenæ Oxonienses*, 4 vols. (London, 3rd ed., 1815), 2:869.
[21] British Library Additional MS. 4820, fol. 98ᵛ.

XX INTRODUCTION

"placed with Sir Horace Vere" and was one of those assigned to guard Johan Van Olden Barnevelt.[22] In 1627 Falkland told the king that Sibthorpe had "had a company in the Cadiz expedition, and kept it for nearly two years in Ireland." Falkland asked that, in the light of such service, the captain "be allowed the command of one of the substitute companies sent over."[23] Sibthorpe himself tells us that he served as "Sarjeant Major & Privye Councellor of the province of Munster" (fol. 73[r]), but about his parents and siblings we can only speculate.

In 1588, payments (fols. 5[r]–6[v]) are made to men whose names suggest a Flemish origin, and the accounts are signed by a John Sibthorpe, suggesting that he is probably the "John Sibthorpe" mentioned in the introduction to the De L'Isle Papers, who had a foot company of men after December 1585 in Ostend.[24] This man may be the "John Sibthorp (baptised 27 February 1546," and married "28 November 1573, [to] Rosamund Bellamy") who had, "with other issue," sons Gervasse and William.[25] The dates are appropriate ones for Henry's father. Sir Christopher Sibthorpe (d. 1632), a "pamphleteer," who was made Third Justice of the King's Bench in Ireland (1607), may also have been a relative. Christopher, Henry, and Anne were at least acquaintances, if not relatives, for Anne's brother Edward was a Chief Justice of Munster.[26] Further, Henry Sibthorpe included the book, *S[r] Chr: Sybthorps booke ag[t] Popery*, in his library (fol. 65[r], no. 22).

---

[22] Chamberlain's *Letters* include John West's petition for Henry Sibthorpe in 1618 (2:166); an expression of gratitude for kindness shown Sibthorpe in his "sickness and distresse" in 1624, p. 557; and similar expressions in 1625, p. 624. *Dudley Carleton to John Chamberlain, 1603–24, Jacobean Letters*, ed. Maurice Lee, Jr. (New Brunswick, N.J.: Rutgers Univ. Press, 1972), 261, refers to Sibthorpe's placement in 1618. I am indebted to Steven W. May for this and other references. See also John Lothrop Motley, *History of the United Netherlands from the Death of William the Silent to the Twelve Years' Truce–1609* (New York, 1879), 4:39, 88, and 239, for references to Sir Horace Vere, and to Olden-Barnevelt, passim; and see Pieter Geyl, *The Revolt of the Netherlands (1555–1609)* (New York: Barnes & Noble Inc., 1958), for references to Johan van Oldenbarnevelt, passim, but none to Sibthorpe.

[23] *Calendar of State Papers Ireland of the Reign of Charles I 1625–32. Preserved in the Public Record Office*, ed. Robert Pentland Mahaffy (London, 1900), 273.

[24] *Historical Manuscripts Commission Report on the Manuscripts of Lord De L'Isle Dudley Preserved at Penshurst Place*, ed. William A. Shaw (London: His Majesty's Stationery Office, 1936), 3:xxxiv–xxxv.

[25] *Burke's Genealogical and Heraldic History of the Landed Gentry*, 17th edition, ed. L. G. Pine, 3 vols. (London: Burke's Peerage Ltd., 1952), 3:2310. I am indebted to Michael Leader for pointing this out.

[26] *DNB*, 18:188–89; Burke, 430.

INTRODUCTION   xxi

Sometime during 1628 Lady Anne and Captain Henry probably returned to England,[27] living in Clerkenwell on the outskirts of London. In 1631 they moved to Acton (according to the dated inventory on fol. 59[r]), where they rented a home on the Steyne River. Fols. 71[r]–72[v] record the payments of the rent to Robert Johnson, a respected composer and court lutenist, and after his death in 1633 to his widow Ann.[28] According to T. Harper Smith, local historian in Acton today, "Acton was having a little Renaissance of its own .... Shakespeare's son-in-law, John Hall, inherited his father's house, 'Butlers,' in the village, which passed to his daughter Elizabeth Nashe. His sisters married into the village. The licensed schoolmaster was Edward Burles, who wrote the standard Latin grammar used for many generations. Lady Conway, widow of Sir John, Secretary of State to Charles I, retired there, followed by Lady Dudley, Robert Dudley's wife and widow who presented the church with plate in 1636."[29]

Lady Anne wrote a eulogy for Robert Johnson, which praises his talents as well as his virtues, describes his death in a highly dramatic way, and says that the curate Roger Cocks conducted Johnson's funeral on 21 November 1633 (fol. 72[r]). Lady Anne also thought highly of the curate of Saint Mary's Church in Acton, for fol. 21[r] shows the poem she had written "in commendations of M[r] Coxe (the Lecturer of Acton)." The Rector was Dr. Daniel Featley, but he was rarely in residence and left most of the parish duties to his curate.[30] No doubt Cocks also conducted the services for Lady Southwell, who died 2 October (fol. 74[r]) and was buried 5 October 1636.[31] He wrote some of the eulogy on fol. 73[r].

"On the right Hand of the Chancel" of Saint Mary's Church a "small

---

[27] See the last payment to Captain Sibthorpe "by the corporation of Cork, and due to him" for the maintenance of his men, on 12 December 1627 in the *Calendar of State Papers Ireland in the Reign of Charles I 1625–32*, ed. Robert Pentland Mahaffy (London, 1900), 1:293.

[28] Johnson is believed to be the composer of "Full fathom five" and "Where the bee sucks" in Shakespeare's *The Tempest*, according to *The New Grove Dictionary of Music and Musicians*, ed. Stanley Sadie (London: Macmillan Publishers; Washington, D.C.: Grove's Dictionaries of Music, 1980), 9:681–82. See also David C. Price, *Patrons and Musicians of the English Renaissance* (Cambridge: Cambridge Univ. Press, 1981), 30, 62, 80, and 127.

[29] T. and A. Harper Smith, "Dr. Featley of Acton, Chelsea and Lambeth" (London: A paper circulated by T. and A. Harper Smith, 1990), 9.

[30] Smith, "Dr. Featley," 9.

[31] I am indebted to T. Harper Smith for a transcript of the Burial Register at Clerkenwell.

xxii INTRODUCTION

Monument of Alabaster gilded and beautified with several Devices" was erected. Mounted on the wall were three plaques, one of black stone with gold lettering still hanging in the church today, and two wooden ones, all "with panegyrical verses" from fols. 73 and 74 about Acton's "Darlinge of the Nine." A small brass plate in Saint Mary's chancel read, "Here lyeth the Body of the Lady *Anne Southwell*." To be buried in the chancel was an honor in itself, one that the minister and parishioners apparently felt was due her.[32]

Since the eighteenth century, all but one of the plaques have come down, and only a few historians have mentioned her. Brief references to her literary reputation appeared in the works of George Ballard in 1775, Joseph Hunter in 1838, and Alexander B. Grosart in 1886. In the twentieth century, Ralegh editor Agnes Latham asserted that twelve lines of "The Lie" are "unique to Lady Anne Southwell." Only her letter to Lady Ridgeway and the booklist of Folger MS. V.b.198 have been published.[33] Although Lady

---

[32] John Bowack, *The Antiquities of Middlesex; Being a Collection of the several Church Monuments in that County* (London: Printed by W. Redmayne, 1705), 51–52; see also Daniel Lyson, *The Environs of London being an historical account of the Towns, Villages, and Hamlets, within Twelve Miles of that Capital: Interspersed with Biographical Anecdotes,* 4 vols., County of Middlesex (London Printed for T. Cadell, Jun. and W. Davies in the Strand, 1795), 2:8; I am grateful to T. Harper Smith for recommending the two books above and showing me the wooden plaque (containing verses from the right column of fol. 73^r) which he has in his possession; and to Robert Rodes for the information about the prestige involved in a chancel interment.

[33] George Ballard, *Memoirs of British Ladies Who Have Been Celebrated for their Writings or Skill in the Learned Languages, Arts, and Sciences* (London, 1775), vii; Hunter, *Chorus Vatum Anglicanorum Collections,* 1:280^r–81^r; Grosart, ed., says, " '*Sir Thomas South-well*'—He was of the Council of Munster, and was seated at Poulnelong, co. Cork. He married Anne, daughter of Sir Thomas Harris of Cornworthy, Devon, and sister of Sir Edward Harris, Justice of the King's Bench. Lady Southwell was a poetess of some merit. She wrote (among others) a Poetical Epistle of 121 lines to Doctor Bernard Adams, Bishop of Limerick, 1604–1636" (*The Lismore Papers (First Series in the Learned Languages, Arts, and Sciences)* [London, Printed for Private Circulation Only, 1886], 2:346). See also Agnes M. C. Latham, ed., *The Poems of Sir Walter Ralegh* (London: Constable & Co., 1929), 158; and Sr. Jean Carmel Cavanaugh, "The Library of Lady Southwell and Captain Sibthorpe," *Studies in Bibliography* 20 (1967): 243–54, and "Lady Southwell's 'Defense of Poetry,' " *English Literary Renaissance* 14, no. 3 (Autumn 1984), on two unnumbered sheets inserted between pp. 184–85. Although Cavanaugh asserts without documentation that Lady Southwell was "a maid of honor to Elizabeth," I find no evidence of this. See also J. Klene, "Recreating the Letters of Lady Anne Southwell," in Hill, 239–52. Since this work has been with the printer, a book by Louise Schleiner discussing Lady Anne Southwell and others has appeared: *Tudor & Stuart Women Writers,* with verse translations from Latin by Connie McQuillen, and from Greek by Lynn E. Roller (Bloomington: Indiana Univ. Press, 1994), chap. 5.

INTRODUCTION   xxiii

Anne's reputation has been a very limited one, it has far surpassed those of her two husbands.

Authorship in a Manuscript Culture

Lady Anne shows her participation in the manuscript culture of the early seventeenth century when she takes a poem like "The Lie,"[34] adds a few lines, and has a scribe copy it into the commonplace book. She may have done the same thing with the first five "sonnets," for three of them appear as the first verse of lyrics set to music in early seventeenth-century songbooks, as the commentary for fol. 1 states. According to the Folger first-line index, Sonnet 1 also exists in a similar version in a 1630 commonplace book, Folger MS. V.a.339, fol. 192. Two other poems were identified in Dobell's 1927 catalogue as "The Exequy" and an elegy for Gustavus Adolphus, popular poems by Dr. Henry King. These two, however, were not altered.

Prose selections by others seem to be included for various purposes. The heading on fol. 68 tells us that Lady Anne "best affects" the "perticulers" chosen from Topsell's bestiary, but about some of the others, no rationale appears. Among the "Apothegmes" on fol. 69 are two identified as the work of "Bushop Kinge" and "Fox." Others, like "A Glutton diggs his owne graue with his owne teeth," have the wit and sarcasm of Lady Anne and may have been composed by her. Most of them show the concerns that recur in her poetry. Coping with affliction, for example, is a constant concern as well as the topic of an apothegm (fol. 69^v, no. 25). She also included excerpts of a tract on how "the Law of the Gospell is more perfect then all other lawes" (fol. 70^r), and from Augustine's *City of God*. The latter may have helped her deal with the fact that "Aduerse and prosperouse fortune are both assistants in ... Saluation" (fol. 67^r).

Twice Lady Anne exploits the well-known elegiac formula, "Like to a lamp wherin the light is dead," to express grief (see fols. 9^v and 23^r and their commentary). Even in the more formulaic poems, however, her distinctive touch appears in at least one or two lines. Death is succinctly labelled "liues midwife" in the elegy for the countess of Somerset (fol. 23^r). When writing a sincere elegy for her good friend Cicely MacWilliams, however, she uses little of the formulaic. Like her pen, she is "choakt wth gall" (fol. 21^r).

---

[34] For a discussion of poems attributed to Ralegh, see Arthur F. Marotti, "Manuscript, Print, and the English Renaissance Lyric," in Hill, 209–21.

xxiv   INTRODUCTION

A search of first-line indices suggests that most of the remaining poems may be by Lady Anne.[35] But the question of authorship for all of the poems will not be settled definitively until all Renaissance verse miscellanies, commonplace books, and songbooks are examined.

Characteristics of Her Writing

Lady Anne's wit and humor are among the attractive features of her writing, and they often emerge, especially when she defends females. The shortest example appears on fol. 16^r, where the speaker sounds like Emilia in Shakespeare's *Othello*, criticizing the double standard (IV.iii.86–103). On fol. 26^v Lady Southwell again argues whimsically for Eve's superiority. Proving her "Grandams cause" partially by insisting on the female's superior creation from Adam's human material over his inferior composition from the earth shows her awareness of the popular topos.[36] She also mocks the "wilfull

---

[35] Margaret Crum, ed., *First Line Index of English Poetry 1500–1800 in Manuscripts of the Bodleian Library Oxford* (Oxford: Clarendon Press, 1969). For their prompt responses to my requests for information about first lines, I wish to thank curators Hilton Kelliher of the British Library, Kathy Schneberger of the Huntington Library, Stephen Parks of Yale University Library, and Steven W. May, who is continuing the indexing of Elizabethan verse begun by William A. Ringler. Although Cambridge has no first-line index, Assistant Keeper of the Archives E. S. Leedham Green contacted individual scholars and checked the first lines of Additional MS. 8684, compiled by editor E. A. Perryman, for an M.Phil. dissertation. Editions that have been checked include Edward Doughtie, ed., *"Liber Lilliati" Elizabethan Verse and Song (Bodleian MS Rawlinson Poetry 148)* (Newark: Univ. of Delaware Press; London: Associated Univ. Presses, 1985); Ruth W. Hughey, ed., *The Arundel Harington Manuscript* (Columbus: Ohio State Univ. Press, 1960); Steven W. May, ed., *Henry Stanford's Anthology: An Edition of Cambridge University Library MS Dd.5.75* (New York: Garland Publishing, Inc., 1988); Helen E. Sandison, ed., *The Poems of Sir Arthur Gorges* (Oxford: Clarendon Press, 1953); and Peter J. Seng, ed., *Tudor Songs and Ballads from MS Cotton Vespasian A-25* (Cambridge: Harvard Univ. Press, 1978).

[36] *The Riverside Shakespeare*, ed. G. B. Evans (Boston: Houghton Mifflin Company, 1974); all subsequent references to Shakespeare are also taken from this source. The topos of female superiority may be a resonance of Agrippa, whose name and book, the *De Occulta*, Southwell mentions in Precept 3 (Appendix 2, fol. 153, stanza 82). She may have known his defense of women from the *De nobilitate foeminei sexus*, trans. by David Clapam and published in 1542 (*STC* 203). On the topos and its derivation, see Linda Woodbridge, *Women and the English Renaissance: Literature and the Nature of Mankind 1540–1620* (Urbana: Univ. of Illinois Press, 1984), 38–44. On Agrippa's efforts to win the favor of Margaret of Austria, see Charles G. Nauert, Jr., *Agrippa and the Crisis of Renaissance Thought*, Illinois Studies in the Social Sciences no. 55 (Urbana: Univ. of Illinois Press, 1965), 26–27.

INTRODUCTION   XXV

herresye" of "thinkinge ffemales haue so little witt / as but to serue men they
are only fitt" (fol. 26ᵛ).

Even more striking is the expression of tension and anger which sometimes emerges, as in the poem beginning,

> Nature, Mistris off affection
> gaue my loue to thy protection
> wher it hath receiued infection
>   and is dying   (fol. 11ʳ)

In the experiment with sapphics, Lady Anne has the speaker cry out against
an unfaithful spouse, one who bears a hatred that "like hell fiare doth
burne." The predominantly trochaic tetrameters of the first six stanzas are
"turnd" in line 1 of stanza 7 to some iambics, as the speaker struggles with
images of opposition like "loue and hate," "Doues and Serpentts in one nest"
and "truth and falshood in one brest." Being "hatefull" in her spouse's sight
causes great pain, yet she asks for her marital "due" and threatens a suicidal
resolution without it. The sense of domestic martyrdom noted by Mary
Ellen Lamb[37] in the conclusion of the meditation against adultery also
prevails in the conclusion of this poem.

Her statements about the position of women vary. As noted above, she
can be harsh in criticizing them, but in other places she emphasizes their
equality with men or wittily exploits the topos of female superiority. Once
she comments wryly that "both turned fooles in Paradise / Which was the
meerest foole is harde to tell" (fol 26ᵛ). Both sexes are cautioned in Precept
4: "when you both are stript out of this clay / there will not bee a difference
in your sex" (stanza 83). In the everyday world, however, she recognizes that
a male hierarchy prevails and cautions women not to forget their "duty" as
the "seconde borne the weaker creture" (fol. 51ʳ⁻ᵛ, 215–58).

In many of the first poems of the volume, Lady Anne explores the book
of human nature, and when she studies it, she sees "How many blotts there
be" (Sonnet 2, fol. 1) in herself and others. Anger, envy, jealousy, betrayal,
and disappointment are topics she pursues relentlessly, and in a passionate
way. The speaker can seem hurt, angry, despairing, and wittily disdainful—
and sometimes all four simultaneously. Emblems of struggle like Cain
against Abel and Jacob against Esau recur. In what seems the most painful

---

[37] At the 1993 meeting of the Shakespeare Association of America in the seminar
organized by Margaret Arnold and Ruth Widmann.

imaginative leap of all, she speaks of Jacob and Esau "wthin the Mother / ... strucgleinge ... to murther one another" (fol. 21^r). This unusual pregnancy image appears in a poem celebrating a book on the birth of Christ. Two poems, one on anger (fol. 9^r) and the other on envy (fol. 22^v), proceed in a dialogue form, with a long line asking a question and then a short one coming down vehemently in a bitter answer. The explorations often proceed in legal language, as a speaker calls someone to the bar, proves a case, or discusses an assize.

A defense of reading poetry appears in Lady Anne's letter to her friend Lady Ridgeway (fol. 3), in an argument that reveals much about the cultural importance of art in their society. The poet sees her medium as something which provides a unity of discourse, and she defines it analogously as the "silke thredd that stringes your chayne of pearle; wch being broken, your iewells fall into the rushes; & the more you seeke for it, the more it falles into the dust of obliuion." Although other statements in the letter show that the writer is probably familiar with Sidney's "Defense of Poesy," she does not use his definition, but creates her own. Examining the commonplace book shows some of the poet's ideas about the art.

Lady Anne's love of wordplay, something she shares with George Herbert (1593–1633), often appears. Note, for example, the cryptic punning in Sonnet 5 (fol. 1^r); the formation of "Francis Quarles" by the first letters of the lines on fol. 17^r; the development of the long poem for Bishop Adams by many plays on his name (fols. 18–19); the apparent experiment in paradox on fol. 25^r, and the shifts in the short poem honoring "Coxe," where she plays with his name. Here her own initials tease the reader (fol. 21^r), as they also do in her notes for poetry: "a worm A:s I am dar*e* not bo*a*st" (fol. 45^r).

The volume also shows more mundane concerns about poetry. A desire for organization appears in a marginal note that Lady Anne wrote: "this must cum next to the sense of last" (fol. 42^v). A meditation like "Thou shalt not steale" (fols. 52–57) nevertheless remains unorganized, as the often corrected and sometimes non-consecutive numberings show. Effective rhyme is another concern, for when told that she has used "wyf / lyfe to ofte," she chooses another rhyme (fol. 49^r) and changes two previous instances on fol. 48^v. But the new feminine rhyme, "dvtye"—"beautye," also becomes over-used—four times within the meditation. The apparently subservient gesture deconstructs itself in its recurrence.

Lady Anne clearly cares about conventional aspects of good poetry. Her rationale for rhyme appears in Precept 4, where she explains that rhyme

INTRODUCTION

xxvii

gives the lines "more fuell" to form "a curious Iewell" and also offers a "help to memorye" (appendix II, fol. 161^r, stanza 49). As Sidney laments mere "rhyming and versing," so she scorns the "amorous Idiots [who] doe disgrace it [poetry] / in making verse the packhorse of theyr passion" (fol. 161^r, stanza 50). Although she warns against the assumption that "caelestiall powers will blesse / Loose ballads or Hyperbolizeinge Ryme" (Folger MS. V.b.198, fol. 17^r), she herself hyperbolizes on occasion. But the commonplace book makes no claim to be a collection of polished poetry.

On the contrary, a major interest of Folger V.b.198 lies in its copious examples of a poet at work. For Lady Anne, the process involves drafting passages (as on fols. 44^v–46^r and 57^r–58^r), dictating poems, reading and rereading them. Sometimes she deletes words and phrases by crossouts or erasures, and at other times, she allows alternative readings to remain. Corrections in her hand are sometimes very interesting, as, for example, when she changes "Voluptuous mynds are neither good nor wise" to "Voluptuous men" (fol. 8^v). In another instance, she changes an original image for the union of man and wife, "as is softe the skin that in an egg shell lyes / our indevyduall loving harts shall cleaue" to the tougher "as is the opticke artire to the ies / our indevyduall loving harts shall cleaue" (fol. 50^v). The reworking of the final stanza concluding the meditation on adultery, with corrections in her hand alongside an undeleted phrase, suggests that the topic was too painful for her to write any more. Sometimes a phrase scratched next to a stanza is almost totally illegible, as on fol. 53^r. The reference to her own poetry as "theise blotted Lines" (fol. 19^v) appropriately describes many lines. Using the commonplace book effectively, as discussed above in relation to the manuscript culture, was also part of Lady Anne's approach to writing poetry.

A profound sense of godliness, deeply rooted in the Scriptures, pervades every composition, regardless of the pain, bitterness, or defiance also expressed. While many of her scriptural models were clever and successful females, like Rahab and Abigail, some had defied tyrants in a violent way, like Jael and Judith. Lady Anne tells us that she identifies with them as she deals with attacks on her own life and writing. Her God was a divine judge—a gloriously transcendent being. She gropes for words to describe the luminous aspects of such a deity and of heavenly inhabitants. Often she uses images suggesting the majestic visions of the Apocalypse, either of God, as "hee cums in a treeis[?] in the day of iudgment" (fol. 34^v) or of a glorified soul as one wearing "the robe of a trancelusantraye" (fol. 32^v). The poet studies God's law theoretically in "How that the Law of the Gospell is /

more perfect then all other lawes" (fol. 70) and pragmatically in the meditations on the Ten Commandments. These compositions resemble a Brueghel painting in that they include all God's people—prostitutes, pedlars, politicians, lawyers, soldiers, servants, parents and children, and beggars—and their mundane activities.

Godliness does not inhibit her questioning; on the contrary, it forces her to ask more questions—like those about unfaithful spouses. Religious doctrine and reality sometimes collide. Perhaps the enigmatic lines on fol. 58^r best illustrate her struggle with religious theories. She even shows an awareness of the accepted use of language itself when she complains, "The man that for gods cause forbears to kill / to sweare, lye, steale or droune his soll in wine / ... / why, hee is scornde and calde a femynine." She insists that such use "abuse[s]" God Himself (fol. 48^r).

When the speaker seems less passionately involved in what is being said, the writing seems to proceed by methods of amplification prescribed in the rhetoric books. Topics are often explored by listing conventional divisions, such as the disciplines of an education. Consider the way she marches through stanzas about philosophy, metaphysics, arithmetic, geometry, architecture, drawing, music, astronomy, rhetoric, ethics, politics, and economics in the meditation on keeping holy the sabbath (fols. 41^r–42^r).

Other Compositions

By 1614 some of Lady Anne's work had been published. Two brief prose pieces—one response to the "Newes from the very Country" by I[ohn] D[onne] and another to Sir Thomas Overbury's "Newes from Court"— appeared in *A wife now The Widdow of Sir Thomas Overburye ...*, 1614 (*STC* 18904). The *Overburye* book was issued in sixteen impressions between 1614 and 1638. "Certaine Edicts from a Parliament in *Eutopia*; Written by the Lady *Southwell*" was added to the sixth impression published in 1616 and renamed *Sir Thomas Ouerburie, his Wife* (*STC* 18909). The "Edicts" are probably by Lady Elizabeth Southwell, the woman John Chamberlain refers to as "Lady Southwell" in his letters to Dudley Carleton, but without other writing by Lady Elizabeth, certainty is impossible. Lady Anne's authorship is suggested by two unusual verbal parallels but they provide too little evidence to confirm it. The question needs further examination. That Lady Anne wrote the response to Donne, however, is certain, and that she wrote the response to Overbury is probable. Because of the notoriety of the Overbury murder and the popularity of the book (and of

INTRODUCTION   xxix

John Donne), Lady Anne's name must have been known by some of the literati.[38]

Although only the initials A. S. are beneath the 1614 "Answere[s]" to the "Newes from the very Countrey" by Donne and the "Newes from Court" by Overbury, similar images appear in the "Answere[s]" and in Folger MS. V.b.198, suggesting that Lady Anne Southwell wrote both. In the answer to Donne, A. S. says that "life, death, and time, do with short cudgells dance the Matachine," and in the letter to Falkland, Lady Anne says, "Yo^r perspicuous eye see's dayly, how Nature, chance, and death / doe daunce the Matechyne" (fol. 4^r). The word "matachine" itself is somewhat rare, for concordances reveal that Shakespeare, Spenser, Sidney, Marlowe, Donne, and Jonson never use it in their poetry. The word "cinque-ports" as a metaphor for the five senses also appears both in the "Answere" to Donne and in the commonplace book (fol. 8^v, "Blessed Life"). Ordinarily the word refers to the five southeastern ports of Dover, Sandwich, Hastings, Romney, and Hythe, as it does in Shakespeare's only use of it (*Henry VIII*, IV.i.48).[39]

---

[38] See Sir Geoffrey Keynes, *A Bibliography of Dr. John Donne, Dean of Saint Paul's*, 4th ed. (Oxford: Clarendon Press, 1973), no. 73; Evelyn Simpson, "John Donne and Sir Thomas Overbury's 'Characters,'" *Modern Language Review* 18 (1923): 410–15; for background information on the Overbury circle, see R. C. Bald, *John Donne: A Life* (New York: Oxford Univ. Press, 1970), 272–79, 290–301, and 313–15; and Arthur F. Marotti, *John Donne, Coterie Poet* (Madison: Univ. of Wisconsin Press, 1986), 205; Marotti points out that Helen Peters's *Paradoxes and Problems* (Oxford: Clarendon Press, 1980) puts the "Newes from the very Countrey" "(for no especially compelling reason) among the Dubia" (p. 336, n. 152). Editions and impressions of *Ouerburie, his wife* are listed in the *STC*, vol. 1. For references to Mrs. E. Southwell, see Chamberlain, 1:64, 70, and 512.

[39] Marvin Spevack, *The Harvard Concordance to Shakespeare* (Cambridge: Harvard Univ. Press, 1973); Charles Grosvenor Osgood, *A Concordance to the Poems of Edmund Spenser* (Gloucester, Mass.: Peter Smith, 1963); Herbert S. Donow, *A Concordance to the Poems of Sir Philip Sidney* (Ithaca: Cornell Univ. Press, 1975); Robert J. Fehrenbach, Lea Ann Boone, and Mario Di Cesare, *A Concordance to the Plays, Poems, and Translations of Christopher Marlowe* (Ithaca: Cornell Univ. Press, 1982); Homer C. Combs and Ray R. Sullens, *A Concordance to the English Poems of John Donne* (Chicago: Packard & Co., 1940); and Mario A. Di Cesare and Ephim Fogel, *A Concordance to the Poems of Ben Jonson* (Ithaca: Cornell Univ. Press, 1978). The *OED* lists uses by others of both "matachine" (such as Webster's in *The White Devil* [V.vi.170]) and "cinque-ports." *The Alchemist*, by Ben Jonson, also contains the word, as Raphael Seligmann has pointed out; Face says that Doll is "our Castle, our cinque-Port, Our Douer pire," indicating her privileged position in satisfying Sir Epicure Mammon (III.iii.18–19, *Ben Jonson*, ed. C. H. Herford and Percy Simpson, 5 [Oxford: Clarendon Press, 1937]).

For attributions of the responses to other women, see James Savage, editor of *The "Conceited Newes" of Sir Thomas Overbury and his Friends* (Gainesville, Fla.: Scholars' Facsimiles & Reprints, 1968). He attributes the "Edicts" to Lady Frances Southwell (p. xl).

In the "Answere to the Court Newes," a brief response to Sir Thomas Overbury's "Newes from Court," less unusual verbal parallels appear. A. S. says that "Titles of Honor, are rattles to still ambition" and Lady Anne repeats this in the stronger line of "ffrayle loue": "Titles are gawdes to still ambition" (fol. 10^r) and in lines 37–40 on fol. 26^v. About goodness, A. S. writes "That *Goodnesse* is like the Art *Prospectiue*: one point Center, begetting infinite rayes." Lady Anne expands the conceit in her meditation on keeping the sabbath:

> And by the arte perspectiue, clymes the lights
> whose lynes of longitude, are immortalitye
> and parolels are rests, and full delights
> that from the optick lynes of maiesty
> doth from one glasse reflect a thousand faces
> and from one poynt, as many lynes and spaces
>
> (fol. 41^v, 273–78)

Many of the ideas in the response to Overbury are also articulated in the commonplace book. A. S. says "That only to refrain ill, is to be ill still" and Lady Anne repeats that "vertue consists in action" (fols. 8^r and 18^v). The idea recurs often, for Lady Anne believes that idleness causes many sins, beginning with that of Eve (fol. 47^v). A. S. asserts that "enuie knowes what it will not confesse"; Lady Anne's entire poem on envy calls for the "foule Monster, at truthes barr to stand" and confess its secrets. Envy must answer the questions of the speaker, who probes into what "enuie knows" (fol. 22^v). Another line by A. S., "That men's loues are their afflictions," is what Lady Anne says of her own love in "Nature, Mistris off affection" (fol. 11^r, 33–34). The word "affliction" recurs twenty-five times in the commonplace book.

The misogyny of the statement "That Man, Woman, and the Diuell, are the three degrees of comparison," may surprise some readers. Could the sentence have been inserted by another? Readers might also wonder whether, because the initials "A. S." after the "Answere to the Court Newes" appear only in 1614, Lady Anne herself objected and asked that her initials be removed. It is certainly possible. Her reputation is not dependent on

---

About the brief articles above the initials A. S. he offers as a possibility Lady Anne Clifford (b. 1590), who early in 1609 became Lady Sackville and three days thereafter countess of Dorset (p. xxxvii). See also V. Sackville-West, introduction, *The Diary of the Lady Anne Clifford* (London: William Heinemann Ltd., 1923), xxxiii; the writing bears no similarity to that in the responses.

INTRODUCTION

xxxi

these eighteen sentences. But those familiar with the many lines from the Folger and Lansdowne manuscripts which uphold the male points of view should not be surprised. A. S. may be repeating a misogynistic commonplace, one containing the same bitterness that Lady Anne occasionally expresses. The printer could have dropped the initials.

As Donne, Overbury, and other players of the "Newes" game often express the social and political criticism common in the early decades of the seventeenth century, so also does Lady Anne. Her poetry discusses human nature in its many manifestations. The context of the activity is usually that of the "State, Religion, [and] Bawdrie," as Ben Jonson describes the subject matter of the "newes" game in his satire, "An Epigram on The Court Pucell." The Epigram censures Cecilia Bulstrode, another contributor to *Ouerburie*, whose death in 1609 sets the date when the coterie competition was probably completed. Lady Anne's poetry also shows the habit of writing conceits, a basic requirement for playing the "newes" game.[40]

In addition to the two letters by Lady Anne in the commonplace book, two others are among the Lismore Papers at Chatsworth in Derbyshire. Both are dated "1623" and sent from Castle Poulnelong. One petitions Sir Richard Boyle, earl of Cork (vol. XIV, fol. 160), and the other Sir Thomas Browne (not the famous writer; vol. XIV, fol. 174) for the land rights of Sir Richard Edgecombe, a friend of her deceased father. They show that she was at ease in addressing the politicians of her own day for a humane purpose. Few would have teased the earl of Cork as Lady Anne did when she declared, "But if you will neither doe mee good in this respecte, nor tell mee why; I must bee forc'd to put vp a petticion against you to the Countesse, who by this tyme I hope [*sic*] is stronge enough to putt you ten thousand pound in debt by the birth of another sonne or daughter." To a man whose wife had already delivered twelve children, this was no idle threat.[41]

Two poems, Precept 3 and Precept 4, on fols. 142–67 of British Library Lansdowne MS. 740, were also written during the Ireland years, for the speaker mentions the possibility of dying "in Hibernia" (fol. 148^r, stanza 41). The unpublished poems are included in appendix II because they provide information for understanding the commonplace book. They begin with a

---

[40] Savage, *The "Conceited Newes,"* xxiv–xxv; the "rules" of playing with conceits on pp. lvi–lxii; see also Arthur Marotti, *John Donne, Coterie Poet*, 204–206 and 336, n. 153.

[41] For a list of the children and their dates of birth, see Nicholas Canny, *The Upstart Earl: A Study of the Social and Mental World of Richard Boyle First Earl of Cork 1566–1643* (Cambridge: Cambridge Univ. Press, 1982), 88.

"Poeticall Dedication to the King" above the name but not the signature of "Anne Southwell" (fol. 142ʳ) and conclude with a poem by Sibthorpe praising his wife (fol. 167ᵛ). They are part of a manuscript well known for its many poems by John Donne.[42] The meditations have as a nucleus two poems in Folger MS. V.b.198: Precept 3 adds many lines to "Thou shalt not take the / name of god in vayne" (fols. 35ʳ–37ʳ) and Precept 4 to "Thou shalt keepe holy the / saboth daye" (fols. 37ʳ–44ʳ). Lines 327–44 (fol. 42ᵛ) in the Folger manuscript praise "that prynce that governs bryttan now" for his books and the pardon he granted "to those that sought his death" and hence must have been written before James's death in 1625. Because those lines were dropped in the Lansdowne manuscript, the dedication was probably written to Charles I.

Many stanzas from the Folger drafts are repeated verbatim or with only slight variations in Lansdowne MS. 740. A few, like the following, are revised:

> Might others deeds my sex or song approue
> victoryous Debora to god did singg
> and Nabals wife by wisdome did remoue
> the vowed vengeance of an angry kingg
> Iehell* and Iudas armes were made the rodd   *Jael
> to scoordge the mighty enemyes of god
>   (Folger MS. V.b.198, fol. 44ʳ, *with deletions omitted*)

In Lansdowne MS. 740, fol. 158ᵛ, stanza 24, Lady Anne focuses more sharply and argues more clearly. Lines 1 and 2 state the problem: "& now mee thinks I hear some wizzard say / how dares this foolish woman bee soe bold"; lines 3 and 4 personify the deadly instruments of two heroic females: "ask Iahells nayle yᵗ Siseraes head did stay / & Iudiths sword that made her hott loue cold"; and 5 and 6 conclude with an explanation of her own empowerment and an exhortation to others: "Hee that enabled them, enables mee. / yf thou seeke knowledge hee'l enable thee." In both manuscripts, however, the stanzas have been crossed out. Either husband (setting patriarchal boundaries?) or wife could have deleted it in the Folger manu-

---

[42] For a description of Lansdowne MS. 740, see Peter Beal, *Index of English Literary Manuscripts* (London: Mansell, 1980), vol. 1, part 1, 250–51. I suspect that Sibthorpe was the collector of Lansdowne MS. 740, for the handwriting of some titles for the Donne poems seems to be the same as some of Sibthorpe's writing in Folger MS. V.b.198.

INTRODUCTION   xxxiii

script, but in the Lansdowne manuscript, Sibthorpe probably did the revising. The secretary hand occasionally making corrections resembles the Sibthorpe secretary hand in the Folger manuscript, though this and other aspects of the Lansdowne manuscript need more study.

The extended meditations add a few enigmatic details to Lady Anne's biography. We learn that she was strongly criticized for her writing (fol. 163^v, stanzas 74–75) and that any "honest harted man" who commended her risked being criticized also (fol. 164^r, stanza 76). The phrase is significant in that the speaker of the love poem on fol. 27^r of the Folger manuscript calls himself an "honest harted man" (line 4). Stanza 69 tells us that the British government had laid "an envious stepdames hand" on her (fol. 151^v), but we are not told how or why.

II. The Manuscript

The Provenance

Folger MS. V.b.198 was purchased in 1927 by Mr. Henry Clay Folger, founder of the Folger Shakespeare Library, from P. J. and A. E. Dobell, shortly after the publication of *Dobell's Catalogue of Poetical Manuscripts*, which described it as a "volume of Papers in various hands, containing a number of Poems by Lady Ann Southwell and a few by other writers." The volume had been sold by Thomas Thorpe (catalogue for 1836, n. 1032) to Sir Thomas Phillipps (Phillipps MS. 8581), and at his sale (London, 1908, n. 699) had been bought by Bertram Dobell.[43]

Appendix I: Lady Anne as Composer and Compiler

Appendix I is constructed to show in brief some of the evidence that Lady Anne Southwell was the person who either composed or compiled most of the selections in Folger MS. V.b.198 along with pertinent information about a few physical aspects. The many repetitions of her name and revising hand throughout the volume show that it is not merely a collection of works by a variety of authors. Column four indicates that Lady Anne's name or initials appear on twenty-eight pages and a pronominal reference on two

---

[43] Seymour De Ricci, with the assistance of W. J. Wilson, *Census of Medieval and Renaissance Manuscripts in the United States and Canada* (New York: The H. W. Wilson Company, 1935), 1:419, no. 1669.1.

pages; an "S" indicates each of the forty-three pages on which her angular hand appears. On fols. 31 through 58, where her name occurs only once, her revising hand appears often, on all but four of the folios. Two of the unidentified long meditations, "Thou shalt not take the name of god in vayne" and "Thou shalt keepe holy the saboth daye," of fols. 35^r–44^r, do have her name on them in their lengthened form at the British Library. Other columns were included for the information about each folio that they offer briefly: column three lists the main scribe of a page, and the last column shows, first, whether a sheet is a full page (F), that is, an original part of the volume or group of folios, or one inserted, that is, tipped (T) into the volume. The sheets tipped into the volume raise unanswered questions about who inserted them. Did Lady Anne, her second husband at a later date, or both of them together? Secondly, the last column gives information about watermarks, but they offer little help in terms of dating the poems. All but the last two are sixteenth-century watermarks. In short, the first appendix contributes to an overall picture of the volume. Many of the physical aspects of the manuscript are discussed below in detail.

Physical Description

Folger MS. V.b.198 is a folio measuring 23.5 by 35.5 cm. It was bound in Russia leather around 1835 and has five raised bands and the words, "Lady Southwell's Works 1626," in gold, on the spine. The covers are decorated with five parallel lines around the edge; the two outer ones are gold tooled. The marbled end papers and two flyleaves at either end were probably added at the same time when the exposed edges of the leaves were gilt. The manuscript itself is made up of seventy-four leaves from several different paper stocks of varying sizes. It was apparently the result of Captain Sibthorpe's and Lady Southwell's attempts to gather her compositions and favored selections into an existing volume which had first been used by John Sibthorpe for recording receipts in 1587 and 1588. The volume is tightly bound and conjugate leaves cannot be safely identified and collated.

Watermarks, Stains, Tears, and Sheets Added to the Volume

The dominant watermark of the original volume, placed centrally between chain lines, is that of "Nicholas Lebe" below a backwards "B" within a shield, similar to Briquet 8080, dated 1578, as indicated in appendix I. Some sheets added to the book also have this and another Lebe watermark, suggesting that the Sibthorpes probably had a substantial stock of Lebe

INTRODUCTION   XXXV

paper. Other watermarks also appear; fol. 3, tipped onto a guard, has the pot watermark, possibly with the initials "OO" and a crescent moon above.[44] Fol. 4, with the Lebe watermark, has a smaller sheet pasted flat onto it, with creases showing that it had been folded into squares of 1 1/4 inches. The copies of the two letters on fols. 3 and 4, which Lady Anne had sent before 1630, may have been inserted by her or, at a later date, the Captain. Four different hands seem to have written the folios thus far; the note at the bottom of fol. 4 is similar to the hand of Henry Sibthorpe on fol. 73. The date of his writing the note, as the commentary suggests, remains a mystery.

A variety of watermarks and hands appear in the volume. The watermark on fol. 10 has the name "C Denise," under "DC" intertwined within a shield (similar to Briquet 9334, dated 1572–1578). Fols. 12–15 and 31–58 have a second Lebe watermark in slightly smaller paper with the "B" facing in the same direction as the name. Fols. 20–23 have a totally different watermark, a dog prancing above "I Nivelle," similar to Briquet 3642, dated 1581. Fols. 26–29, with either the first Nicholas Lebe watermark or none at all, have sheets with other watermarks tipped onto them. Tipped onto fol. 26 is a sheet containing a horn and baldrick with a trefoil above; tipped onto fols. 27 and 29 are sheets with no watermarks; and tipped onto fol. 28 is a sheet with two pillars and grapes above. The added sheets are brown and have strong creases; where they are torn, as the sheet tipped onto fol. 27 is, they have been mended with narrow strips of paper. Fol. 30 has the first kind of Nicholas Lebe watermark; fol. 31 has none.

Fols. 32–58 and all but fol. 53, possibly tipped into the book, contain the same large brown—not ink—stains on the bottom third of each sheet. Fol. 53[r] has two stanzas on a rectangle of paper (with the same brown stains) pasted flat on a blank leaf. The meditations written on these folios (except for fols. 44–46 and 57–58 in Lady Southwell's hand) seem to be in the same hand, resembling in some ways that on fol. 27.

The only seventeenth-century watermarks appear on the sheets tipped onto the last two folios. The sheet tipped onto fol. 73 has a rose over M and an illegible letter, similar to Heawood 1902[A], dated 1656; that tipped on fol. 74 has another version of the watermark with two pillars and grapes

---

[44] See C. M. Briquet, *Les Filigranes* (1907), ed. Allan Stevenson (Amsterdam: The Paper Publications Society, 1968); and Edward Heawood, *Watermarks, Mainly of the 17th and 18th Centuries* (Hilversum [Holland]: The Paper Publications Society, 1950).

xxxvi INTRODUCTION

above, similar to Heawood 3509, which is ascribed the date "16 ... ". The full fol. 73 has the "Claude Denise" watermark, and the full fol. 74, no watermark.

The volume is in remarkably good condition. Neither tears nor stains often interfere with the legibility of the writing. A few pages, however, have been trimmed, so that letters or the tops of letters in the titles and sometimes letters or numbers at the ends of lines on the right-hand side are missing.

The Scribes of Folger MS. V.b.198

Chronologically, John Sibthorpe comes first, for he signed in an italic hand the receipts for money spent in the Dutch wars in 1588 on fols. 5^r, 6^r, and 6^v. The writer of the body of the signed receipts (fols. 5^r, 6^r, and 6^v) and the six unsigned receipts (fols. 62^r, 63^r, 64^r, and 65^r) of the 1580s shows a distinctively secretary but unidentified hand, and is labelled X-80. The other hands in the volume are those of Lady Anne, Captain Henry, and, it seems, members of their household.

Several characteristics make the hand of Lady Anne the most difficult to read. First, she forms many letters with one or more downstrokes, often with only slight variations. An *r* can also be a *u* or *v*; a *t* an *e*; and an *m* a *w*. The bowl of a letter, like that of an *a* or a *d*, is often open, and at times these two letters can be distinguished only by taking into account the adjacent letters. An *m* is sometimes shortened to an *n*, a *w* to a *u* (as in "pour" for "power"), a *c* is used for an *s* and vice-versa, and sometimes a *b* and *p* are interchangable and occasionally one is written over the other. When consonants are juxtaposed, such as a *tr*, *st*, *gn*, or *mb*, one is often omitted; "ignorance," for example, is spelled "innorance." Judging by the spelling and spacing, she must have written some words as she heard them. Very often the *e* or *t* is omitted, probably because she did not hear the letter. In some places, however, she does write both correctly and legibly, as for example on fol. 40^r, lines 165–70. There is very little punctuation in any of her lines although she knows what it is and refers metaphorically to the "Comma, Colon, & Period" as essentials (fol. 3^v). The sometimes indecipherable lines illustrate how a woman could know little about penmanship even though she was very well read. After quoting the one sample the British Library has of handwriting by the prolific Margaret Cavendish, Elaine Hobby concludes, "The figures concerning people's ability to write

INTRODUCTION

are the subject of some controversy, but all sides agree that men were far more likely to be able to write than women."[45]

A third hand is that of Captain Henry Sibthorpe, who signs and dates fols. 73^r and 74^r in 1636, so all variations of his hand are compared with these, but even these two differ. Fol. 74^r is predominantly a cursive and modern italic hand with only a few secretary formations, but fol. 73^r contains predominantly secretary letters, written in a cursive, cramped, and rapid way; one distinctive feature is the occurrence of the modern j, rather than the i, which appears in lines 23, 26, and 31, and nowhere else in the book. The styles vary according to purpose: fol. 73^r was probably meant to be a first draft and read by no one but Sibthorpe and perhaps Roger Cocks, who contributed some of the lines. Fol. 74 is much more carefully written, with its two centered and column-like passages. What seems distinctive about his secretary or italic hands, here and earlier in the volume, are the frequent convex strokes and the thin downstrokes occasionally above a capital letter, as in the D beginning line 16 of fol. 74^r.

Members of Lady Anne's household may have served as scribes, both in Ireland and England. Joseph Hopton, who signs as a witness to two accounts in an italic hand with clubbed ascenders and descenders (fol. 72^v), may be the one who wrote "The Lie" on fol. 2^r, with its uniformly clubbed ascenders and descenders. Two signatures, however, offer insufficient evidence for certainty. Another witness to the six Acton receipts on fols. 71^r–72^v, Samuel Rowson, may also be the one who wrote some of the pages—those in the upright style with serifs forming right angles as they

---

[45] For discussions about what was taught to women, especially those outside of London, see David Cressy, *Literacy and the Social Order: Reading and Writing in Tudor and Stuart England* (New York: Cambridge Univ. Press, 1980), especially 112, 115, 128, 145, and 146; and David Cressy, *Education in Tudor and Stuart England* (London: Edward Arnold, 1975), 109–10, quoting Richard Mulcaster on schooling for girls in 1581. Qualifying Cressy is Keith Thomas, "Literacy in Early Modern England," *The Written Word: Literacy in Transition: Wolfson College Lectures 1985*, ed. Gerd Baumann (Oxford: Clarendon Press, 1986), 97–132. Elaine Hobby, *Virtue of Necessity: English Women's Writing 1649–88* (Ann Arbor: The Univ. of Michigan Press, 1989), 5. See also Herbert Schulz, "The Teaching of Handwriting in Tudor and Stuart Times," in *The Huntington Library Quarterly*, vol. 6, no. 4 (1942–43), 381–425; and Foster Watson, *The English Grammar Schools to 1660: Their Curriculum and Practice* (Cambridge at the Univ. Press, 1908), chap. 11, explaining that "written work had not ordinarily played any considerable part in school practice" (p. 186). Writing, "in the earlier part of the 17th century, in the Grammar Schools, . . . if taught at all, seems to have been regarded as an extra and paid for by a special fee" (p. 192).

xxxviii INTRODUCTION

end an *n*, *m*, or *h*, and sweeping descenders in letters beginning a line, as, for example, on fol. 11ʳ. John Bowker, the first name in the inventory heading on fol. 59ʳ, may be the one who wrote pages resembling the writing here, as, for example, fol. 4ʳ; on the other hand, another person may have been writing for Bowker, who is named as the one in charge of the inventory. The hand resembles that of Sibthorpe.

Other hands also appear. In addition to those already mentioned as witnesses to the receipts for the rent, Thomas Warburton, Robert Johnson, Ann Johnson, and Mary Phillips also signed them. Occasionally throughout the manuscript a few lines are written by a totally different hand, or at least in a different way, and the changes are indicated in the textual and paleographical notes.

III. Editorial Method

The edition is made up of a table of contents, introduction, diplomatic transcription of most of the manuscript (with facsimile reproductions of fols. 44ᵛ–46ʳ and 57ʳ–58ᵛ containing Lady Anne's drafts), two appendixes, bibliography, commentary, textual and paleographical notes, and an index of the first lines of poems. Folger MS. V.b.198 seems to be a private document in that some of its poems are neither finished nor meant for publication. I follow the argument made by Thomas Tanselle and repeated by D. C. Greetham that "false starts, cancellations, insertions, and slips of the pen are important characteristics of these documents and that an editor who eliminates such features is altering the nature of the document and is obscuring evidence of motivation."[46] Decisions which Lady Anne or Captain Sibthorpe would have faced, had they published the commonplace book, have not been made here. I have concentrated primarily on the textual content of the original, reproducing as closely as possible the exact spelling, punctuation, and capitalization of the document (although instances of all these are often debatable). Letters or words added above or below a line are so placed in the text. The font of the corrections and additions below or above a line has

---

[46] Thomas Tanselle, "Textual Scholarship," in *Introduction to Scholarship in the Modern Languages and Literatures*, ed. Joseph Gibaldi, 29–52 (New York: The Modern Language Association of America, 1981), 34, and "Reproducing the Texts of Documents," in *A Rationale of Textual Criticism*, 39–66 (Philadelphia: Univ. of Pennsylania Press, 1989); and D. C. Greetham, *Textual Scholarship: An Introduction* (New York: Garland, 1991), 350–51.

INTRODUCTION   xxxix

been reduced here although, in the manuscript, they are the same size as other words.

Because of the quagmire into which one is led in transcribing the folios written by Lady Anne, the editing of those few pages differs from that in the rest of the volume. Fols. 44^v–46^r and 57^r–58^v have been reproduced in facsimile; on the right side of each reproduction is a somewhat modernized version, in that spacing is silently regularized and an italicized letter is occasionally added for easier reading. Lady Anne used no tildes or loops to indicate an additional letter, so no underlined letters appear here. Where a word cannot be made comprehensible by the addition of one or two letters, the word which may have been intended is sometimes added in brackets, immediately juxtaposed. What looks like "theugh," for example, must have been intended for "Thyatira," judging from the proximity of two other biblical cities, Smyrna and Ephesus, all three of which appear together in the Book of Revelation 1:11. The transcription reads: "theugh[Thyatira]" (fol. 46^r). Several times a word that seems to complete the sense of a line is added within unattached brackets, as, for example: "shall not [be] forsacen."

Aspects of the volume's format which can be transferred are kept. The indentation of lines and the placement on the page of titles, signatures, and catchwords follow the layout of the manuscript page. The number of lines on a folio is often much greater than the number possible in print so no page-for-page correspondence is attempted. Deletions of letters or words by erasure or by being crossed out in the manuscript are indicated by angle brackets: < >. Only two words in the manuscript do not have the deletions included because of the puzzling transcription (much more confusing than the manuscript itself) which the use of too many brackets creates: "<t>h<e>y<re>" is transcribed as "hy" (fol. 38^v, 102) and "b<ȯ>t<h>" as "but" (fol. 49^v, 206). Both are explained in the textual notes. When deleted letters are decipherable, they are included within angle brackets; when they are not, hyphens appear to indicate the amount of space occupied by the letters. Where no hyphens appear, an erasure has been made in the manuscript. When a whole stanza as well as words and phrases within it have been deleted, the angle brackets are doubled before and after the stanza. Occasionally conjectured letters are provided within brackets, such as at the end of the line when the right-hand side has been cropped on fols. 68 and 69. Three meditations have titles (on fols. 32^v, 35^r, and 37^r) which were probably inserted after the poem was written, for the space between the last line of the preceding meditation and the first line of the new meditation is the same as that between other stanzas. The space for each has been enlarged here.

xl INTRODUCTION

Textual notes also record letters that were inserted and those that are corrections, whether by reshaping original letters or writing boldly over the earlier letters or over an erasure of previous ones. If discernible, the deleted letters are noted as those written *over*; if not, the letters in the text are noted as *corr.*, that is, corrected. The placement on the page of a number, word, phrase, or line, if different in the manuscript than in the text, is also recorded in these notes.

An "[S]" in the right margin shows Southwell's hand. When her initial follows a word that she added above or below the line of text, or a whole line that she wrote, no additional note appears. When the amount she added needs to be made clear, her contribution is stated in the textual notes.

The paleographical notes, which are combined with the textual notes, record other changes in the hands writing the lines, as well as significant changes in the nib of the pen; unusual flourishes which underscore meaning (as on fol. 4^r), changes in the size of the letters when the change seems to indicate an emphasis (as on fols. 18^r–19^r and 25^r) and significant variations in the formation of letters or words (such as the abbreviation for "etc." in the booklist of fols 64^v–66^r). These notes also record apparent attempts to reinforce meaning by appearance, as on fol. 4^r.

Foliation is indicated by arabic numbers within square brackets on the right hand of the pages; line numbers for each composition are in brackets in the left margin, at five-line intervals, except for a few instances where including something in the manuscript's left margin, like a number or a word, prevents putting the number in that space. The numbers indicate the number of lines in a work considered by itself, except for the few pages of receipts when the numbering begins at the first line and continues through the last line of the receipt or receipts on the page. Otherwise, new items begin with new numeration. A number between stanzas is not given a special line number but that of the line of text above which it appears. The lineation of prose passages follows modern conventions rather than the number of the line in the manuscript. Dropped in the prose passages are hyphens or tildes serving as line fillers, apparently to justify right-hand margins (as on fol. 4^r).

Occasionally appearing in the margins is an asterisk, an "X," or a pointing finger. All seem to function as modern asterisks, calling attention to a passage. On fol. 10^r, 11, for example, the "X" calls attention to lines written to the right that need insertion; on fol. 47^v, 25, to a topic also discussed on fol. 26^v, Eve as our "grandome." In the inventories, the "X," completed by a short line extending to the right, suggests the completion of a list with

INTRODUCTION   xli

items "sent" (fols. 59ʳ and 60ᵛ). The numbers and lines occasionally in the
left margin and those somewhere around a stanza were retained in the text
even though what they mean is often unclear. Where the tilde functions as
a decoration in the title, as on fols. 1ʳ, 8ʳ, and 74ʳ, or to emphasize closure,
as on fol. 1ʳ after Sonnet 4, and that on fol. 9ʳ, 22, it is retained as such.

Short and long pen lines indicate various things. A short horizontal line
functions as a caret on fol. 19ᵛ, 26, and the word "caret" is deleted. A short
line under a line of poetry or prose shows the completion of a unit, that is,
a poem (fols. 1ʳ, 9ʳ⁻ᵛ, and others), stanza (fols. 10ʳ and 54ᵛ), section (that is,
of an inventory [fols. 59ʳ and 60ᵛ] or bestiary [fol. 68ʳ⁻ᵛ]), or entire work
(like the line under a receipt, separating it from the booklist which follows
[fol. 65ʳ]). Lines often underline dates, as on fol. 4ʳ, 23, or occasionally in
the receipts. In one instance, lines have been ruled for the text of a stanza
(fol. 32ʳ, 79–82), just as they seem to be for the stanzas throughout the
meditations, but only the first line was used. Lady Anne probably meant to
come back to the stanza, but apparently lost interest in completing the lines.
These horizontal lines are the only ones which have been given individual
line numbers.

Braces often separate one unit from another, as on fols. 5ᵛ (around the
three columns) and 7ʳ (to the right of "Dauids … afliction"). Sometimes
they call attention to the insertion of a line or two of poetry (as on fol. 10ʳ,
leading from line 14 up toward the X before line 11; and fol. 19ᵛ, 25). Braces
are also drawn to the right of receipts (even though line 12 on fol. 6ʳ runs
through and beyond the brace). Short braces around two or three lines may
also call attention to a topic, as the brace seems to do on fol. 26ᵛ, 35–37. It
may also emphasize closure when placed around the last two lines of a
poem, as on fols. 8ʳ, 49–50, and 8ᵛ, 49–50 and 13–14.

The mark for the accent grave has also been retained as a reversed
apostrophe and placed after the word it stresses. Occasionally the mark
follows the letter it seems to be above or immediately after. Southwell uses
the accent grave often but not exclusively in poems where she seems emo-
tionally involved, such as the poems for Lady Ridgeway (fols. 19ᵛ–21ʳ) and,
to a lesser degree, for Dr. Bernard Adams (fols. 18ʳ–19ʳ). Occasionally an
accent grave also appears where she does not seem personally engaged.
Punctuation always follows the mark for an accent or an apostrophe although, in the manuscript, it may appear to be directly underneath.

Abbreviations with superior letters are retained, that is, "oʳ" for "our," "Sʳ"
for "Sir," "Mʳ" for "Master," "yᵉ" for "the," "yᵗ" for "that," "yʳ" for "your,"
"agᵗ" for "against," "wᶜʰ" for "which," "wᵗʰ" for "with," "Bᵖᵖ" and "B:" for

"Bishop," "D^r" for "Doctor," and "K^g" for "King," an elevated ^{t} for words ending in "ent," "aint" for "ainst," "^{g}" for "ing," "^{r}" for "er," "ro" or "re," and sometimes slight variations of these. Where a period is included, it follows the superscript letter, even though the dot often seems to be directly below the elevated letter in the manuscript. Because of occasional uncertainty about the placement of final letters in the abbreviations y^e and y^t on fol. 21^v (with its 121 lines in two columns), I have regularized them to superscript letters. Common scriptural abbreviations also appear, like "Gen:" for "Genesis," "vers." for "verse" and "Cha." for "Chapter." Abbreviated proper nouns include "Io." for "John," "And:" for "Andrew," "Robt" for "Robert," "Chr" for "Christopher," "Tho:" for "Thomas" and "R. C." possibly for "Roger Cocks." Other abbreviations, for which there are no keyboard equivalents, are expanded and the missing letters underlined, like the downstroke for *es*, the different strokes through the descender of a *p* for p*er*, p*re* or p*ro*, a *q* for q*ua*, and the tittle or loop to indicate a missing letter or letters, as in "le*tt*re" or "Impr*imis*." If letters from a word have been trimmed or scraped off, the conjectured letters are sometimes added within square brackets.

Titles have been taken, for the most part, from those in the text or from the first one or two lines. A few titles have been formulated from the content and are put within brackets in the Table of Contents and in the text.

The edition is, for the most part, a diplomatic transcription of a document not intended for print. The spelling and punctuation of the manuscript are preserved as closely as computer equivalents can transcribe them. Marginal notes and numbers are kept in the text, even though their purpose is often unclear and an explanation not always possible. Where letters are indecipherable, dashes suggest the space occupied but not the number of letters, as, for example, on fol. 53^v, lines 73–74. The pages in the hand of Lady Anne are edited in a slightly different way as a tentative solution to the difficult problem of the author's hand.

Appendix II: British Library Lansdowne MS. 740

Fols. 142^r–67^v from British Library Lansdowne MS. 740 are included here as supplementary material for the understanding of Lady Anne, Captain Henry, and aspects of the commonplace book. Captain Sibthorpe composed the final poem and signed the initial "H"; he was probably also the book-maker who collected the various works of the manuscript. Lady Southwell's hand never appears in these folios. The lines are not glossed. The tran-

INTRODUCTION

scription is presented as closely as possible to the way it appears in the document. Where the scribe used a tilde or loop to indicate another letter, the letter is added with underlining. In the rare instance where a letter is indecipherable, a hyphen substitutes for the unknown letter; and where the folio is torn (as on fol. 167[r]), the letters of a word appear in the place that they occupy in the manuscript.

The workes of the Lady Ann Sothwell:.~ [1ʳ]
Decemb: 2° 1626°:.

Sonnett: 1ª.

ffly from the world, ô fly, thow poore distrest
Where thy diseased Sense infects thy Soule
And where thy thoughts doe multiply vnrest
Troubling with wishes what they strayt Controle
[5]   O World betrayer of the mynd
      O Thoughts that guide vs being blynd:.

Sonnett: 2ª.

When I sitt reading all alone that secret booke
    Wherein I sigh to Looke.
How many blotts there be,
    I wish I could not see, <or from my selfe might fly>
    or from my selfe might flee,
[5]   Heauens I implore, that showes my Guilt
    To hell I dare not goe
The World first made me rue, my selfe my woes renue
    To whom then shall I sue.
Is there no hope in death? yes: Death ends all our woes.
        from   Am
[10] Death me <will> ME <vnlose> will lose, myselfe<from> all my foes:.

Sonn: 3ª:

ffarewell fond World, the onely Schoole of Error,
The Chaos whence all stormes and tempests rise:

2 THE WORKS OF THE

Mount thow my Soule vnto that Sacred mirror,
That showes menn are but fynite Sommer flyes:

[5] And there wth piety bewayle their Cares:
Whose fond Laborious Webbs are their owne Snares:.

Sonnett 4^a.

If in the flesh where thow indrench'd do'st ly
Poore Soule thow cold'st lift vpp thy lymed Winges
Carry thy selfe vpp to that azur'd Sky
And wash them in those sacred-Cristall Springes

[5] Where Ioy and requiem the holy Angles singes
And all Heauens Vault wth blessed Eccho ringes:.~

Sonnett. 5^a:

Shall I sublyme my Soule to frame a letter
And to the Sisters proue a nedy Debter
No spritefull muse on Hierogliphicks mount
And tell the World I skorne their bose accompt

[5] Let Scriueners seeke that <iustly falls> fame that ioyntly falls
Vppon the keper of Romes Capitall.

[1^v is blank]

[Ralegh, "The Lie"] [2^r]

Goe sole the bodies guest
Vpon a thankeles arrand
feare not to touch the best
The truth shalbe thy warrand

[5] And yf they dare reply
boldlie giue them the lye

Goe tell the Court yt gloze
And shines lyke rotten wood
Goe tell the Church it shewes

[10] Whats <is> good but doth noe good
If Court or Church reply
Giue Court and Church the lye

Tell potentates they liue
Actinge but others actions

LADY ANN SOTHWELL

[15] Not loued unles they giue
    Not strong but by their factions
If potentates reply
Giue potentates the lye

    Tell men of high Condition
[20] That rules affayres of state
    Their purpose is ambition
    Their practise onlie hate,
And yf they doe deny
Then giue them all the lie

[25] Tell those that braueth most
    They begg for more by spendinge
    And in their greatest Cost
    Seeke nothinge but Comm<u>e</u>ndinge
And yf they doe deny
[30] Then giue them all the lye

          ar not sounde
    Tell schooles <they want> profounde<nes>   [S]
    And onelie liue by seeminge
    Tell artes they want true grounde
      thriue
    And <liue> but by esteeminge   [S]
[35] Yf schooles or artes reply
Giue schooles and artes the<y> lye

    Tell phisicke of her boldenes
    Tell nature of decay
    Tell Charitie of < > Coldenes
[40] Tell iustice of delay
And yf they doe deny
Then giue them all the lye

    Tell beautie it is a flourish
    Tell tyme it steales a way
        thoughts
[45] Tell <faults> they all must p<u>eri</u>sh
    And fortune doth betray
And yf they this deny

Then giue them all the lye

[50] Now when thou hast as I—Comm̄aunded thee done blabbinge
Allthough to giue the lye—Deserues noe les then stabbinge
Stabb at thee he that will—Noe stabb the sole Can kill
                         Anne Southwell   [S]

[2ᵛ is blank]

To my worthy Muse,   the Ladye Ridgway.   [3ʳ]
that doth these lines infuse.

How falles it out (noble Ladye) that you are become a sworne enemye to
     Poetrie; It being soe abstruse an art, as it is, that I may say, The other
     artes are but Bases & Pedestalles, vnto the wᶜʰ this is the Capitall. The
     meere Herald of all Ideas; The worldes true vocall Harmonye, of wᶜʰ all
5   other artes are but partes, or rather, may I iustly say; It is the silke
     thredd that stringes your chayne of pearle; wᶜʰ being broken, your iew-
     ells fall into the rushes; & the more you seeke for it, the more it falles
     into the dust of obliuion. You say; you affect proze, as your auncestors
     did; Error is not to bee affected for antiquitye. Therefore, (Noble &
10   wittye Ladye) giue mee your hand, I will leade you vpp the streame of
     all mankind. Your great great grandfather had a father, & soe the last,
     or rather the first father, was God; whose neuer enough to bee admired
     creation, was poetically confined to 4. generall genusses, Earth, Ayre,
     water & fire. The effectes wᶜʰ giue life vnto his verse, were, Hott, Cold,
15   Moist & Drye, wᶜʰ produce Choller, melancholye, Bloud & flegme. By
     these iust proportions, all thinges are propagated. Now being thus
     poetically composed; How can you bee at vnitye wᵗʰ your self, & at
     oddes wᵗʰ your owne composition: It may bee, you will say, that Poesye
     is a fiction, & fiction is a lye. O but, Rahabs concealing the spyes, was
20   more to bee approued, then Doegs truth. But heerein, Poesye seemes to
     doe more for nature, then shee is able to doe for her selfe, wherein, it
     doth but lay downe a patterne what man should bee; & shewes, that
     Imagination goes before Realitye. But hee is not worthy the name of a
     phisitian, but of an Emperick only, that giues one potion to all manner
25   of diseases. for it is as great an error to giue purges to one in a con-
     sumption, as it is to giue cordialls to one in a Repletion. Therefore it is
     necessarye to knowe how the humor aboundes, that soe wee may the
     boldlyer applye. Then, since all are eyther fooles, or phisitians, to escape

LADY ANN SOTHWELL

the former I will take vppon mee to knowe, what hath soe distasted [3ᵛ]
your palate against this banquett of soules, devine Poesye. Some wanton
Venus or Adonis hath bene cast before your chast eares, whose euill
affyre; disgracing this beautifull Nimph, hath vnworthyed her in your
opinion & will you, because you see a man madd, wish your self wᵗʰout
Melancholye, wᶜʰ humor is the hand of all the soules facultyes. All
exorbitant thinges are monstrous; but bring them agayne to theyr
orbicular forme & motion, & they will retayne theyr former beautyes.
Our Reason ought to bee the stickler in this case. who would not
skornefully laugh wᵗʰ Micholl, to see the old Prophett daunce; but when
wee knowe hee daunced before the Arke, must wee not thinke the Host
of heauen was in exultation wᵗʰ him, as well as that of Ierusalem. To
heare a Hero & Leander or some such other busye nothing, might bee
a meanes to skandalize this art. But can a cloud disgrace the sunne? will
you behold Poesye in perfect beautye. Then, see the kingly Prophett,
that sweete singer of Israell, explicating the glorye of our god, his power
in creating, his mercye in redeeming, his wisedome in preseruing;
making these three, as it were the Comma, Colon, & Period to euery
stanzae. Who would not say, the musicall spheares did yeeld a cadencye
to his songe, & in admiration crye out; Ô neuer enough to bee admired,
devine Poesye. It is the subiect, that commends or condemnes the art.
But noble Ladye, I will trouble you noe further now; yett when I haue
your honorable word of reconciliation, I will then delineate out euery
limme of her, & how shee is envelloped vpp wᵗʰ the rest of the artes. In
the meane time I rest more then thankfull for your noble louing letter,
as the louer of your virtues.

Anne Southwell

vera Copia per Io.

prvto turi

Do: An: o: /

[A letter to Falkland]   [4ʳ]

Thrice honored Lord

Will yow <yow> vouchsafe a pardon if I play the Critick wᵗʰ this one
word in yoʳ letter. Wherein yow say yow are depriued of all, Is the Sun
bereft of his beames because a cloude interposeth betwixt him and oʳ
watrye balls, Could a banis'ht Philosopher say vnto him selfe, Omnia

mea, mecum porto? And can yow loose anythinge as longe as yow enioy
yo'selfe, What', though yow hould not the sword & Scepter of a Kingdome still! rather a losse to the nation then to yow, This was but a guift
of ffortune, and such is hir nature, y' shee were not, if shee weere not
fleeteinge, Sure' yo' soule is of a higher strayne then to valew any thinge
w^{th}in hir reach, or to giue one Inch of grownd to hir purloyneinge
hande, soe', that shee can but make a lame sally out against yow, Yo'
perspicuous eye see's dayly, how Nature, chance, and death doe daunce
the Matechyne about all Mortalls till they haue stript vs of those borrowed plumes y' begett admiration onely in Ignorance, Soe y' <shee can
but make> while theise Triumviri conglomerate about vs, wee must
looke for noe stabilitye noe faelicity here. It is yo' goodnes noble Lord,
that hath made mee honnor yow, not yo' fortunes, for hir despight and
my disdayne haue euer beene æquipollent, your perseuerant fauor begetts
my acknowledgment and humble thanks, And this is the plus vltra of
my request, that yow wilbee pleased to inrolle Captaine Sibthorpe and
mee in the nomber of yo' seruants.

1628
The coppie of a lettre writt by the
Lady Anne Southwell, to the Lord
deputye ffalkland of Ireland. /

[4ᵛ is blank]

     [A signed receipt of the 1580s, number 1]   [5ʳ]
The .6. of february 1588
Reconed wth my Captaine for Aryan Ba ⎫
stians and Peter Pluce, and the chardges ⎬   5ⁱᵍ —15ˢᵗ /
of them Amountes to _____⎭
       Iohn Sibthorpe

[5]

A Hym to Christ

Alpha Omega, O^h thow first and Last
Restorer of fallen man, Prist, Profett, Kinge,
Blest Virgines sonne, who only able haist
subdued all thinges, shalt iudg euery thinge.
Trwe santifer of this holly Land

LADY ANN SOTHWELL

by Natiue beirth, Lowe nourture, filiall Caire,
patternes, precep<u>tes</u>, merickell<u>es</u> of thy hand,
doth, resurection, after buriall heere,
Breathe on me God and man, inspire thou me
[10]   <inspire thou me>, wth <har>free Confession, harty penitence
trwe Loue, feirme hope, and perfect Charity
that so by merrett of thy bloud<u>es</u> expence
I liueinge by thee, in thee may p<u>er</u>seuer
approtch vnto to thee, wth the rest for euer. /

[5^v]

5 {predicables} The general worde   io: predicaments: [S]

The kinde	The Substance:
The difference	The Quantite
The properte	The Qalitie
[5]	The thing chauncing or	The Relacion
cleuing to the substance	The Maner of doing
	The Suffering
	When
	Where.
[10]		The Settelling
	The Apparailing

[Signed receipts of the 1580s, numbers 2, 3 and 4]   [6^r]

The secound of Ianuary 1587

Reconed wth my Captayne ffrome the
xvjth of December vntill this secound
of Ianuary ffor all thes prysonars
[5]   Wose names ar vnder wrytten and p^d
him all ther Charges, Constantin an
Itallyan Iohn Debe hauig Cornelyvs
Corman. Lymnering. Iane Adryanes
Henricke Petters Lawrance Petterig
[10]   Walter Tyrrowe Petter De Peares   144^g’ —5st /
Willi<u>am</u> Van men Iozen ffredericke
Henricke Turlewe and all other <—> souldgiours of this
garrison

prysonars that have byne Comytted
since the Daye abowe Wrytten

8 THE WORKS OF THE

[15] vntill this secound of Ianuary 1587 ⎫
Iohn Sibthorpe

The 4 of Ianuary 1587

Reconed wth my Captayne for Iame
Iacobe prysoner and payd him his
[20] Charges dewe ffrome the 16. of December ⎫ lviij^s vj^d
vntill the .3. of Ianuary. the some
beinge ffyfte eyght shillinges six pence
more for Grygory Bure Charles
Kelker the Charges of them beinge
[25] twenty one Gildars
Iohn Sibthorpe

The <4> 12 of Ianuary 1587
Reconed wth my Captayne for Glawde
Bratte Charles ffreinge mathyas
[30] Lootte and ij solcgiars of steue bargayne iiij^{li'} ij^s ⎫
The Charges amovntinge as apeareth by
the booke to ffowre poundes ij shillinges <sta>
Iohn Sibthorpe

[Signed receipts of the 1580s, numbers 5, 6, 7, 8 and 9] [6^v]

The xiijth of Ianuary 1587

Reconed wth my Captayne for Iacobe
mavrice and hance De Grave the ⎫ 69. gild' v sti^rs
Charges amovnting as apeareth by the booke
[5] Iohn Sibthorpe

The xvijth of Ianuary 1587

Reconed wth my Captayne for Clewken
Damond. Bonettes Peter. Poweles & his
mother. Serinson Hovenias and the ⎫ 187 gi^{l'} 12. sti^rs
[10] Charges of theim all amovnteth vnto
187 gild' . 12. sti^rs

LADY ANN SOTHWELL

Iohn Sibthorpe

_____

The xxv[th] of Ianuarye <u>1588</u>

[15] Reconed wth my Captaine for Ioyce Cop
perman, Peter Pegin', Ettane Ianne Iohn
Millane, Iohn Bowdowe, and Twoe more   } 61 gild'/
and the chardgis of them all, Amountethe
vnto / lxj gilders _____
       Iohn Sibthorpe

_____

[20]   The xxix[th] of Ianuary 1588

Reconed wth my Captaine for Iohn Mallow
Ioche Boyle Ernewe Deroue, hance   } gild' — sti'
Bashe, and the Pape, And the char-   }157—15 —
gis of them all Amontethe vnto, 157–gil'
[25] &—15 styvers _____
       Iohn Sibthorpe

_____

The 2 of Februarij—1588 /
Reconed wth my Captaine for Anthonye moe
myans and leonarde Vander haide and G   } gild[r]—st
[30] Gilliam Cattaies and xxvij souldiors of Steue }152—10
Bargaine, And the chargis of them all Amontes
to—152 gilders and 10 styvers, _____
       Iohn Sibthorpe

       [Psalm 25, to the Earl of Castlehaven]   [7[r]]

Dauids Confidence in ┐   Writen by the ladie A[nne] B-------------
prayer he prayeth for | to ye first Earle of Castle hauen
remission of sinne and {
for helpe in afliction. ┘

    To thee my soule I rayse.
    my God I trust in thee
    Let not my life wth shame be stayned

nor foes triumph on me
[5]   let none y^t on thee wayte
be of theyre hope ashamd
Let those y^t causelessly transgress
be rightfully infamd
Iehouah shew thy wayes
[10]   me teach thy pathes most strayght
Lead mee in truth; my saueing god
on thee I dayly wayte
Thy louing kyndness lord
thy mercies manifold
[15]   recal to mind wch thou dist power
on mee in tymes of ould
fforgett my sines of youth
of faults no <t>notice take
but lord in mercye think on me
[20]   euen for thy goodness sake
vpright and good is god
he sinners wil enstruct
in wayes of life, and all the meeke
in Iudgment will conduct
[25]   The footesteppes of the lord
are truth and mercy still
to those that doe his counant keepe
and witnes of his will
Now for thy holy name
[30]   Iehouah I intreate
vouchsafe mee pardon for my sin
for I confess it great
who so doth feare the lord
shall learne to chuse his way
[35]   his soule in goodness shal be lodgd
his seed on earth shall stay
To those that feare the lord
his misteries are showne
his gratious counant vnto them
[40]   he maketh clearlye knowne
mine eyes are humblye bent
the lord still to behould

LADY ANN SOTHWELL

      for he shall pluck my tangld feate
      from nets that them infould
[45]   with mercye turne to me
      for I am desolate
      the troubles of my heart increase
      redress my woefull state
      O lord behold my payne
[50]   aflictions and distresce
      forgiue my sines consider well
      the hate my foes express
      ffor great theyre number is
      they hate wth. violence
[55]   discharge my soule, preuent my shame
      I trust in thy defence
      Integritye and truth
      let them preserue me still
      I wayte one thee o God redeeme
[60]   thine Israell from hell

     A Paraphrase vppon Lucius Anneus Seneca   [8^r]
          on his booke of Prouidence: ~

It is an easy taske to pleade the Cause
off him that rules this Machyne w^{t}h his Lawes
And out of nothing, made this glorious ball:
And by his prouidence supporteth all.
[5]   He that beholds the motion of the Starrs
The setled Center and the Ocean Warrs
Whose wynd-swollen Billowes mustering rank on Rank
Doth w^{t}h pale Tremblings kise the bounded bank
May seing, knowe, there is a hand doth tye
[10] This various fforme, this Contrariety:
And w^{t}h his reason neuer Liue at odd.
But still be reconciled to his godd.
Yet some will say! How doth it happen then?
Calamity befalls the best of men?
[15] Those thinges w^{c}h ffortune giues & can dispose
A wise man cares not, whither wynn or Loose
Riches & honor they cann so contemne
As thinges possessd^t but not possessing <t>him

12   THE WORKS OF THE

Children & freinds, health, Life, or Liberty

[20] Hee Counts the Ending of a Tenancy,

And thus resolu'd, in height of fortunes Skorne

He cannot dy So poore as he was borne.

But wold yow se a warr pleasing to Ioue.

That ioyes the Angles, and their smiles approue

[25] A Goodman wrastling w{t}h Calamity

Giuing no Inch of ground to Ieopardy

         cuninge
And from Affliction hath this ∧ \<pleasure\> gott

For euery poyson his trewe Antidote

God makes no fondling of those men he chuses

[30] But hardens them, the Dasterds he refuses

Fortune herselfe doth Skorne to through her sheild,

To those that at first shock doth fly the feild

Rather she laughes, to see such Cowards fly

Hatchyng on Soll, and doting till they dy

[35] By which vnhappy rest they neuer knowe

Themselfes, \<-\>or Harmes, before they feele the blowe

So all the stroakes that Goodmen doe endure

Are as the fyre that makes the gould more pure.

Theise Diamonts by Cuttyng giue best splendor

[40] Theise Gumms by beating Sweetest Odour render.

Vertue consists in Action: and the wise   [8{v}]

Hould all Afflictions, vertues exercise

To shake the Lazy rust from off their mynd

For ease & welth makes ignorant & blynd

        rest
[45] Who is benumbd w{t}h \<ease\> and delectation,

May iustly haue a feare of his saluation

The worldes allurements fraught w{t}h all Dissemblyng

Debarrs the blisse, wrought out w{t}h feare & trembling

  Wellcome the worst of Ills: in Seas of Gall ⎫

[50]   My patience is resolu'd to laugh at All ⎬
                 ⎭

      Blessed Life:

Seest thow a man that's vassaliz'd to pleasure

Hould hym a foole, a Coward, and a slaue

That doates on gaudes which hold's so little treasure

LADY ANN SOTHWELL

That dares not looke on danger, or the graue
[5]   Whose handes are bound in Cordes of delectation
    Doth quite forget the end of his Creation

That life is death wch pleasure wholly barrs
To vertue then a handmayd she may Serue
Yet wisest myndes will Count her dimples skarrs
[10]   And like to Sodom Apples feede and starues
    For he that onely liues for Senses sportes
    Makes Sathan Cheiftayne ouer his Cinque portes

Voluptuous men\<ds> are neyther good nor Wise
Nor neuer shall a blessed life comprise

Anger

Anger proceedes from a surcharged Gaule
Yet See! This Embrion setts the frame on fire
The onely Bane that on the world doth fall.
Confusions Dam, Iniquityes Grandsire
[5]   And they that haue it hold a torturing hell
    From whence God flyes: & damned furyes dwell.

Dialouge: [9^r]

Sonnet.

Anger what art thow? Hast thow treuth to tell:
    A flame of hell.
Where is thy Dwelling? or thy tutring schooles?
    The Hart of fooles.
[5] What is thy hopes in all thy fierce intrusion?
    Confusion:
Who did begett the? or who gaue the place.
    The want of Grace.
Where wold'st thow place the Tropheyes of thy Euills?
[10]   With the Diuills.
What dost thow gayne (think'st thow) in thy vexation?
    Damnation
What might I call so monstrous an Elfe?
    Madnes it selfe

14 THE WORKS OF THE

[15] Who are thy fellowes in the Earth or Ayre?
    Hell & despaire
What wold'st thow leaue behynd the in thy moode?
    Teares woundes & blood.
When will the fury of thy Source be turned?
[20]   When all is burned.
Mapp of confusion and the worlds disturber
Being plac'd in hell, who wold pursue the further:. ~

Sonnet

Beauty, Honor, yeouth, and fortune
    I importune
None of yow to be my freind
    Theise gambols end.
[5] And I haue gaynd a Rosy bed.
    vppon your head
Trod out of thornes and cruell Cares
    And now yor wares
Semes noysome trumpery to my thoughts
[10]   Things good for noughts
O happy state that dijing liues
    And reason giues
A iust accompt of her disdayning
    By her lost gayning:

Sonnet: [9^v]
Like to a lampe wherein the light is dead
Or as a Ring whose Ruby out is falne
Or as the nest from whence the byrds are fled
Or as a Shryne where is no Saynt at all
[5] Or as a well when Dried is the Spring
Or as a Hiue the Honey hyd away
Or as the Cage wherein no Bird doth sing
Or as the world depriued of the day
Or as the Limbes when life hath taken flight
[10] Or as the Spray when as the Rose is Reft
Or as the Moone Eclipzed of her light.
Or as the Hart wherein no Ioy is left

LADY ANN SOTHWELL   15

>
Such to my sence all worldly Pleasures be
When bitter Absence reaues thy selfe from me.

Sonnett.

O how happy were I dearest
ffar aboue all tonges Expressing
If thow wert as thow appearest
Neuer Queene had such a blessing
[5] In the Pride of ffortunes dressing

Thow hast sworne might I beleeue the
Ill do I deme my suspition
And to say so much, Doth greiue me
That I see thy bad Condition
[10] And my faults are thy Addition.

ffrayle Loue is like faire flowrie fields   [10']
pursued by Autume at the heeles,
And beautie men soe stellefie
are lamps for fooles to studye by,
[5] Since all things perish vnder heauens orbs.
these to my thoughts Contempt affords.

Longe life is like a fooles discourse,
tyreinge it selfe is heere or worse.
And strength of body is an Asse
[10] that beares about corruptions Masse
    X Those vaine delights men pleasures call
     are drops of honey smerd wth gall
Sith all things perish vnder the Orbes ⎤
theise to my thoughts contempt affords. ⎦

---

[15] Quick witts are like quick-siluer balls
that vnto dotage hazard falls
Titles are gawdes to still ambition
death, tyme, and fame change theyr condicion.
Sith &c'.

---

16   THE WORKS OF THE

[20] Seruants are Traytors, theiues, and Spies
that for o^r Pelfe in Ambush lyes
And in o^r vice wth smiles Doe stroke vs
to gaine the stronger chords to choke vs.
Sith &c'.

[25] Children are ofsprings of o^r blood
that often choke theyr founts wth mudd
And gould that worldlings make theyr God X
beinge abus'd it proues theyr rodd.
Sith &c'

[30] ffreindshipp is but a masse of words
lesse ‹tyme›
this fayth ‹this›∧ tyme nought elce affords.

Each man his owne Acts doth approue
and makes a goddesse of selfe loue
but wth detraction crownes his freind
[35] thus all things to priuation bend.
Sith &c'.

[10ᵛ is blank]

Nature, Mistris off affection
gaue my loue to thy protection
Wher it hath receiued infection
and is dying

[5] Fame, the daughter great of wonder
brekeing ffrom thy mouth like thunder
rendinge truth and me assunder
all with lyinge

Loue, that looked through mine eyes
[10] neuer borowed beam ffrom lyes
or Sofft passions of disguise
or Estranged.

But all this serues not thy turne
thy hate, like hell fiare doth burne

LADY ANN SOTHWELL 17

[15]
and at all my best acts Spurne
and near Changed

Eue to Adam, was his Crowne
and can baldness, be renowne
this thou pullst thy owne state downe
[20]   O meere maddness

Much like, to Pandoras purss
turne heauens blessing to a Curss
which I feare will still wax worss
      To my saddness

[25]
Thou hast turnd, my daye to night
putst my aged plumes to flight
that am hatefull in thy sight
      as all men see.

Can loue and hate, together rest
[30] Doues and Serpentts in one nest
truth and falshood in one brest.
      It canot be

I See that loue, and deere affection
is the nurss, off my affliction
[35] the eye of truth giues this direction
      to my sick brest

Am I a yookffelowe, or slaue
what is my due I looke to haue
or elce Ile digg my selff a graue
[40]   and ly at rest.

[11ᵛ is blank]

Honor thy father and mother that the   [12ʳ]
    dayes may be long in the lande wᶜh the lord thy god
          gyveth thee.

If to be borne the Image of the Lord
if to be made the temple of<or> his sperit
if to have eares to heare his sacred woord
a soule that shall his heavenly seate inherit

18   THE WORKS OF THE

[5]   and singg a requiem wth his saynts on High
        not for a tyme but in eternyty.

        If to liue long in this all glorius woorld
        crownd wth rich Iemes of soonn of moone & starres
                         blew
        ore wch a <crimsen> white crimsen vale is hurlde
[10]   swelling in pleates bounde in wth goulden barres
        paved with perfumes of party colored flowers
        cooled with windes and moystned wth sweet showers

        If to have censes served wth delectation
        the pleasing props vnto the frame of nature
[15]   if to a witt which tendes to preservation
        and to subdue all other kynde of creature
        if this and more be woorth a dear respect
        gyve honor to the cause of this effect

        Behould those things wch are inanimate
[20]   having but being, sans life reason sence
        they never from this presept derogate
        vnlesse constreyned at wch they take offence
        throw vpp a stone by force into the ayre
        how soone it will vnto the earth repayre

[25]   Lock vpp the light wingyd ayre in some close cave
        how will it toyle to come vnto its syre
        how lyke a frantick fury will it rave
        till it have gaynd its dutious desyre
        rending the earth and wth a voyce like thunder
                                        make
[30]   make infants tremble and ∧ ould men woonder.

        The siluer streames that in the channell slyde   [12ᵛ]
        pressing each vshering dropp to hash away
        doe in theyre pretty murmuring seeme to chyde
        and frett the earth as causer of ther stay
[35]   and by theyre swift and never ceasing motion
        expresse theyre duty to theyre mother Ocean

LADY ANN SOTHWELL

The fyre wee keatch from flynts and fyx in oyle
and flatter it with wood with flax and straw
how angry doth it looke how doth it toyle
[40] and into peramytes doth vpward draw
indures noe touch but all to ashes turnes
and in a clooud of thick black smoke it moornes

<Behould the censytyues innumerable>
Behould the vigitabels wanting cense
[45] with rootes and stringgs they doe imbrace the grownde
and being puld away by vyolence
<do>they chaundge theyre hew and in a deatfull sownde
fruteles and leavelesse evermore they moorne
vntill vnto the mother earth they toorne

[50] Behould the censytiues innumerable
(by them) in the greate glasse of nature looke
to oure dull sence more comprehensible
then the two <s> volumes of the sacred booke
the littell lambe to pay her duteous fees
[55] doth never suck, but humbly on her knees

Man that is graste wth being lyfe sence <&> reason
oh let his reason wth its selfe dispute
let not corrupted <ay> will ay woorking treason
make him inferyor to the plante and brute
[60] in derogating both from god and nature
defacing of so fayre a compleate creature

Obey and have thy dayes long in the lande   [13^r]
not in the lande of thornes, and bitter toyle,
but there, where blessed Abrams seede shall stand
[65] wch doth oreflow wth hony mylke and oyle
the promisd lande wherein thou arte to lyve
       thy god
which land the lord ʌ him selfe doth gyve.

     koyn
Not as he gave the <purse> to Iudas hand   [S]
not as he gave Achan the wedge of goulde
[70] not as raboam hadd his fathers land

or Iesabell did Nabaths vynyard hould
but you in peace in ease in pomp shall dwell
              over   sraell
greate lord & Iudges <ov of> I<erusalem>

                       on
See how the lord invites ∧ this presept

[75]   he gyves you all the woorld wth out desert
in lew therof he bids you gyve respect
to those wthoute <> whome you can have noe parte
and from his <b> presence he doth still exclude
fowle disobedience and in gratitude.

[80]   The noblest faculty with in the mynde
is frendship and by parents most exprest
for toe shrowde turnes they common_ly are blynde
and quickly can an iniury disiest

                                   [13v–15v are blank]
All.maried.men.desire.to.haue good wifes: [16^r]
but.few.giue good example. by thir liues
They are owr head they wodd haue vs thir heles.
this makes the good wife kick the good man reles.

[5]   When god brought Eue to Adam for a bride
the text sayes she was taene from out mans side
A simbole of that side, whose sacred bloud.
flowed for his spowse, the Churches sauinge good.
This is a misterie, perhaps too deepe.

[10]   for blockish Adam that was falen a sleepe

                                [16^v is blank]

F<w-> ayne would I dye whil'st thy braue muse doth liue   [17^r]

    Quaintest of all the Heliconian traine
Rays'd by thy arte-full quill, t'hat life<ht> doth giue
                 s
    Vnto the Dullest things, thy fy'ery straine
Adds Immortalitye, <and --------------> maugre priuation

[5]   And by thy power brings forth a new Creation.
Vnhappy they that poesye professe
    Rayseinge their thoughts by any starr but thyne

LADY ANN SOTHWELL

Nor lett them thinke cælestiall powers will blesse
  Loose ballads or Hyperbolizeinge Ryme<s>
[10] Curst bee those sulphrous channells that make stincke
  Each christall dropp y^t in theyr cranyes sincke
In throne thy Phœnix in <Hi> Iehouahs brest
  Since shee aproue's hir selfe bird of that nest
Soe shall she liue immaculate and blest.

[17^v is blank]

A Letter to Doctor Adam B^pp of Limerick by the Lady A:S: [18^r]

Adam first preist, first Prophet and first Kinge
greate Lord of euery vegetable thinge
true Image of his God whose awfull brow
made euery creature wth Obedience bow.
[5] A heauen on Earth a litle world of wonder
Ah' where's the power can bringe this Monarch vnder.
And doth hee still theise rich endowments hold!
more worth then mynes of purest pearle and gould
Noe' hee is falne turn'd meere Antipodes
[10] and more then subalterne to each of theise
Yet not soe falne as to his endlesse harmes
but slipt from Iustice ire, to mercyes armes
If this extent of paper could suffice
to show how Adam fell how hee might rise
[15] Good reuerend Father I will doe my best
and where I fayle doe yow supply the rest
A songe of eight tymes three parts I would singe
assist my feeble Muse heauens mighty Kinge
And grant my pen portraict true harmony
[20] wth out a discord in Diuinitye
First the createinge Trinitye diuine
whom all men must adore, none can define
In man beloued a Trinitye created
whose power a fiuefould trinitye rebated
[25] and headlong threw him from fælicitye
to this deaths confines where wee grouelinge lye
Opprest wth greife, calamitye dispayre
to wch each sonne of Adam now is heyre

	The trinitye this litle world did fill
[30]	was vnderstandinge memory & will
	A type of that greate Trinitye aboue
	to deck Gods darlinge Man and show his loue
	That beinge adornd wth this especiall grace
	hee might supply the fallen Angells place
[35]	whoe wth a (fiat) fram'd this < > worlds huge masse
	might if hee would bringe greater things to passe
	Three tymes fiue Vultures sett uppon this Swanne
	this marble Architect this braue-made-man
	And soe defild the soules cheife facultyes
[40]	That shee (poore Queene) wth lamentable cryes
	bewayles theyr treason, and heauens ayde implores
	Mercy waytes euer at repentance Doores
	See theise six monsters that wth irefull stinge
[44]	did almost wound to death o^r Quondam Kinge
1	Suggestion, consent, and custome brought
2	weaknes, and blyndnesse, and defiled thought
	whoe like to Cadmus teeth did still increase
	hatchinge more Babells to disturbe mans peace
	A threefould species of this horrid crue
[50]	inuade man's memorie and its power's subdue
	Opinionated, idle, burthensome
	whose fond chymæra's doe surchardge the roome
	where figures of creation & redemption
	should fixe to tell the Soule, of Gods intention
[55]	Loe now tis but the Magazine of scrappes
	wch foolish obseruation neately wrapps
	to make a signe at doore of some rich masse
	where inly dwells a poore and blinded Asse
	The busy memory < >beateinge the rocks
[60]	gathers but foame from theyr hard-curled locks
	Much like to Chimicks dreames in So'ls perfection
	whose coabations neuer gaine proiection
	Though vrgd wth Vulcan 'gainst cucurbite glasses
	draw but a fowle Witch from fayre virgin Ashes
[65]	Uppon the will a threefould Monster lyes
	concupiscence of flesh, lust of the eies
	the worlds tormentinge fury (pride of life)

[18^v]

LADY ANN SOTHWELL

the will is now become theyre passiue wife
Leeseinge their power as by theise traytors bounde
[70] wills wth out power, gett's noe inch of grownde
Tis well depraued Will, hir first power misses
least Midas like wee choake o^rselues wth wishes
But see the Prince of the soules facultyes
is one of theise deprau'd Triumviris
[75] The Iudge and high distinguisher of causes
is falne' into inextricable Mazes.
The vnderstandinge whose high dignitye
hath lost the truth of perspicuitye
Tos't, and turmoyld and rackt on Ixions wheele
[80] still Tantalized and doth euer reele
Twixt truth and falshood, t'wixt ye good and ill
profitt, disprofitt, crawleinge upp the hill
For beinge blinde and falne ^ <to> a Meander
in tremblinge feare, and terror hee must wander
[85] Or elce lye still as dead as in distraction
But Adam rise', virtue consists in action
Open those euerlastinge gates whose Center
leades to thy heart & lett Iehouah enter
heare and reioyce what truth to thee hath sayd
[90] The womans seed shall breake the serpents head
Behould thy Scala Cæli to thy blisse
whose toppe 'boue Cælum Empiræum is
Behould three thrones directinge thy ascension
[94] gainst whome Infernall Dis hath noe preuention.
1 The first is fayth whose eies like burneinge tapers
whose fyery wings disperse these foggye vapours
Ore-walkeinge fyery Ouens, like flowry feilds
playeinge wth Lyons, as boyes play wth keeles
This is the hande that houlds the promisd grace
[100] the eie that lookes redemption in the face
2 The next is hope, the sick soules skilfull leach
that cures as fast as <fast as> folly makes a breach
builds bravely vpp what Tyrants doe destroy
counts all Aflictions in the world a toy
[105] takes upp the widdowes teares, & Orphanes cries
and makes them heauens accepted sacrifice

[19^r]

THE WORKS OF THE

3   The third is loue, (oh' all sufficient loue
exhalleinge earth to crowne the Orbes aboue
Drawes God from heauen to earth where mortalls dwell
[110]   whoe wing'd wth loue flyes through the gates of hell
strange Metamorphoser whose high power can
make man a God, and make a God a man
high handed Elohim built loues sacred nest
feathringe hir younge in the Almightyes brest
[115]   whose Topographick hee y^t can surprise
may hould his state aboue the Hierarchyes
Now Adam out of Edens place of pleasure
I leaue thee in more high more happy treasure
expectinge there wth ioy to heare thee singe
[120]   An Halleluiah to heauens glorious Kinge
whose sweete resultance cordinge wth the spheres
may wth delight rauish o^r mortall eares. /
        ffinis

An Elegie written by the Lady A: S: [19^v]
to the Countesse of London Derrye.
supposeinge hir to be dead by
hir longe silence.

Since' thou fayre soule, art warbleinge to a spheare,
from whose resultances, theise quickned weere.
since', thou hast layd that downy Couch aside
of Lillyes, Violletts, and roseall pride,
[5]   And lockt in marble chests, that Tapestrye
that did adorne, the worlds Epitome,
soe safe; that Doubt it selfe can neuer thinke,
fortune, or fate hath power, to <breake> ^{make} a chinke.
Since', thou for state, hath raisd thy state, soe farr,
[10]   To a large heauen, from a vaute circular,
because', the thronginge virtues, in thy brest,
could not haue roome enough, in such a chest,
what need hast thou<ght>? theise blotted Lines should tell,
soules must againe take rise, from whence they fell,

LADY ANN SOTHWELL

[15] From Paradice, and that this earths Darke wombe?
is but a wardrobe till the day of Dome?

To keepe those wormes, that on hir^r bosome<s> bredd,
till tyme, and death, bee both extermined,
Yet in thy passage, fayre<,> soule', let me know
[20] what things thou saw'st in riseinge from below.?
Whether that Cynthia regent of the flood
wth in hir Orbe admitt of mortall brood?
Whether the 12 Signes serue the Sun for state?
[24] Or elce confine him to the Zodiaque!
   <caret> And force him retrograde to bee the nurse
———(whoe circularly glides his oblique course)
Of Alma Mater, or vnfreeze the wombe
of Madam Tellus? wch elce Proues a tombe,
whether the starrs be Knobbs uppon the spheres?
[30] Or shredds compos'd of Phœbus goulden hayres?
Or whether th'Ayre be as a cloudy siue?
the starrs be holes through wch the good soules driue?
whether that Saturne that the 6 out topps
sitt euer eat<>inge of the bratts of Opps?
[35] Whose iealousye is like a Sea of Gall
vnto his owne Proues Periodicall<,>?
But as a glideinge star whoe falls to earth
Or louers thoughts, soe soules ascend theyr birth,
wch makes mee thinke, that thyne had noe one notion,
[40] of those true elements, by whose true motion;

All things haue life, and death, but if thy_∧ ^{ne}<nine> eyne',
should fix a while uppon the Christalline. /
Thy hungrye eye, that neuer could before,
see, but by fayth, and faythfully adore,
[45] should stay, to marke the threefould Hierarchye,
differinge in state, not in fælicitye
How they in Order, 'bout Iehoua moue,
In seuerall Offices, but wth one loue,
And from his hand, doe hand, in hand come downe,
[50] till the last hand, doe heads of mortalls crowne.
Fayne would I know from some that haue beene there?
what state or shape cælestiall bodyes beare?

For' Man, to heauen, hath throwne a waxen ball,
In wch hee thinks h'hath gott, true formes of all,
[55] And, from the forge howse, of his fantasie,
hee creates new, and spins out destinye.
And thus, theise prowd wormes, wrapt in lothsome rags,
shutt heauens Idea upp, in letherne baggs.
Now' since in heauen are many Ladyes more,
[60] that blinde deuotion busyely implore,
Good Lady, freind, or rather louely Dame,
if yow, be gone, from out this clayie frame,
tell what yow know, whether th' Saynts adoration?
will stoope, to thinke on dusty procreation,
[65] And if they will not, they are fooles (perdye)
that pray to them, and robb the Trinitye,
The Angells ioy in o[r] good conuersation,
yet see vs not, but by reuerberation,
And if they could, yo[w] s[ts] as cleere eies haue,
[70] if downe yow looke to earth, then to the graue,
Tis but a Landkipp, more, to looke to Hell
in viewinge it, what strange thinges may yow tell?
From out that Sulphrous, and bitumeous lake,
Where Pluto doth his Tilt, and Tournay make,
[75] Where the Elizium, and theyr Purgatorye
stande, like two suburbs, by a Promontarye;
Poets, and Popleings, are æquippollent,
both makers are, of Gods, of like descent,
Poets makes blinde Gods, whoe with willowes beates them,
[80] Popelings' makes Hoasts of Gods, & euer eates them.
But let them both, Poets & Popleings, passe
whoe deales too much wth eyther, is an Asse,
Charon' conduct them, as they haue deuised.
the Fall of Angells, must not bee disguised,
[85] As', tis not tirrany, but loueinge pittye,
that Kings, build prisons, in a populous Cittye,
Soe', the next way, to fright vs back to good,   [20[v]]
is to discusse the Paynes, of Stigian flood.
In Eue's distained nature, wee are base,
[90] And whipps perswade vs more, then loue, or grace,
Soe', that if heauen, should take a way this rodd,

LADY ANN SOTHWELL

God would hate vs, and, wee should not loue God,
For as afliction, in a full fedd state,
like vinegar, in sawces, doe awake
[95]   dull Appetites; and makes men feed the better,
soe when a Lythargye, o^r braynes doth fetter,
the onely way, to rouse againe o^r witts,
is, when the Surgions cheifest toole, is whips,
Brasse hath a couseninge face and lookes like gould
[100]   but where the touchstone comes it cannot hold.
That Sonne of ours, doth best deserue our rent,
that doth $\overset{\text{w}^{\text{th}}}{\wedge}$ Patience beare, o^r chastisement,
Each Titmouse, can salute the lusty Springe,
and weare it out, wth ioyllye reuellinge,
[105]   but yor pure-white, and vestall clothed swan,
sings at hir death, and neuer sings but than,
O noble minded bird, I envy thee,
for thou hast stolne, this high borne note from mee.
But‘ as the Prophett, at his M^{rs} feete,
[110]   when hee ascended, up, the Welkin fleete
Watcht'; for his cloake, soe euery bird, & beast,
When princely Adam, tumbled from the nest,
catcht, from his knoweinge sowle, some qualitie,
and humbly kept it, to reedifye
[115]   theyr Quondam kinge, and now‘, man goes to schoole,
to euery Pismire, that proclaymes him foole,
But stay my wandringe thoughts? <a>’las <whether>$\overset{\text{where}}{\wedge}$ wade I?
In speakeinge to a dead, a sencelesse Lady
Yow Incke, and pap_er_, be hir passeinge bell,
[120]   The Sexton to hir knell, be <Answer’d well,> Anne Southwell.

An: Epitaph vppon Cassandra MackWilliams wife to Sr Thomas [21^r]
    Ridgway Earle of London Derry. by y^e Lady A: S

Now let my pen bee choakt wth gall.
since I haue writt Propheticall
I wondred‘, that the world did looke,
of late, like an vnbayted hooke
[5]   Or as a well whose springe was dead
I knew not‘, y^t her soule was fledd

28   THE WORKS OF THE

Till that the mourneinge of hir Earle
did vindicate, this deare lost pearle.
           starr gasears
Yo <> ‘∧ <Astronomers> that view the skyes?

[10]   saw yow of late a newstar rise?
Or can yow by yor Art discouer
hir seate neere‘ the Cælestiall mouer?
She is gone, that way, if I could finde her,
and hath not left, hir match behind hir,

[15]   I'le prayse noe more, hir blest condic_i_on,
but follow hir, wth expedition. /
               A: S:

Written in commendations of Mr Coxe (the Lecturer of Acton) his
booke of the birth of Christ.

Thou faythfull Harrold of the morne
Peters remembrancer, the Lyons terror
The blessed'st babe y^t ere did wombe adorne
is by thy pen pourtray'd a curious mirrour

[5]   Embellished wth Lillyes whose support
are verdant pedestalls & doe import
Goodnes & constancye must grow together
If eyther part asunder, both doe wither
              A:S:

[10]   But like Rebecca's Twins wthin the Mother
doe strucgleinge seeke to murther one another. /

          [Henry King, "The Exequy"]   [21^v]

An Elegie Writen by Mr Barnard brother to M^{r}es Jernegan
                       y^t dyed at
                           Acton

Accept thou Shrine of my dead Sainte
Instead of Dirges this complainte
& for sweete flowers to crowne thy hearse
receiue a strow of weepeinge verse

[5]   from thy greiu'd freind whom thou might see
quite melted into teares for thee
Deare loue since thy vntimely fate
my taske hath beene to meditate

LADY ANN SOTHWELL

On thee, on thee thou art ye booke
[10] the library whereon I looke
though almost blind for thee lou'd clay
I languish out not liue the day
vseinge noe other excersise
then what I practise wth my eies
[15] by wch wett glasses I finde out
how lazeilye tyme creepes about
to one y^t mournes, this onely this
my excersise & busines is
soe I compute ye weary howers
[20] wth sighes dissolued into showers
nor wonder though my tyme run thus
backward & most preposterous
Thou hast benighted mee thy Sett
this Eue of blacknes did begett
[25] whoe wert my day thou ouercast
before thou hadst thy noonetyde past
And I remember must in teares
thou scarce had seene soe many yeares
As day tells howers by thy blest Sun
[30] my loue & fortune first did run
But thou wilt neuer more appeare
folded wth in my hemisphere
Since both this light & motion
like a fledd starr is fallen & gone
[35] & 'twixt mee & my soules deare wish
an earth now interposed is
wch such a strange eclipse doth make
as nere was read in Almanack
I could allow thee for a tyme
[40] to darken mee & my sadd clyme
weere it a moneth, a yeare or ten
I would thy exile wayte till then
And all y^t space my mirth adiourne
soe thou wouldst promise a returne.
[45] And puttinge of thy ashy shrouds
at last disperse this sorrowes cloude
But woe is mee the longest Date

to narrow is to calculate
Those emptye hopes, neuer shall I
[50] be soe much' blest as to Descrye
A glimpse of thee till y^t day come
wch schall ye earth to Cinders dome
And a feirce feauer shall calcine
the body of this world like thine
[55] My litle world, that fitt of fyer
Ouer our bodyes shall aspire
To our soules blisse then wee shall rise
& view o^r selues w^{t}h clearer eies
In y^t calme region where noe night
[60] can hide vs from each others sight
Meane tyme thou hast hir earth, much good
may my harme doe thee, since it stood
wth heauens will I might not call
hir longer myne, I giue thee all
[65] my short liu'd right & interrest
in hir whoe liueinge I lou'd best
most freely though thou see mee weepe
I giue thee what I could not keepe
bee kinde to hir & pray thee looke
[70] thou write wthin thy doomes Day booke
Each parcell of this raritye
wthin thy Caskett shrynde doth lye
see y^t thou make thy reckoninge straight
& yeeld hir back againe by waight
[75] for thou must audit on thy trust
each grayne & atome of hir dust
as thou wilt answere him y^t lent
not gaue thee my deare monument
Soe close ye grownd & touch hir shade
[80] black curtaynes drawne my bride is layde
sleepe on my loue in thy could bedd,
neuer to be disquieted
my last good night, thou wilt not wake
till I thy fate shall ouertake
[85] till age or greife or sicknes must
marry my body to y^t Dust

LADY ANN SOTHWELL

31

It soe much loues & fill ye roome
my heart keepes emptye in thy tombe
Stay for mee there I will not fayle
[90]   to meete thee in y^t hollow vale
& thinke not much of my delay
I am all ready on ye way
And follow thee wth all ye speede
Desire can make or sorrow breede
[95]   Each minute is a short Degree
& euery hower a step towardes thee
At night when I betake to rest
Next morne I rise neerer my west
Of life, almost by eight howers sayle
[100]   then when sleepe breath'd his drowsy gale
Thus from ye Sun my bottome steares
& my dayes compasse downewards beares
nor labour I to stem ye tyde
through wch twards thee I swiftly slyde
[105]   Tis true wth shame & greife I yeeld
thou like ye Van first tooke ye feild
And gotten halfe ye Victorye
by this aduenturinge to dye
before mee, whose yeares might craue
[110]   a iust præcedence in ye graue
But heark my pulse like a soft drume
beates my approach, tells thee I come
And slow how ere my marches bee
I shall at last sitt downe by thee
[115]   The thought of this bidds me goe on
& wayte my dissolution
wth hope & comfort, deare forgiue
the cryme, I am content to liue
Deuided wth but halfe a heart
[120]   till wee shall meete & neuer part
      Finis. /

What if I wante the dross of Tagus Strann   [22^r]
That doth becrampe the mvddie minde of man
It is some ease to scape those hungrie flyes

That ever haunte the doore wheare treasure lyes
[5] Wante I those beames; that Hellin Could discover.
What have I lost; some base addulterouse lover;
O tis a happie blest necessitie;
That frees the soule; from hell bredd aggonie;

A letter to ye Duches of Lineox; from the
Ladie Anne Southwell:

Vouchsafe this fauor; as to tell me how;
your princes fares; to whom all hartes doe bow
Not for her tytles; or her giftes of fortune
But for her humble Sweetness; doth importune
[5] Shes a Temple; where the blessed trine;
Inthrone themselves; and make her glorie shine
Nor shall I faile; to let the world $_\wedge^{\text{to}}$ knowe
How much vnto; her gracefull grace; I owe

An Epitaph vpon the king of Bohemia; written
by the ladye Anne Southwell:

Here lyes a king, and gods anoynted
by fate a Pilgrim poore appoynted
Who liued his death; and dyed his life
now pittie leads vs to his wife
[5] Whose many griffes; and good desarte
makes eich man weare a wounded harte.
For he with reason is not blesst
that pitties not (goodness) distrest

An Epitaph vpon ye king of Swede /

Maliciouse fate enuyinge humaine glorie
hath rent the Dyadem from Chiuallrie
Leauinge the subiect of a woeful storie
to fright the eares of all possteritie
[5] Mars wee haue lost thy only sonne and heire
See thou him stelifyed in highest Sphere
Blew eyed Bellona teares her amber tress

LADY ANN SOTHWELL   33

to see oure Champion, and her darrlinge Quelld
And vowes his like the earth shall near rebless
[10] but he shall liue and dye vnparalleld
    Fame swoulne with greeff, resoundes his prayes so lowde
    that nothing but eternitye Can Clowde
The widdowe earth Imbalmes his Corpes in teeres
and on her Coutch of Ibbonie lyes Mourninge
[15] Hopeing to frame a deludge for her feares
    inraged with greefe against all Coumforte spurninge
    Each eye doth hate that light that letts him see
    gloriouse Gusstauus sadd Catastrophe.

Come forth foule Monster, at truthes barr to stand   [22ᵛ]
hould vp thy leperose, and Infected hand

Enuie, what arte thou answer me, and tell
    A flame of hell

                    and   [S]
[5] Whoe tippt thy tounge with Infamie <of> ∧ euill
    O The diuell
That ould false Mvrtherar throne from the Skye
    Euen such am I
From what brutte beast, may I thy name decline
[10]   a filthie Swine
In curiouse feelds of flowers which please thy sence
    Some excrements
Flyst thou all sweetness; sure thy breth doth stinck
    Worss then a sinck
[15] In good, Societie, how dost thou rest
             as doth   [S]
    <I breed> ∧ the pest
What antidote, against thee must be worne
    Contemte and Scorne
        may thy blacke   [S]
But what <shall thy> Charectars deface
         e   god and his   [S]
[20]   <euen -arb of> ∧ Grace
Dost thou know this, and willt thou still acost
    Shame found, is lost
How many feet, may such a monster mooue
    Pride, and selff loue

[25]	Hast thou no winges, to raise thy<r> horrid frame	

[25] Hast thou no winges, to raise thy<r> horrid frame
                    yes, Spotted fame
                                           dies   [S]
      What help hast thou when her false ecquode <eyes>
                    Imp them wth lyes
      What dost thou gaine, by this the worlds vexation
[30]   Hell; and damnation

      Thou rack of honor, and of Innocence
                                        <Thou Imp of hell, & nurss of all offenc.>
      Thou Imp of hell and nurss of all offence

      Thou damm of wrath, of hatred, and of murther
      being placed in hell, who would pursue thee further
[35] hence from the barr with all thy damned traine
      to fflagidon, and there for aye remaine
      To shew the Iustice of this Condemnation
      read but a little of the accusation
      T'was he in Paradise gaue God the ly
[40] telling, rebelliouse Eue; she should not dy
      T'was he that lent to cruell Caine the darte
      to wound his brother Abels tender harte
      T'was he that filld the world with such, sedition
                                of
      that God repented ∧ oure Composition
[45] And in his anger Sent a mightye flood
      turninge the stream of Mankynd (back) to mudd

              An Epitaph vpon the Countess of   [23^r]
                    Sommersett

      To tell the shrine that its faire saint is gone
      alass tis Deff<-nes> & <like> deaths Compannion
      Since shee fled hence see how ye world doth looke
      naked, and poore, like an unbayted hoocke
[5]   Or‘ as a ringe, whose Diamont is lost
      Or as an euidence‘, whose lines are crost
      Or as a lampe, wheras the light is dead
      Or as a nest, from whence ye birdds are fled
      Or as a hiue, the hony hid awaye
[10] Or as the world depriued of the daye
      Or as the moone Eclipssed of her light

LADY ANN SOTHWELL

Or as the limmes when liffe hath taken flight
Or as a Well, when dryed is the springe
Or as a Cadge, wherin no birdd doth singe
[15] Or as a spraye from whence the rose is refft
Or Quiuer where, there is noe arrowe lefft
Such is the world, such to my sences bee
all <her> worldly gaudes since shee was refft from mee
Death thou art nothinge but a meere preuation
[20] yet bringest allthinges to anighillation
Hadst thou bine aught thou hadst not bine thus Cruell
to rend ffrom earth, Natures admired Iuell
But shall I hate, or fly thee for this deed
O thou liues middwife (no) bouldly proceed
[25] Thou art that Laudenum that layes in steep
all oure afflictions in the lapp of slee'p
Now her Immortall and well tempored soule
viewes thy defyence as an ydle scrole
Nor doth shee feere, or hate thee, for in Ioue
[30] All her affections are transformed to loue
Thou didst her good; tis wee retaine the sorrowe
wee haue the night, and shee hath gained the morrowe
All peace attend my deere, till that assise
when He shall see thee, in true glorie ryse
[35]   Her Epitaph
    Heere lyes Interrd a Princly Dame
    the Fenix of great Hawardes name
Francis the faire, Spouse to Earle sommersett
to whose true worth all penns doe ly in dett

*   Only eight soules, the waued tost Church did keepe   [23ᵛ]
    and yet to one of them, this beast did Creepe
In Curssed Cham enuye, disdaine, awaik<t>ed
    and made him scorne, his adged father naked
[5] And thus with Iron hooffes he trots the round
    and may almost in euerye place be found
But shall I tell you, where he takes deep roote
    the trinitie; will neuer sett in foote
Can enuye, and true loue, liue in one brest
[10]   can Doues and Serpents harbour in one nest

One heaun in peace, hould Michell and the Dragon
    one house, giue rest vnto the Arke and Dagon
One tounge Confess Iehoua, and base Melchon
    Iacob and Esau wrastled in one wombe
[15]   So truth and falshood Cannot hould one Roome
    but Eich to other giues Consumtion
Let Carnall men, ly snoreinge as secure
    and scorne Gods Iudgments, in their acts Impure
The are asleepe, what trumpett can awake them
[20]   to tell as death doth leaue them, Iustice thakes them
Tell them of God or heauen, you h<ad>r as good
    tell them of Skogine, or of Robin Hood
Their Cammell sines, <seem> to them seemes little flyes
    bycause the Diuell hath put out both their eyes
[25]   Sometymes to Church their giddie feet doe wander
    and hear the preachar tell (gods) sloe to anger
Then their presumption doth on tipptoes stand

[Henry King, "An Elegy upon ... Gustavus Adolphus"]   [24ʳ]

Like a cold fatall sweat which vshers death
My thoughts hang on mee, and labouring breath
Stopt vp with sighs, my phantsy bigg with woes
feeles two twinnd Mountaines struggle in their throwes
[5]   Of boundless sorrow one, to'ther of Sinne,
for less lett no one rate it, to beginne
Where honour ends in great Gustavus flame,
That style burnt out and wasted to a name
Does barely liue with vs, as when the stuffe
[10] Which fedd it, failes, the taper turnes to snuffe
With this pore snuffe, this ayrie shadowe wee
Of fame and honour must contented bee
Since from the vaine graspe of our wishes fledd
This gloriouse substance is, now hee is dead
[15]   Speake it againe, and lowder, lowder yett
Least whilest wee heare the sound wee shall forgett
What it deliuers lett hoarce rumor crye
Till shee so many ecchoes multiply
Those may like numerouse wittnesses confute

LADY ANN SOTHWELL

[20] Our vnbeleeuing soules, that would dispute
And doubt this truth foreuer; this one way
Is left our incredulity to sway,
To waken our deafe sence and make our eares
As open and dilatate as our feares:
[25] That wee may feele the blowe, and feeling greiue
At what wee would not faine, but must beleeue,
And in that horrid fayth behould the world
From her proude height of expectation hurl'd,
Stooping with him, as if shee stroue to haue
[30] No lower Center now, then Swedens graue.
　　　　O could not all thy purchas'd victories
Like to thy fame thy flesh immortalize
Were not thy vertue, nor thy valour charmes
To guard thy body from these outward harmes
[35] Which could not reach thy soule? could not thy Spiritt
Haue somewhat which thy frailty might inherit
From thy deviner parte, that death nor hate
Nor Enuies bulletts ere' could penetrate
Could not thy early trophees in strong fight
[40] Torne from the Dane, the Pole, the Muscouite
Which were thy triumphs seeds, as pledges sowne,
That when thy honours haruest was ripe growne
With full summ'd wing thou Falcon like wouldst fly
And cuffe the Eagle in the German sky,
[45] Forcing his Iron beake, and feathers feele
They were not proofe gainst thy victorious steele
Could not all these protect thee [&] preuaile
To fright the Coward death who oft grew pale
To looke thee, and thy battailes in the face:
[50] (Alas) the could not, Destinye gaue place
To none: nor is it seene that Princes liues
Can saued bee by their prerogatiues!
Noe more was thyne: who cloas'd in thy cold lead
Thus from thy selfe a mournefull lecture read
[55] Of mans short dated glory: learne you kings
you are like him but penetrable things.
Though you from demy-Gods deriue your birth,
you are at best but honourable earth,

And how ere sifted from that courser branne
[60]   which doth compound and knead the Common man
Nothing's immortall, or from earth refin'd
About you, but your office and your minde
Heere then breake your false glasses which prent
You greater then your maker euer meant
[65]   Make truth your mirrour now, since you finde all
That flatter you, confuted by his fall
          Yet since it was decreed thy liffes bright Sun   [24ᵛ]
Must bee ecclip'd ere thy full course was runne,
Bee proud thou did'st in thy black obsequies
[70]   With greater glory sett, then others rise
For in thy death as life: thou heldest one
Most iust and regular proportion
Looke how the Circles drawne by compass meete
Indivisibly ioyn'd from head to feete
[75]   And by continued poynts which them vnite
Growe at once circular and infinite
So did thy fate and honour now contend
To match thy braue beginning with thy end
Therfore thou hadst in stead of passing bells
[80]   The Drummes and Cannons thunder for thy knells
And in the feild thou did'st triumphing dye
Closing thy eyelidds with a victory,
That soe by thousands, who there lost theire breath
King-like thou might'st be waited one in death,
[85]   Liu'd Plutarch now and would of Cæsar tell
Hee could make none but thee his paralell,
Whose tyde of glory Swelling to the brimme
Needs borrowe no<ne> adition from him
When did great Iulius in any clyme
[90]   Atcheiue so much? and in so small a tyme,
Or if hee did yet shalt thou in that land
Single for him, and vnexampled stand
When O're the Germans first his Eagle towr'd,
What saw the legions which one them he powr'd
[95]   But massy bodyes, made their swords to trye
Subiects not for his fight, but slauery.
In that so vast expanded peice of ground

LADY ANN SOTHWELL

(now Swedens Theater and Tombe) hee found
Nothing worth Cæsars valour, or his feare
[100] No conquering Army, or a Tilly there
Whose strength, nor wiles, nor practise in the warre
Might the fierce torrent of thy triumphs barre;
But that thy winged sword twice made him yeild
Both from his trenches beat, and from the feild
[105] Besydes the Romaine thought hee had done much
Did he the banke of Rhenus only touch
But though his march was bounded by the Rhyne,
Not Oder, nor the Danube thee confine
And but thy frailty did thy fame preuent
[110] Thou hadst thy conquest strecht to such extent
Thou migh'tst Vienna reach, and afte spann
From Mulda to the Baltique Ocean
But Deat hath spann'd thee nor must wee deuine
What heire thou leaust to finish thy designe
[115] Or whoe shall thee succeede as Champion
For liberty, and for Religion
Thy taske is done, as in a watch the Spring
Wound to the height relaxes with the string;
So thy Steele nerues of conquest from their steepe
[120] Ascend declin'd, ly Slackt in thy last sleepe,
    Rest then triumphant soule, foreuer rest
And like the Phenix in her Spicye nest
Embalm'd with thyne owne merritt, vpward fly
Borne in a Cloude of perfume to the skye,
[125] Whilst as in deathless vrnes each noble mynde
Treasures thy ashes which are left behinde
And if perhaps noe Cassiopean sparke
which in the north did thy first rising marke
Shine on thy hearss the breath of our iust praise
[130] shall to the firmament thy vertues raise
Then fix and and kindle them into a starre
Whose influence may crowne thy glorious warre. /

The more my soule doth shrinke from loue, ye more, loue doth   [25^r]
    inflame her
  and when I seeke to finde the cause, t'is, Cos: amoris amor

I sett my reason Centenall, that passions may<ht> not shame her
who tells mee they like shadowes pass, for Omnia Vincit amor
shee fly
[5]   If with Angellick winges from hence, ∧ can mortalls blame her
since from heauens lampe comes all her light, for Cos: amoris amor
Then let her mount, with faith, hope, loue, where sine nor death can
lame her
where all afflictions end theire rage, for Omnia Vincit amor.

My loue from Cherubs soueraintye, was in a manger laid
[10]   the second of the Trinitye did soiorne with a maide
Went from the Cratch, vnto the Cross, from Cross, to graue and hell
only to free my guiltye soule, that there was Iudg'd to dwell
Now is the hand writt cancelled, the debt it trulye paid
the Iudge is fullye satisfyed; My soule be not dismaide
[15] Now death, and hell haue lost theire stinge, the graue's ye bed of rest
Or gate to let the ffaithfull in, to Christ for euer blest. /

Behold the purchase, true loue doth Inherit,
Christ Iesus is the price of o^r: saluation,
And for a pledge he leaues his holye Spiritt
[20] him selff a full rewarde, (Oh) hy donation
Then let no other loues, my soules loue waite,
but to thee, in thee, and for thy deere sake. /

[25ᵛ is blank]

Vnless himselfe against himselfe weare bent   [26ʳ]
and gaue the wound by breach of testament
Or doth he still theise high Indowments hould
more rich then Tagus Strann, or Ophirs gould
[5]   No he is fal'n, turned meere Antippodes
and more then Subbalterne to each of theise
Gen: Cha 3.
yet not so fal'n, as to his endless harmes
vers 15.
but slippt from Iustise Ire to mercies armes
If this extentt of papar could suffice
[10]   to show how Adam fell, how he must rise
My noble Neighbour I will doe my best
and wheare I faile, please you supplye the rest,
Whoe hath a minde and hoards it vp in store
is poorer then a beggar at the doore

LADY ANN SOTHWELL   41

[15]   Let your cleare Iudgment, and well tempored soule
        Condemne, amend, or rattifye this scrole
   Twi'll prooue your fairest Monument and when
        your Marble ffailes, liue with the best of men
   If you haue lost your fflowinge sweete humiddities
[20]   and in a dust disdaine theise quantities
   Pass it to oure beloued Docter Featlye
        his tongue dropps honnye, and can doe it neatlye
   Meanetime a Durge of aight times three I singe
        assist my ffeeble muse, heauens mightie Kinge
[25]   And grante my penn portraite true harmonye
        Without a discorde in deuinitye,
   ffirst the creatinge trinitye diuine
        whom all men must adore none can define
   In Man beloued a Trinitye Created
[30]   whose power a fiuefoulde trinitye rebated
   And headlonge threwe him from ffelicitye
        to this deaths Confines where wee grouelinge lye
   Oprest with griefe, Calamitie dispaire,
        to which each sonne of Adam now is heyre
[35]   The Trinitye this little world did fill
        was vnderstandinge, Memorye, and will,
   A type of that great Trinitye aboue
        to deck Gods darlinge (man) and shew his loue
   That beinge adorned wth this especiall grace
[40]   he might supply the fallen Angells place
   Whoe with a (fiat) fram'd this worllds huge Masse
        might if he would bringe greater things to passe
   Three tymes fiue Vultures sett vppon this Swanne
        this Marble Eddifice this braue-made-man
[45]   And soe defyled the soules Cheife facultyes
        that shee (poore Queene) with lamentable cryes
   Bewayles their treason, and heauens ayde implores
        Mercy waytes euer at repentence doores
   See theise six Monsters that with irefull stinge
[50]   did almost wound to death our Quondam Kinge
   Suggestion, consent, and custome brought
        weaknes, and blindnesse, and defiled thought
   Whoe like to Cadmus' teeth did still increase

THE WORKS OF THE

hatchinge more Babells to disturbe mans peace
[55] A threefould species of this horrid crues
inuade Man's Memorie and it's power subdues
Opinionated, idle Burthensome
whose fond Chymæras doe Surcharge the roome

S^r. giue mee leaue to plead my Grandams cause.   [26ᵛ]
and prooue her Charter from Iehouæs Lawes.
Wherby I hope to drawe you ere you dye.
resolu'd
From a \<peruerse\> and wilfull herresye.
[5] In thinkinge ffemales haue so little witt
as but to serue men they are only fitt,
Wee haue one birth, one death, one resurection
one god, one Christe, one lawes subscribtion
Our bodies are as gould tane from your earth
[10] and soe are of a more refined birth
ffrom that read claye where Adam did resyde
precipitated, and well dullcifyed:
God tooke a Marble Piller and did build
a little world with all perfection fill'd
Gen: 2 Cha.
[15] And brought her vnto Adam as a bride
vers ye 22.
the text saith shee was taken from his syde
A symbolle of that syde from whence did flowe
Christ's spouse (the Church) as all wise men doe knowe
But Adam slept, as saith the historie
[20] vncapable of such a mistarie
And they sleepe still that doe not vnderstand
the curiouse ffabrick of th'almighties hand.
Gen: Cha: 2
God made a helper meete and can you think
vers. 18
a foole a help, vnless a help to sink
Gen: Cha: 5
[25] \<God called them Adam both, and did vnite
vers 2
both male and ffemale one hermophradite
And beinge one ther's none must dare to seuer
without a curss, what God hath ioyned together\>
Soe either count her wise, or him a foole
[30] or else Creation fail'd in a true rule

LADY ANN SOTHWELL

As they are one, I not account her wise
    for both of them turned fooles in Paradise
Which was the meerest foole is harde to tell,
    without Christs ayde, that must be knowne in hell.

[35]   Want wee the witt for stratagems of state
    those are but Anticks vnto time and fate
Or wante wee skill to purchase Crownes and thrones
    to ordaine lawes, vnite deuissions
Theise are but guades that makes men proude and iollie
[40]   damm'd in their skill prooues all but emptie follie
ffor whats our purchase if the world wee gaine
    and loose our soules in hells eternall paine
O 'tis a happie blest necessitie
    that barrs the soule from hell bredd aggonie
[45] Haue wee firme ffaith and hope of our saluation
    wee haue the happiest end of our Creation
But O poore Adam this thought makes mee sadd
    thy lefft syde is turned ffoole thy right syde madd

Gen: Cha 1th
    How comes thy glorye thus to be rebated,
verse 31
[50]   that weart at first so perfectly created
Thou wast a Priest, a Prophet, and a Kinge
    great lord of euery vigitable thinge
Gen. Cha. 1th
    True Image of thy god, whose awefull browe
vers. 27.
    made euerye Creature with obeydience bowe
[55]   A heauen one earth, a little world of wonder
a'h wher's the power could bringe this Monarck vnder

In this frayle worlde, where soules in earth are cladd,   [27^r]
& through the sences are made safe or sadd.
what greater honour or more comforte can
bee giuen to an honest harted man.
[5] then heauen-like virtue in like beautye sett
Without or feare to keepe, or paynes to gett.
Shall I that am assured to hold, & haue
both these in one, & all that I can craue
Shall I, deere life, that cannott liue without thee
[10] not rest content, but lett worse fortunes flowt mee?
O noe; I am not to my self soe cruell,

as to refuse soe rich, soe rare a iewell;
not blinde to see, nor sencelesse to regarde it
am I, though yett vnable to rewarde it.
[15] faultes of my will, Deere, though thou mayest impute,
to such as are not mine, thou must bee mute.
Thy truth, with truth, I can, & will repay,
vnto thy worth, I yeeld vnwilling way.
freely to mee, what others cannott hire,
[20] thou giuest in deede; I giue more in desire,
though not in worth; & is not this as much?
my gift is all I haue, thine is but such.
Thus am I fayne to lende my weakenes proppe
of argument, to match thy matchlesse toppe.
[25] which I am bold to doe, because I knowe
my soule in loue, is sett beyond the showe.
parte for respects & partely through feare
it lookes the lesse sett in soe high a spheare.
But when as time shall bringe loue neere thy center
[30] that it may safely bide the sweete adventure
then will it bee the fayrer much in seeming
yf it may looke soe in thy fayre esteeming.
When fate shall all the putt-betweenes remoue
then shall our deedes fullfill the face of loue.
[35] Till when, like to the master that attends   [27ᵛ]
the happye windes which masters all his endes
with patience I will readye rigged abide
for first advantage of the winde & tide.
to bringe mee to the longe desired porte.
[40] which once attayned, shall make my life a sporte.
yf once I cast but anchor in thy brest
Ile stoe my treasure all within that chest.
A voyage that will recompence in gaynes
all former hazardes, patience & paynes.

The ffirst Commandement.   [28ʳ]
Thou shalt haue noe other gods before mee

Raise vp thy ffacultyes my Soule ti's time
to Wake ffrom Idleness the Childe of death

LADY ANN SOTHWELL

Mount to the heauens, and ther thy wings subblime
wheare bodies liue, not bound to hassard breath
[5]   And being dipt in heauens Selestiall Springes
         My penn shall portrait Supernaturall thinges

All your respects of earth, O$_\wedge^r$ earthly wightes
encampe your selues in reareward of this battle
And when I will historifye your knights,
[10]   Echo and Parratt, ayd mee wth your prattle
         ffor yor traditions are of power enough
         to Magnifye such momentanye stuffe,

Now as a ladder which on ground is fixt
whose topp leades to the topp of some high tower
[15]   Soe shall my knees of earth, with earth bee mixt
         my soule with reuerence shall ascend gods bower
              fayth, hope, loue, zeale, assist my limber winges
              you climax terræ to the kinge of kinges.

And ere I further goe, I heauens Implore
[20]   that wth artes proude carieers I doe not mount
         but humbly pace by clensing Iordans shore
         least pride for zeale stand in thy iust account
              nor for vayne glorye of historian fame,
              crowne Ouids Idolls with wth Iehouaes name.

[25] A sicknes to, to much infecting paper
         to mix heauens milke with aconite of hell
         wee leaue the sunne and wander by a taper
         forsake gods worde and on vaine fables dwell
              Trye Seneca and Paule with one touchstone
[30]   Way Aristotle with wise Solomon.

Who wrott the grauest, Smoothest, highest style   [28ᵛ]
or who diues deepest in the sea of nature,
yf cloudes of error doe not truth beguile
Our reason quickly will resolue this matter
[35]   why those, whose eyes did neuer see the light
              should want the skill to hitt the marke aright,

Knowledge is a fayre vsher in the way
to happines, and mans eternall rest

but if fayth helpe not out, it's lame essaye
[40] oure deepest reach is but a fruitlesse iest
    fish, beastes, and birdes, not fayling in y^t parte
    haue bine mans schoolemaster in many an arte,

Presumptuous knowledge was the angells fall
presumptuous knowledge wrought poore Adams woe
[45] O sacred wisdome, iudge and guide of all
true limiter, how farre ech witt should goe
    with mediocritye asist my flight
    as free from fogges, as farre from winges to light

With feet of claye to enter the most holye
[50] or watterye balles to stare against the Sunne
alas it is but blinde presumptuous follye
a porchase sought, by which wee are vndon
    let mee be of ^{thy}ᴧ Court, there will I rest
    leauing thy secrets, to thy sacred brest,

[55] Tis not my ayme to make a flight soe large
a lower strayne my humble thoughts intend
only to giue the eares a frendly charge
and tell how farre theyr facultyes extend
    for whose sake only are these verses framed
[60]   wherin I will aduenture to bee blamed.

Of those fiue handmaydes that attend the soule   [29ʳ]
by whoose embassage, shee the world doth knowe
full fraught with subiects to her high controule
ther's none that doth more faithfull seruice showe
[65] then doth the eare, through whose incircletts runne
the knowledge of our neuer setting sunne.

Now since the obiect to the eare is breath
first breath that pearc'd the eare was breath deuine
the next the serpent, breathing breathlesse death
[70] O eare why did thy tunnell shape incline,
    broad to receaue and narrowe to retayne,
    th'infectiouse dampe, that poisond euery vayne

How canst thou cleere thee to thy wronged mates
whose bondage is of equall weight with thine

LADY ANN SOTHWELL

[75] that they were actors in their fatall states
foreseene, <by eye diuine> before 'twas done by eyes diuine
   this framed a way for iustice, mercye, grace
   and for lost earth, giues vs a better place.

Yf soe, why should the sonne, (whose father gaue
[80] a tenancye, or land in seruice held,
(which not performed, the childe becomes a slaue)
refuse to giue it back for freer feeld
   now wee haue lost our freedom in this earth
   god giues vs heauen by Christ in a new birth

[85] But stay, there are tenne steppes to this high throne
which are empau'd with tenne orbes or spheares
our reason reacheth but the Horizon,
fayth vnto cælum Empyreum beares
   Those are tenne precepts by Iehouah spoken
[90]   of which noe Iod or tittle may bee broken,
         esau -----   [29ᵛ]
Thou eare, the doore of euerlastinge life,
through,which the king of glorye is to enter,
who, like a bridegroome with his loued wife,
[95]   the pure thoughts, seated in thy hartes center
   who, when hee came, like tongues, downe from the spheares
   it was to meete, salute, and deck the eares

Lift vpp thy gates, and let th'almightye Ioue,
his sonne and spiritt, all one god eternall
[100] enter, who is the prince of peace, and loue,
fountayne of ioy, and shield from greefes infernall
   yet ere thou entertayne this gloriouse guest
   See that thy house bee cleane and purely drest

Then learne to knowe that sacred god aright
[105] who in his couenants, hath his will exprest
To knowe god
         and in mans knowing him, doth take delight
B e
   and for his knowledge doth pronounce him blest
      but them that know him not, his dreadfull ire
      doth threaten vengence with consuming fire

48   THE WORKS OF THE

[110]   Then next to knowinge god <it doth>, it doth behoue
          with all our soules, our heartes, our strength and powers
To loue god
           his sacred Maiestye wee deerely loue,
          giue him his due, that duely giues vs oures
             who sayth thou shalt adore noe gods but mee
[115]   t'was I that out of bondage sett thee free,

          Loue him for this, loue him with all thyne hearte
          for his rewardes, none but himselfe can tender
          and knowe hee doth reiect thy loue in parte,
          hee must haue all the loue thy hearte can render
[120]   Corriualls or Competitors with him
           in his owne creatures hee doth much contemne,
                     A: S

                                      [30ʳ is blank]

                                      [30ᵛ]

An abstract of The liues of the Romaine Empourers; as the haue bine
          related vnto vs by Plinie Plutarch; and Suetonius
          and first of the first;

          Fortie twoe yeares; before oure sauiours birth
          liued Iulius Ceasær greatest prince on earth
          Nature and fortune; stronglye did combinde
          to make this hero; darlinge of mankinde
[5]   In fiftie battles; he the Conquest wonn
          Iuli his daughter; made Pompeye his sonn
          but not his frend; for twixt them was such hate
          That eich did seeke; to ruine others state
          The kinge of Egipt; great Ptolamie
[10]   he slue; and gaue his sister soueraintie
          Faire Cleopatar; whoe bare him a sonn
          Cæsario h<a>ight; Egipts sucsession:
          Fiftie six yeares he liued; his peacfull breth
          Was but fiue monthes; then; treators gaue him deth
                bastard
[15]   Brutus his ∧ sonn; Cassius his frend
          Did in the Senate; giue; his glories end

          Who euer sawe himself but in a myrrour   [31ʳ]
          tis others eyes not ours weare out our vestures

LADY ANN SOTHWELL

and selfloue deemes all others actions error
then doth this sicknesse breede but these impostures
[5] pryde in our selues, envye to those looke on her
theft to all anymalls, to god dishonoure

for stately pallaces and sumptuous towers
in which wee are but tenants for a tyme
let not the eye with louinge lookes deeme ours
[10] since euery day doth witnesse oure declyne
man's but a passenger sent on an errand
that may not stay or steay^r beyond his warrant

When Ionas once tooke pleasure in his guoorde
which was but lent him for necessytye
[15] a woorme devourd it sent by his loude lorde
to make him knowe his h[ar]te was sett a wrye
god is a Iealous god and may not brooke
his loue vppon an other lou[e] shoulde looke

Why should the intellect in orbe of claye
[20] like to flesh flyes which some glasse bottels houlde
with lumbringe noyse, disturbe lyues quyet day
since all life is but one day often toulde.
this doth the sence the purer parte infect,
whose fervent loue, can harbour noe suspect

[25] Esteeme not goulde though colored like the soonne
of greater woorth, then it gaynes by opynion
the wise ‹man› slaue; that on his arrants runn
the fooles commander and his best loued mynyon
tis but the master bowle, in the woorlds game
[30] and yet men runn ‹with› sweate to touch the same.   [S]

Goolde takes the teares from oute the widdowes eye   [31ᵛ]
it gladds the soonne to digg the fathers graue,
it turnes all frendshipp into trecherye,
it makes the freest harte, become a slaue
[35] it is the actiue, to the passiue will
begetting vypers, that theyre parents kill'

God plaste this moulde in darke obscvrytye
and sure I thinck twas made the barrs of hell',
which men brake vp, with whome sprang all impuritie
[40]   for it this dust the servind now doth   [S]
        <and now for loue to it, in hell doth dwell,>
        <when Sallomon had spread his house with goulde>
        <Idolatrye waxt strong, his fayth grewe coulde.>
        Seing his shap was hat ful to mankind   [S]
[45]   he frams an obyect fittor to his mind   [S]

        Behould not troopes of servants with delyghte,
        if they bee good, they bee thy humble frends
        if badd, bee sure they will woorke the but despyghte
        they serue not thee, but theyre owne pryvate ends
[50]   they'll tosse thy honoure like a tennis balle.
        and beinge full, like leechese off they falle

        Thy woords must bee imprysoned in thy harte,
        thy wealth must searue, but theyre necessitye,
        as for theire loues, expect the poorest parte.
[55]   mans nature is, to hate servyllytie.
        and in thy vice, with smyles they'le seeme to stroke thee,
        onely to gayne the stronger cords, to choke thee.

        Thus is thy freedome, by thy follye bounde.
        thy thoughts confused, to gouerne theyr confusyon.
[60]   if thou bee sterne, that is theyr hatreds grounde.
        thy kindenes breeds contempt, and base intrusion,
        thy sinnes are doubled in thy sauiours sight,
        whoe doth commaund thou governe thyne aright.

        The vniuersall Church w^{c}h they assume
[65]   By their owe word is not Confynd to Rome

                                            as
        His couenants are twoefolde, $_\wedge$ woorks, and grace,   [32^r]
        on which his Iudgment and his mersy stands,
        and for his will, in lawe, must take full place
        hee in his soonne, doth pay and quitt the bands,
[70]   and wee in him made good, by imputation
        are set agayne in state, of our creation.

LADY ANN SOTHWELL

51

His sonne a seede, sent forth in tyme, to take
oure flesh, to satisfye, for flesh, offendinge.
as man for man did satisfaction make,

[75] as god to god his power in it extendinge.
this soonne, this sacryfice, doth pleading stand,
a preist, a Iudge, a savyoure, at his hande.

Yet neyther preist savyoure nor sacryfise

————————————————————
————————————————————
————————————————————
————————————————————

Whoe knowes him doth renew that perfect forme,
which knowledge of oureself, did first deface,

[85] his facultyes in woorking doth adorne,
and perfect good, doth make the vyle and base.
whoe to the darke confused Chaos, sayde.
bee bright, and vnyforme, and it was obeyde,

Knouledge the genus, or the primatiue

[90] of this all knowing power, that sitts aboue.
hath to his speties or deryvatiue.
feare, hope, and trust, service, and perfect, loue.
for whoe woold feare, serue, trust, or loue, that weight.
hee never k\<e>new by letter fame or sight

[95] Then next to knowinge god, it doth behooue,   [32ᵛ]
with all oure souls, our harte, our strenth, and powers,
his sacred maiestye, wee deerely loue
gyue him his deew, that deewly giues vs ours.
whoe sayest thou shalt adore noe god but mee,
          him   [S]

[100] gyue \<mee> thy harte, that gaue a harte to thee.

    I am thy god thatt brought
    thee oute of the house of bondage thou shalt haue noe others g[od]
                                        but mee.
  god   [S]
  \<I> tooke thee oute of claye, and gaue thee lyfe,   [S]
            his   [S]
  and shape like \<myne>, repleate with maiestye.
  those elements that in them selues haue stryfe,

in thy Compotion, houlde sweete simpathye.

[5] thou arte the abstract <or Epytomy ⌃of this glrious ball⌃ of his full> creasion   [S] [S]

the trw epitome of this grett all   [S]

<of all the others beauties made by mee>

his glolious [lot] but fore sins priuasion   [S]

Thou art the glasse, wherin <I> ⌃god⌃ doe behould,   [S] [<S>]

[10] <my> ⌃his⌃ full creation, and <my> ⌃his⌃ sperits face.   [S]

and though poore earth doe <my> ⌃his⌃ Idea hould.   [S]

that earth by it shall haue, immortall grace.

<the soule of plants and beasts remayne in thee,>

<one comprehending. both, was breathd from mee.>

[15] <when in an instansei from this hear mator>   [S] [S]
⌃cas n⌃

When that in fused part now bound inclaye   [S]

or <when shall be exchandid to ⌃an⌃ ⌃⌃ manie raye>   [S] [S]

Shall war the robe of a trancelusantraye   [S]

Which is a forming ⌃<thar>⌃ substance and doth moue,   [S]

[20] quicken and fill with life the bodyes parte.

it diues to hell, and scales the heavens aboue,

and yet it doth not from the body starte.

to know thy shape aright, doth passe thy witt,

<I> ⌃god⌃ and the woorld, are simbolisde in it.   [S]

[25] And though thy ⌃that⌃ soule, to formall dust bechayned   [S]

it hath noe forme, and yet all formes it taketh.

it <all> ⌃much⌃ conteynes, and yet it is conteyned   [S]

it moueth not, that all thy motion maketh.

thou as a mortall god, with ⌃god⌃ mee doest walke,   [S]

[30] god as immortall man, with thee doth talke.   [S]

he set the soonn, a loft the firmament   [S] [33ʳ]

gaue thee an eye, encountering that soonn.

<my>self ⌃him⌃ thy obiect, for <my soule> ⌃his <loue> will⌃ was bent   [S]

to loue thy face till thou away dids runn.

[35] and being gone my ⌃his⌃ onely soonne was slayne.   [S]

LADY ANN SOTHWELL

in going forth to fetch thee backe agayne

of loue he forth did sende [S]
the cumfrtor we [S]

his   <loue> [S]
<My> holy sperit <also I did send>
like to an humble doue, to bee thy staye.

to   he [S]
<and> tell thee I with mersy did attende

[40]   thy coming, and woold meete thee on the way.

he is   he [S]
<I am> thy god and <I> the woorde haue spoken,

his [S]
come and come safe, my woorde cannot be broaken

him   him [S]
Loue <mee> for this, and <mee> with all thy harte,

his   him [S]
for<my> rewards, none but <my> selfe can tender.

hee   th [S]
[45]   and know <I> doe reiect thy loue in parte,

he [S]
<I> must haue all the loue, thy harte can render.

hime [S]
corryuals or competitors, with <mee>,

u
<of my> owne creatures,<phy it> m∧<a>st not bee.
in his   he doth much conteme [S]

If< >wealth, ease, pleasure, honour. thou prefer,
[50]   more then thou doest Christ, and him crusifyed,
thy loue is loathsome, and thy soule doth err,

god [S]
thy voues are mocks, and thou to <mee> hast lyed,
thou sacrifisest to thyne owne delight;

god [S]
thou seruest not<mee>, but thyne owne apetite.

[55]   feare followeth next, which perfect loue doth breed,
but not that feare which sathan hath in hell',
which from the feare of torment doth proceede
but feare for loue, as louinge to doe well.

r
such feare is wisdome, and shall haue rewa< n>de,
[60]   as righteousnes in oure great gods regarde.

<feare him that oute of Eden Adam turned.   [33ᵛ]
feare him that into hell the Angels hurlde.
feare him that Sodom and Gomorah burned.
feare him that in his anger dround the woorld.

54   THE WORKS OF THE

[65]
feare want of feare for tis a fearefull thing
to fall into the hands of heauens great king,>

Then trust in him and florish like the spring,
or like the Cædar, by the ryver syde,
increase in corne, wyne, oyle, and each good thing,
[70]
thy store augmenting, like a swelling tyde.
whoes current, though it ouer flow the banckes,   [S]
thou shalt returne for all, but humble thanckes.
                              all   [S]

<God by his prouidence, his owne doth keepe;
[75]
strenthning theyre harts, in ever doing well',
though Iacob went to keepe his vncles sheepe,
that shepperd was, the chosen Israell',
opprest by Laban, <thretned> by his brother, hatid   [S]
                              is firmely statid   [S]
yet still his trustes in god, <and in noe other>   [S]

[80]
                 A note of <for> gods providence
                 freewill and predestenation
                 taken out of Saynt Augusten

Next serue him, none but him, and him aright,
false service, to the trew god doth displease;
[85]
trew service, to the false god, dyms his light.
whoe hath exprest himself, his woords are these,
(I am thy god,) thou shalt haue none but mee
t'was I, that oute of bondadge sett thee free'.

Then to that god whose power <he> each place doth fill
[90]
can saue, can kill, can make, and bringe to nought,
even for his greatnesse sake, obserue his will,
which hath in mersy, and in terrour taught.
come all and learne at oure Iehouahs scoole,
whoe hath an other god, is but a foole.

                 Thou shalt not make to thy self   [34ʳ]
                 any graven Image nor the likenes of anything

Noe man may see the face of god and liue
his back tipt Moses <f>vysage with a flame
then what symylitude shall uee him gyue

LADY ANN SOTHWELL

1   that yet want woords ^{for} to expresse his name

[5]   <w>h<o>e <on Mount> Horeb <made> it smoke and trembled [S] [S]

    it shewed noe forme; that <man> might <none> resembled [S] [S]

What base accounte make wee of this great lord

that carue our blockes <to immitat> his forme to immitate

    <to paynte or hew his Image like a snake>   [S]

[9]   heauen, earth, sea, hell, and all can not afforde

2   a forme that may his gloryes predicate

whoe loues his prince and makes a beastly creature

the heroglyfficke of his goodly feature

forbeare you blocks to forme you gods of woodd

the holy arke shall make youre Dagons fall,

[15]   you priests of Ball that swallow soe much bloodd

youre lyvers shall conuert it into gall'

3   noe flame shall fix vppon youre sacryfise

dead ashes shall bewray youre vyllanyes;

[19]   In terror for the hardnes of your harts

4   god wroght the lawe in the imparatiue moode

<1>   afflyction beating on youre steely parts

must tame your wanton thoughts and make them good

that rebell Sall agaynst all presepts spurned

from Sall to Pall gods terror quickly turned

[25]   sons   [S]

whoe cryes what shall I doe Ile preach thy lawes

Ile bee thy souldier and fight on thy syde

5   Ile bee thyne advocate and plead thy cause

my plea shall bee christ Iesus crusified

[30]   <this can the finger of thallmighty Ioue>

    <turne loue to hate and hate to perfect loue>

    the pas uis of our ^{natur} dulls our wite   [S] [S]

    that whipes perswade us mor then benifet   [S]

[34]   do thow for fear what the haue dun for   [S][34ᵛ]

    <Then for afflyction sake if not> for loue

6   venter with Dannyell to the Lyons de<nn>

and with those three that walkt afflyctions stoue

disdayne the Idoles made by hands of menn
hould them accursd that counte them laymens bookes
that teach but lyes and are but snarlinge hookes

[40]   thes four uersic cum in hear   [S]

looke not on Idoles lest they breed infections
and hurte with eying like an harlots eye
when chosen David fought with the Philistins
7   hee tooke much care to burne theyre Imagery
[45]   the Edomits was by Amazyah slayne
yet theyre lost pupitts conquerd <t>hym agayne

bow not vnto these mamitts with thy knee
hee that made all let him all woorship haue
[49]   tis all hee seeks it is thy keepers fee
8   deny it not if thou thy flocks wooldst saue
and shooldst thou offer it abroad to sell
thers none woold bye it, but the princ of hell'

the Angels will not and the saynts on hygh   [S]
[54]   theyre eyes and eares are filde with admyration
9   which allwayes doe gods glorey gloryfie
and cannot thinck on dusty procreation,
only the god that made it houlds it deere
and for his labour sake bids it come neere

too whome then will you giue your bowing graces   [S]
[60]   to your affections, wills, passions, or lust,
will you advance these Idoles in hygh places
are these the gods on whome you put your trust
will these releeue you in that dreadfull daye
when you each thought and notion must beewraye

[65]   hee cums in a treeis of the day of iudgment   [S]
Will now   [S][35ʳ]
        <then> youre gould your charets or your horses
your lands, alyes, tytles or strength, preserue you
nor   [S]
    then all your loued Idols turne to croses
                                              r
and from the mersyes of your god shall staᴧue you
[70]   then loue which is the pylot of youre harte
armes your affections with afflyctions darte

LADY ANN SOTHWELL 57

man is the best of things eare, made in tyme [S]
yet doth hee beare the rust of his consumption
what blinded madnes hath begott this cryme
[75] or what all daring ignorant presumption
makes him with draw deeu honoure from his kinge
and on his slaue bestowe his woorshiping

the foole hath sayde within his secret harte [S]
ther<s> is noe god yet sparks of adoration
[80] is in his soule wherfore hee cleaues to arte
      c
and <fm>arues the Idole of his owne creation
wherefore come learne at oure Iehouahs scoole
whoe woorships Idols proues him selfe a foole

Thou shalt not take the
name of god in vayne

              is
In this our hartes corruption most exprest [S]
and spreads its selfe more then in any other
those faults that are by temporall lawes supprest
euen for afflictions sake wee seeme to smother
[5] but to blaspheme or take gods name in vayne
is helde a sporte because tis freed from payne

Know you not that the lord his cause will take
into his owne hand and for his renowne
and to him selfe will satisfaction make
[10] and headlongly will throw blaspheamers downe
this precept stands before (thou shalt not kill)
as being more reguarded in his will

Looke but at home into thy secret harte [35ᵛ]
if men doe slander or abuse thy name
[15] wilt thou alowe or take it in good parte
nay wilt not kill him that hath wrongd thy fame
to saue thyne honoure thy owne vaynes shall bleed
these sparkels come from god therfor take heede

Whoe is as Iealous of his name as you
[20] and though to right the wrong'd hee bid you sweare
take heede the cause you paune him for bee trewe

or els twere better that you did forbeare
you must not or you cannot blynde his eyes
or thinck to parolell his treuth with lyes

[25] <Oure pryvate thoughts god from the saynts haue hidden
to haue them to himselfe whoe houlds them deere
when men haue cause to knowe them hee hath bidden
bounde with his name they shoold in treuth appeere
and for that man hath turnd this treuth a wrye
[30] what troops of slaues stands watchmen to this lye>

<All guilt with goodly styles and loftye lookes
they guarde indeede but guarde to fortefye
and sheathe vpp weapons for it in theyre bookes
Sophissems and eulings at this warde they lye
[35] this in a hew and crye the theef hath cryed
oh stopp the theefe and soe gone vnespyed.>

<Alas poore gipsyes all your iugling tricks
cannot before that knowledge stand for holye
whoe laughs in scorne at all your apish witts
[40] and all youre deepest counsayles counte but follye
you cannot cosin him, youre selues you maye
and them like you, whose eyes are but of claye>

<Tis not the sober gate or the graue looke   [36ʳ]
the robe of state or toong ay taught to glose
[45] the eyes cast vpp or fixed on a booke
or thousand such like formall tricks as those
these vysards of the vnregenerate
doe but gods heavye wrath accumulate>

<How many wayes take wee his name in vayne
[50] kings breake theyre lawes subiects neglect theyre duty
husband wrong wiues, wiues doe the like agayne
children, theyre parents all deface gods beautye
all these haue sworne by his sacred name
and all in vayne all doe his wrath enflame>

[55] Hee that denyes the orphant of his right
doth wrong the widdowe or oppresse the poore
hee that walkes proudly in the almighties sight

LADY ANN SOTHWELL

59

or spurnes his owne afflictions oute of dore
forgets the humble savyoure that was slayne
[60]   mocks at his patience takes his name in vayne

<If any to the king or queene be lye thee
accusing thee with what thy soule doth hate
make use of this affliction sent to trye thee
and sent from god for thy salvation sake
[65]   what doest thou know but that thy princes grace
may in thy harte gods Image quite deface,>

<If wicked men doe take away thy wealth
plentye may make thee wanton, kick at god
thinck this impostume lancht for thy soules health
[70]   doe not repyne att the almightyes rodd
whoe were more rayld vppon or whoe more pore
then the apostels of oure savyoure.>

100   [S][36ʳ]

<The wealthy man is gods embassadore
the wittye man gods stewarde to provyde
[75]   his errant is gladd tydings and not warr
to comforte and not cosin all his trybe
for soe hee cosins god whose hande can pull
the borrowed perewigg from his balde scull'>

                                    stet   [S]
<Stryue not by wicked means to fill thy lapp
[80]   but trust in him whose care hath ravens fedd
starue noe mans chylde to pamper thyne owne bratt
the righteous seede shall never begg theyre bredd
choose rather to be cosinde starue and dye
then damme in hell for thy posterytye>

[85]   Oure breth doth hang on mynits, and the graue
doth make noe difference twixt the king and clowne
all's one with god, the Hero and the slaue

                   e
all shall bee crownᴧd with a clayey crowne.
the generall asize shall trye the cause
[90]   of the least frogg that sticks in the storkes iawes.

Alas poore man <poore> poore ayre poore water booble
thou arte but slyme, but dew, Ielly possest,

a house of <o>skinn whose basese stands on trouble
a hell of thoughts a pilgrim voyd of rest
[95] sinnes camping ball the obiect of afflyction
the praye of death knowledge of selfe eviction

A barque, twixt Sylla and caribdis fleetinge
of troubles present and ensuing sorrowe
where hope<s> and feare<s> are like twoe crosse windes meeting
[100] a foole that for the stage his <l>robe doth borrow
and in the tyring house is quickly strypt
and for not acting well is suerly whipte

The purest thinges receyue the fowlest spotts [37ʳ]
                                    the
now man hath made his soule sinnes amphy ∧ ator
[105] forsa'en his pylot runn agaynst the rocks
deface the Image of his deere creator
all things but hee stands in theyr first creation
hee fallen from that, is but a meere pryvation

Then o thou less then nothinge doe not dare
[110] to wrastle with almighty hand to hand
         sacrod   [S]
to take his name in vayne <doe thou> forbeare
least fretting leprosy o<v>erspread thy land
and doo not slepe as secuer In this cryme
gods vengance is defeard but for a tyme

[115] May wee not say hee is a foole or madd
that sheaths his swoord in his owne harte or brayne
whoe tells a lye doth giue his soule the stab
nay kils it quite that takes gods name in vayne
then come and learne at oure Iehovahs scoole
[120] whoe takes gods name in vayne is but a foole

               Thou shalt keepe holy the
                    saboth daye

In six dayes god made this admyred balle,
this verdent coutch, with lyllyes over spread:
ingrayld it with a liquid christall walle,
and hungg a double valence over headd.

LADY ANN SOTHWELL

[5] of fyre and ayre, frindge rounde with starry lights
vnder whose fabrick, walkes all lyvinge weights

There this immortall, mortall prince hee placed
whoe had freewill and free commande of all
this all compleate and with all grases graced
[10] the voyce of voyces to his type doth call.
laboure six dayes but keepe the seventh day holy
when hee bids rest, all labours ar but follye

In this day rest from all thy woorldly paynes   [37ᵛ]
take oute the harrowe from the plowmans hande
[15] refresh his wearyed limmes and faynting braynes
and free thy oxen from theyre yoaked band
t'is six to one, then having so much ods
t'were badly doone, to steale the day that's gods

In this day svmmon vpp thy weeks expence,
[20] that from thy lord, thou mayest acquittance haue
and heape not vpp offence, vppon offence
ingraue thy sinnes, before they thee ingraue.
mersy is for the lyving, not the dead
when life is gone, iustice her power doth spredd.   [S]

[25] This sacrilegious theft drawes on a curse
and doth defyle what god did sanctefye
and <sh> knits vp fyre and flax all in one purse
this stolne tyme eats downe tymes treasury,
and robs vs of that holy saboth rest
[30] which christ the lord of saboth hath exprest

Christ doth commande, that his desiples pray
that fayre Ierusalems foreknowne destruc<k>tion
fall not uppon the holy saboth daye.
least feare of death might pull on liues corruption,
theyre enemyes blood
[35] the Iewes this day <from fighting had> refrayne<d>
theyre feare to god chose rather to be slayne.

If Iewes kept holy that same blody signe
<heu>
that s<aₐu>ed the blood of theyre first borne babes
that killed lambe whose glorius face did shyne

[40] to saue all soules from hels all darkesome shades
      then if thou wilt example oute the best
      knowe god and christ <o>ₐn this day chose to rest

      Christ sayth they make my house a theevish denn   [38ʳ]
      not for th y sould, but stole the daye of god
[45] Mary refused to enbalme oure savyoure then
      the Isralytes on that day sought noe foode
      the sanctuary tooe <h>is left vnbuilt
      he that pict sticks his blood for it was spilt

      full six dayes thou shalt labor sayth the lord
[50] heere is Aadams curse chaynd to necessitye
      and these thy labours plenty shall afforde
      which doth agayne sweeten calamytye
      all thyne owne woorke in six dayes thou maist doe
      though not soe much as sinn invites the tooe

[55] But if thy woorks in these six dayes be bad
      or left vndoone the seventh day is defased
      for woorldly cares will make thy vysage sad
      and guilt of ill will in thy harte be placed
      then to keepe holy this high day of rest
[60] thou must woorke faythfull in all the rest

      Nor art thou bid to sleepe oute this high day
      to sing game dance or goosell out the tyme
      but in gods vynyarde thou arte bid to stay
      to cut downe thornes that over top his vyne
[65] for thou must never rest whilst thou arte heere
      yet in this day thy rest doth most appeare

      Nor art thou bid to labour heere alone
      but thou art bound to bring thy famyly
      thy wyfe and thee twoe loving harts makes one
[70] christ and his church explaynes this simpathy
      thy children and thy servants are exprest
      by thee and them gods vynyard must be drest

      Then know what in this day, is to bee doonn   [38ᵛ]
      by thee, and thyne, and what thou mayst not doe;

LADY ANN SOTHWELL

[75] how farr thy travels strech and where begoon
that all thy famyly are bownde untoe
first wake with god; with god lye downe to sleepe
whoe is the sheppard, that thy soule must keepe

And know a Iorny for the saboth day
[80] is from Mount Oliues to Ierusalem,
where Paule untill the euen with zeale did pray
and all that were asotiates with him
and then they tooke the lo holy sacrament
a seale vnto theyre sacred intente.

[85] Goe to gods borde, there, reape the bread of lyfe
and make thy famyly woorke in thy sight
let none looke back towards Sodom with Lots wife
but laboure faythfully till it bee night
X with as mush care as thou wooldst saue thy corne
[90] to house it vpp from an insuinge storme

Thy children modelize thyselfe (and these
haue littell mynes and like an argent feeld,
beare neyther, motto, emblem, or empreese
but like blanck paper to thy scribling yeeld.
[95] take the more care, what characters thou place
least being blazde, theyre pedegree proues base.

And know this duty thou to them doest ow
to feede them clothe them and instruct them well'
provyde for them that they thy loue may know
[100] and thou escape the name of Infidell'
and bee not like a lyon to thy chylde
hardning hy harts nor yet be thou toe mylde

But chasen him, if hee inclyne to Ill [39ʳ]
least with Elysha god doe breake thy neck
[105] for gyving him the raynes of his vayne will
make his whole motion coming at thy beck
least ₍with₎ proude Absolon hee seeke thy crowne
and then thy swoord beforst to cut him downe

fyrst make him know that hee was made of nought
[110] by that great god which hee must gloryfye

that his soonn christ hath his redemtion wrought
whose holy sperit dyd him sanctephye
and that these blessings tendes to none but them
that humbly weares christs yoake and follows him;

[115] Let him not play at passage with his tyme
nor daunce before the calfe on Horebs hill'
nor let his harte be over drencht with wyne
nor glootton like, his belly over fill
so will he be unfite for this hy mistory   [S]
[120] the which the holy saboth doth imply   [S]
folly un to the unglings hart is bound   [S]
corecetion is the salue for shuch a wound   [S]

                     thats
Thincks thou his face, ∧ like a boonch of grapes
with purple swolen knobes hanging the head
[125] shalbe exchanged into Angells shapes
for being over drunck or over fedd
noe rather thinck that Sathan shall haue power
to brayne hym with Iobs children in thy tower.

Let him not here a wanton parrit pratte
[130] that ietts in coorte and gloryes in hir snoute
whose soule was never coppyed by hir shape
but walkes as if shee bore noe soule aboute
this dalida when shee hath shred his locks
cals the Phillistins in, to giue him knocks

[135] And though shee say hir voues are fully payde   [39ʳ]
know hir perfumes are as the damps of hell
hir sylent eloquence hath oft betrayde
hir guifull toongg is his fames passing bell
hir curled locks are snares vnto his heeles
[140] hir kisses woounds him dead that noe payne feeles

Marke hir that leaues hir lord and laufull mate
to daunce to paynt to bee the stamp of fashions
forsakes hir famyly to liue in state
and getts infection by hir wanton passions
[145] know this is shee that watcheth in the street
and with a fly blowne kisse the youth dyd greet

LADY ANN SOTHWELL

Nor let him spend his tyme or coorse of lyfe
in any thing that may corrupt his mynde
for sinn and vertue allwayes are at stryfe
[150]   and all by nature are to ill inclynde
yet coostoome to doe good may habit proue
and outewarde forme may breed an inward loue

Then let his vertues bee (thy, sacryfise)
gyue his vnspotted youth vnto the lord
[155]   shall hee in glorye thinck with christ to rise
that onely doth his crippell tyme aforde
noe preist deformd, noe kidd spotted or lame
cam to the Alter to im ploy the flame

To morrow is the voyce of high presumtion
[160]   pardon for sinn doth beare the present tence
goodnesse deferde doth proue goodness consumtion
and in the interim theeues breake downe the fence
as the tree falles so shall it lye eternal
a doome pronounced by the all paternall'.

[165]   since Idlenes is sathons chear of state   [S, to l. 170] [40ʳ]
and that the restlis thofts ar euor working
our arms being crost our harts conglomerate
a web in which the enemie Lyes lurcking
try thy suns wit see to what faccallty
[170]   he is inclinde: to that his labors ty

Make him noe tradesman, least falce oaths deface him
nor yet a coortyer least a parasite
nor in the arte of killing doe not place him
because the lord doth hath a homisite
[175]   an advocate is ill, his rise is Iarr
yet not so bound to sinn, as those three are

for say, the law like a Monopoly
were all ingrosed into one<s> mans hand
bounde vpp with brasing barrs in chancery
[180]   where none but guilding favorites might stand
his honest labours yet might finde him bread
though not like hell maude kitchin groomes o'er fed.

66   THE WORKS OF THE

Thy Iosephs vertue may advaunce him, Iudge,
and by his care thy trybes from famin saue
[185]   let him not to his avarise bee drudge
or slaunderous toong his betters borne depraue
because he hath advantage of the place
such slavish acts will shew, his hart is base

But if thou mayest dispose of his vocation
[190]   make him gods souldier and this armor choose
place on his browe the helmet of salvation
brestplate of fayth, and ever peacefull shooes
and with the kingly David let him fight
agaynst the prince of everlasting mighte

[195]   And let his ensigne bee the holy lambe   [40ᵛ]
victorius over sinn and death and hell
whoe from eternyty in blest tyme cam
as ˄ the holy prophets did fore tell
     all
to chace away the shadowes of the night
[200]   and rend the curtaynes that did cloude his light

That sits vppon the kingly <t>bordered throne
and from his hand doth take the seven seald booke
whose color like the glorius Iasper stone
the prophet into deathfull terror strooke
[205]   this lambe, this lyon, of a princly bed,
hath power, of heaven, of hell, of quick of dead

Draw oute a souldyer of this woorlds makeing
how like a petty pedlers pack, hee walkes,
his raggs, ropes, hornes, and pouder, boxes shakeing,
[210]   and like, a feend, with blood and fyre hee stalkes,
kennells all night in durt, and in the day
getts often knocks, but seldome getts his pay.

Poore wretched mapp of princese tyrrany,
were not his slauery guilt and fynely drest
[215]   and all his vyle and barberus butcherye
by courage valoure fortitude exprest;
this hellish trate woold fall, and hell woold misse
a member to accommodate theyre dis

LADY ANN SOTHWELL

Whoe fights for god, shall never misse his pay,
[220] nor shall hee taste of death, or tuch corruption
that is noe life that in the nostrells playe
nor can the graue be counted a destruction:
for good men duck, lyke diuedoppers in earth
but till the Iudgment day, and second byrth

[225] Then bee gods souldyer, conquering every where   [41ʳ]
commande the mountaynes move, and walke the rounde?
the soonn stande senternell, seases fly for feare?
thy horne shall levill sittyes, to the grounde.
the king<s> of kings shall bee thy generall
[230] thy fellowes souldyers saynts, and Angels all

[A s]ouldyer is the skillfullest reth‸ᵐ <an>atitian
[thou]ghts woords, deeds by which the<s> somes <must> [mount]ᵈᵒᵉ
[ ]tions siphers that doe giue addition
whose fractions sumde brings god a full accou[nt]
[235] his hands the ballance are of equitye
to add substract devyde and multeply.

In this vocation sits, all other arts
philosophy reall, and rationall
phisicks, and all mathamatick parts,
[240] and methaphisicks supernaturall;
theyre theorick incampe within his harte,
his actiue hands, performe, the practiue parte

<The Methaphisicks, figurde in gods booke,
was not fyrst gotten by the ayde of penn.
[245] those that had only skill to bayte a hooke
were in an instant made, fishers of men
all that was theyrs (and more) was fyrme desyre
god meets with it, and doth thir soules inspyre>

<But ‸ᶠᵒʳ that part which Stoicks haue acquyred
[250] the Academicks Skipticks and the rest
of Parrapateticks how haue they beene tyred
and yet how littell treuth have they exprest
one dreames oute lyes, how oracles first fell,
an other dyes, to see the Osean swell,>

THE WORKS OF THE

[255] Arethmatick belongeth to his arte
to add, substract, devyde and multeply   mount
        <on>
to tye vpp fractions and devyde in parte
doth best befitt the hande of equitye   nt
besides the goulden number numbred three
[260] is best expressed in the holy trynatye

By geomettrick arte hee doth prepare   [41ᵛ]
weapons and instruments for holy Syon
his harte the harpe, his eyes twoe cannons arre
full charged with zeale and corage of a lyon
[265] his voyce the trumpet and his brest the droom
that beats heavens march vnto the day of doome

Which Syon top by archytecture placed
of polisht thoughts and passions rectefyed
so pleasing to the lord and so well grased
[270] as what you aske there, cannot be denyed
his fervent loue congleutenates the frame
his fayth the basese, that supports the same

And by the arte perspectiue, clymes the lights
whose lynes of longitude, are immortalitye
[275] and parolels are rests, and full delights
that from the optick lynes of maiesty
doth from one glasse reflect a thousand faces
and from one poynt, as many lynes and spaces

Musick is in his soule which styll doth sing
[280] god is his clife, his scale, his scala celi<e>
from the base earth his Dorion strayne doth ring
discorde with sinn, concorde, with pyetye
fayth, hope, loue, feare, are double dyopasanse
humylitye and zeale, his perfect vnisons.

[285] Astronamy shewes hee is a globe that roules
aboute the axell tree of destynye
his byrth, and death, artick antartick poles
the frosen zones are his necessitye<s>
his soule the middell orbe wherein doth runn
[290] vppon the lyne of fayth the glorius soonn.

LADY ANN SOTHWELL

By which the twoo all temperate trophicks sitt   [42^r]
Iudgment and reason his brayne woorking notions
his will, immagination, and his witt
are signes that crosse the zodyacks with swift motions
[295]   when will and witt in opposition stand
they breed eclipsis and makes darke the land

His vertuous deeds are knoobes vppon the sphears
and by the soonn inkindell starrs) whose splendor
are guilt with arts which his greate memorye beares
[300]   so that this littell heaven, this vnfixt center
let him but take survay of his owne creature
he is made a good Astronymer by nature.

This doth he runn the Mathamatick<s> rings
then to the phisicks, as Geographye
[305]   to span the earth and know the cause of things
as lyfe, breath, motion, sence and memorye
and by his power, in heavenly speculation
he doth devyne vppon the earths mutation

for those fower springs of rationall philosophy
[310]   his treuth with retorick is sweetly grased
his thoughts a grammer of congruitye
all logicks arte is in his reason plased
2   his actions bounde as rules of poetrye
1   his moods, tropes, figures, deeds of charyty

[315]   The actiue parte whose Ethicks rules his passion
and polyticks preserues the common weale
and Economicks puts his trybes in fashion
and the monastick his owne coorse doth seale
these branches doth his iustise comprehend
[320]   his factiue hands, with bounty doe extend

This doth he governe like a heauen on earth   [42v]
and this all arts doe by his motion moue
and from his breast all vyrtues haue theyre byrth
his courage conquereth with peace and loue
[325]   that all these grases hangg vppon one pole
and all these gloryes sit in one mans soule

70   THE WORKS OF THE

Witnesse that prynce that governs bryttan now
that blest Augustus that all peacefull king
as knees and harts, so all witts to him bowe
[330]   whose toong doth flow like a selestiall spring
whose powerfull sperit speaking from the lord
makes admyration wayte on every woorde

Witnesse his books, his woorks, his pyety
whoe pulls noe neyboure princese by the ears
[335]   but Immytates that threefolde deytye
and governes gratiusly in his owne sphears
whose godlike mynde hath sent from his blest breath
pardon of lyfe to those that sought his death

Long liue this faythfull steward to the lord
[340]   his champyon of trew fayth myrror of kings
heaven cannot earth a greater blisse aforde
then to preserue this fowntayne and his springs
and let the day of Iudgment change his shape
so shall his subiects halfe theyre fears escape

[345]

Heere stay my thoughts while I doe heaven implore
that with arts proude career you doe not mounte
but humbly pace by clensing Iordans shore
[350]   least pryde for zeale stands in the lords accounte
nor for vayne glory of historyan phame
crounde Ovids Idols with Iehovahs name;

this must [S]
cum next [S]
to the sense [S]
of last [S]

As sicknesse tooe tooe much infecting paper   [43ʳ]
to mix heavens milke with hellish aquinet
[355]   wee leaue the soonn and wander by a taper
and this gods wisdome wee addubyate
try Seneca and Paule with one tutchstone
waygh Aristotell with wise Salomon

Whoe wroghte the ∧ graue <or most accutest> style   [S]
wisest   smothist
[360]   or whoe dyude deepest in the sea of nature
if cloudes of errour doe not treuth beguile
oure reason quickly will resolue this matter
why those whose eyes did never see the light
shoold want the skill; to hitt the marke aright

LADY ANN SOTHWELL

71

[365] Shall' Pethagoryans put our soules to graze
(no over Shall', my over our)

or Varro make vs thinck tis made of ayre
(me over vs)

or shall greate Plato with this error paze

that sayth the forehead doth mans sperit beare

what need such vayne philosophy bee sought

[370] by those whome god and christ themselues haue taught

[S]

Whoe say if Angels doe from heaven desend

and teach you other doctrin; (it detest)

whose woord hath shewed oure cause our coorse oure end

and makes oure peryod in Abrams breast

[375] yet Infidelyty desyres a signe

by which frayle reason onely seekes to clyme

Smale acrons growes to oaks of mighty stature

and budds of trees, wax feathered fowles that flye

and shapelesse things more strange are shapte by nature

[380] beyonde conceypt if Plynny doe not lye

then if gods handmayde can such power expresse

what naturall can thinck, his owne power lesse.

If ∧ twoe <owlde men but> whith a sheephoock armed
(thowes over ∧, brothors over owlde men but)

[S][43ᵛ]

coold overcome all Pharoes' mightye hoast

[385] and a smale wand but with a fewe woords charmd

coolde spread affliction over all theyre coast

if the woord; (fiat) formd the 'whole woorlds masse

if so smale meanes brought such great things to passe

Why shoold wee thinck gods powerfull arme can fall

[S]

[390] or let oure deerest <t>hopes<ts> in the dust lye
(ashes over hopes)

most myserable were a rationall

if that his soule shoold with his bodye dye

let fayth stande vpp since reason groueth madd

to tell each soule shall with his corpes bee cladd.

[395] The righteous soules are safe kept in gods hands

whoe is the god of lyving not of <th> dead

christ giues accquittance for ould adames bands

and hath the land of rest discovered

the grayne wee sow doth dy, rott, loose his shape,

[400]	before it doth an other body take,

Had all those holy fathers of owld tyme
beene oute of hope of an immortall crowne
affliction stepps by which poore man must clyme
had not beene taen before the woorlds renowne
[405] as seeming holynes shoold have suffysed
in which theyr passions might have gone disguised

But stay weake female whether doest thou wander
how dares thy waxen plewmes approtch the soonne
thy better sex are lost in this meander
[410] in which thy ignorance presumes to roonne
pardon deere savyour pardon my presumtion
and let my fayth relye one thy assumtion;

Might others <sex my> deeds my sex or song approue   [44ʳ]
victoryous Debora to god did singg
[415] and Nabals wife by wisdome did remoue
the vowed vengeance of an<o>angry kingg
Iehell and Iudas armes were made the rodd
to scoordge the mighty enemyes of god

Weakelings and babes gods woonder shall reveale
[420] to giue the greater looster to his deede
which from the woorldly wise he doth conseale
least men might thinck they doe from men proseede
this cause barde Moses from the promisd lande
and bids retreate toe most of Gydeons bande

[425] Then since this Iealoius god cannott endure
that flesh and blood shoold steale his fame away
how can that fellon thinck to scape secure
that robs him of the holy saboth daye
the daye of parlyament where hee is speaker.
[430] [t]he burges sayntes: the holy gost the cryor.

<   gost is cryor>   [S]

[Southwell drafts, #1]   [44ᵛ]

euill

why doth she buid us haue thim still in mind

LADY ANN SOTHWELL

as if from them we should sum cumfort find,
<w   >
since noe[Noah] daniell Iobe[Job] the three
[5]   if presant all they could not succor thee

If from the fathors she her youcke[yoke] propoundes,   [45ʳ]
why do her horrid bul*s* brecke doune thar boundes

---

dare she launch out unto gods sacrid word
<thie>
<god> angil guards it with a flaming sword
the
[10]   to cutt down <herisi and or> sofisticke foull disgise
             all <this could fit dis>gyse
as ground themselues on fuirious auorise
          discus
which to co<tnt> in dor[depth?] would requuir
a longer <like> life than I seeke or desier
this shall sofise for me by gods mere grase
[15]   I haue the Ies to see har monstrous fase
the angells fron the toplis heauen ditt fall
<and aur firse parrant taste>
and all turned opostitan [opposition? apostate?] whose thrall
[has] guvyn us arurs[errors] of <weacknis blindnis eruor>
                  profits [prophets]
[20]   the pratriarcke <profits> apostell <from>of all
<haue *sh*pped away from truth thrould[through] blindid tarror>
by blinding ignnorance haue falens away
And for the want of grase to giue them staye
tharfore a worme A:s I am dare not boast
         ust
[25]   only my tr is that the holy ghost
                  dear
the cumfortabell sperit of gods grace
      <bl-ud> foull   off
will keep the beast's marke from my fase
<nor>so that a facket[facet] of the Life in blude
     not afright   ferm
shall <fright> my resolusions <from th--- good>
[30]   <that our trew>
the flocke of christe and protestants <I proue>
           *pro*poses

thar is one god one truth, wan trew serues[service]
nor from christs flou [of redeeming blood] to be deseuorid

<whi god>

[35]   <the pouristan[protestant] fayth>

whi by gods bounty is dincouorid[discovered]

unto the protystance which still I pray

our
<the> golden candelsticke take not awaye

<   > for our neglect or coldnis in devosion,

[40]   nor drownnon not in ignnorance's darke osion[ocean]

but Hes our cheer aund her her lord for us

her
<and> us for hee and for us all Ieisus

we invocate no othor <pouer but the>
                        deity

but the all pouerfull sacrid trenity,

[45]   hating thatt anti christianity

[tha]t do with saynts committ oblityy[apostasy?]

all you that liue and haue the shapes oft men

know lite struke one in but ten sisti ten

then muste you to the dust whence your war taken

[50]   but you haue souls that thae shall not [be] forsacen

by gods desperit if you will aply

your liues to truth for trew felisity

let not the grieatling bomp[pomp] so roman[Roman] preate

that --

              with luv
[55]   bewitch your Ies saleuious seat   [45ᵛ]

<de chere>   more
but [a] chirch more sobor <is> and temporate

        thos   st   like   houros
than like <to> minicke [minutes] geting <ore> aparte

when god requirs a brocon contrite harte

<---------->

[60]   If man had Ies to se his owne foul soul

and for her state

and how the case <he het sibh> to couet gold

    foe robs
his <backe> shol not <----- did ----- >
              his iutisuce [justices] fiue floute

like <giu did> tomes <that hold proufs in ----> doubte

[65]   <to ones> hiding <that couor> gaping in a raeor
gold

<so do their ropes thar in to sectines floute>

LADY ANN SOTHWELL

but with a reuorantsed case of desem*b*ling
working salluasion out with fear and trem*b*ling
*th*at at the polings perhapes will conclude

[70] <that wie ar> workes <our> must be saluasions untorlude that
<but clay to loue the lord our naybor as ion*e*self
w*h*ere we grant in part yet hauing dun our bes*t*e>
shur we ar*e* bound to Lou*e* god above all
our napors[neighbors] as oursselues which <yett>if we shall

[75] good workes will follo*w* <if yt[that] do we our best>
do we what we will.

we ar unpr*o*fitubell seruancs[servants] still

orr
nor can we pay <the> de*b*t then much les*s* merit
<bet in cris*t*e Iesus>
only in Iesus we shall he*a*uen inheritt
and by no athar[other] in he*a*uen or earth

[80] ca*n* man be freed from his sin of berth
much less <from proud puisant sion[Sion] o*u*r iury lette>
much ses les from thos prou*d* babels[Babel's] spires
chris*t*aill
that dar*e* approch heu*e*ne's <sacrid> a*e*theriall fires
re*velation* xiii 4u*erse*

[85] but it must be so that *t*he <fuss>world may prate
who's like the be*a*s*t*e for glori pou*e*r and state
pleat   [46']
this egip*t*s first borne brat doe <boste> that she
asum*e*s her glori from antiquite
so cursid cane[Cain] and bannished esmayle[Ishmael] might [plead]

[90] and ruggid esa[Esau] hat*e*full in gods sighte
could she this recordidly aproue
but < shuld> we yelde to this <recordidly>
ha*t*h befo*r* he*r* t*r*us*t*s*t* loue
she <arth for -- her first> loues feollty
re*velation*   ephesus
with <smernase[Smyrna] theugh[Thyatira]> <but
blindig[blinded] kings ar*e* thaye>
ii*chapter* 4u*erse*   upe
that hold her <depe> but thay shall se*e* the daye

[95] and have har to wlus[unloose?] manie of blasfame
ar written in her fas*e*
<wit*h* cyrases[Cyrus's] she hat*h* durnd[turned] her soall awry>
breaking the bond of motity[modesty] and duty
pr*e*suming on her pou*e*r and forgid be*au*ty

76   THE WORKS OF THE

[100]   or ^{the} <w-> pou*e*r which ^{de*a*d and} blindid kungs <do ^{do giue} s----y>
but the*y* must hate her when the*y* see and live
for thos*e* ten crounid hor*n*s most gor*e* her Ies
<----ser us>   ·
whos*e* all and everipart is blasfemies

         <Its> tis time
<the> for god to lay <his> hand on thes*e* men
[105]   plates that do distray his lawes his word contemne
in her sucesion He doth proudly
<In s*u*ce*s*sion> is anothor of har bo*a*ste*s*
<but> ^{yet} whil*e*s pope Io*a*ne lay in that brag wase loste
<besedes the profit> elias did^{that gre*a*tt}cumplayne
[110]   <   > that all gods saynts besids himselfe was slayne
       which shoues [shows] gods cherch was not perspecious then
         thow knoue to <god>, ^{aim} it hild no state mong*s*t men

[46ᵛ & 47ʳ are blank]

Thou shalt not commit Adooltery

                               [47ᵛ]

                               [S]

God doth <the> ^{with} doggs <and> ^{<the> a} dulterate weights exempte
as noysome carryon, they may not come neere
theyre soules and bodyes are in such contempte
as flaming hell must theire infection cleere
[5]   theyre marrow fryse with paynfull agonye
theyre leprous fame infect socyetye;

Theyre portion in this woorld, is beggery
contempte and scorne W thoughts that still accuse
and yet provoke them to that slavery
[10]   as to theyre flesh black poyson doth infuse
theyre hartes like Etnean topps are all on fyre
with never to be quenched fowle desyre

But let vs draw this twoefold monsters face
this double damning vyle Hermophradite
[15]   whose feloship doth fly from state of grace
and when theyre cankred sores, are brought to light

LADY ANN SOTHWELL

the surgion christ the medson must apply
whose balsome take and, liue, forsake and dye.

The Sodomytes had land that with smale toyle
[20] did yeeld such plenty that they need not woorke
but see; this plenty turnd vnto theyre spoyle
for in theyre lazy harts the dyvell did loorke
soe flynty feilds with a laborious hande
makes men more happy then a frutefull land

[25] Oure lazy grandome Eve in $\overset{X}{}$ paradyse
had shee had weeds to pluck or wooll to spoone
her yeelding eares to newfound vanytyes
had not beene yeelding to the serpents toongg
so honest laboure is one remedy
[30] to cure this iust contemned maladye

What is ₍it₎Adams quarell ₍that₎ you take   [48ʳ]
from whome all fooles must predycated bee
that makes this poore excuse to god. the mate
thou gavest gaue the cursed fruite to mee
[35] coolde this have serud so had he scapte the curse
yet I confesse the womans bonde was woorse

for since that Adam is the slaue to evill'
and shee <is> commanded to obey his will'
how fares that state thats governd by the devill
[40] shewerly theyre woorship is for feare of ill.
then thinck what ever seeming face wee <show> carry   [S]
tis betor dy a vergin then to marry   [S]
<wee hould youre sex oure soule and bodyes foe>

The man that for gods cause forbears to kill
to sweare, lye, steale or <be made drunck wᵗʰ> in wine [S]
                         ᵈʳᵒᵘⁿᵉ ʰⁱˢ ˢᵒˡˡ   [S]
[45] and in a woord to bee the woorst of ill'
why, hee is scornde and calde a femynine
well, you that dare abuse youre maker thus
well gyue you leaue to scorne and rayle at vs

Was christ a swaggerer in deede or woord
[50] or did his life contemne at modestye
he sayes whoe stricks shall perish with the swoord

his doctrine houlds with yours noe sympathye
what is yours iendors honour or renowne
is it in strength, to pull all honoure downe

[55]   Had strength of body held prehemynence
the Elephant had beene the prince of nature
and strongest bodyes governd are by sence
and corrupt sence defyles the soules puer matter
yet must you have your deew the actiue devill'
[60]   takes place in hell before the passiue evill'.

You that haue eares to heere and eyes to see   [48ᵛ]
that know the soule is farr the better parte
and that soule _∧ that is from most sinns free
gyue iudgement from the iustise of your harte
[65]   whether the ravening woolfe <bee> that hunts the pray
bee better then the lambe he beares awaye

Thou onely strongg in ill: thy lost renowne
the second Adam will agayne repayre
take houlde of it and with it take thy crowne
[70]   that sinne pulls off and le<f>ues thy forehead bare
so shall ∧ <a> female as be<hioues a wife>   [S]
houlde thee hir lord <and> comforte <of this lyfe>   [S]

free denysens haue pryvyledge in Cytty
which is not to be graunted to a slaue
[75]   a wife vngratious wilfull and vnwitty
god' sends to clogg a bad man to his graue
but <th> a wisewoman is a good<s> mans hyre
whose plentious breast incleewds all his desyre

The single man doth walke like one that moornes
[80]   and like a robber every way doth runn
and with that wretch the restlesse stone hee turnes
and where chaunce throwes him, hee sitts as with the soonne
<wherfore the anchor houlde of a good life>
in this presept woulds thow liue fre from blame   [S]
<is to be Ioyned to a vertuous wife>
in holy wedlocke tacke sum uertious fame   [S]

LADY ANN SOTHWELL

79

[85] <Then> marry in thy youth and strength of tyme [S]
    The daughter of some honest parentage [S]
    and let hir love, thy wanton thoughts confyne
    so may that state be calde thy merry age
    and having gaynd a chylde of Israell
[90] tis a ritch portion, see thou use it well'

    But if thou doest not take thy ayme from god [49^r]
    but for some other end doest choose a mate
    one shall bee gyven to the, but for a rodd
    and as a corsiue she shall frett thy state
[95] as clyminge sands are to the aged feete
    so shall her Ianglinge toongg, thy cominge greete

    If thou doest wed for natures rarytes
    thou sets a naked swoord vnto thy brest
    and rushing forth amongst thy enemyes
[100] by theyre vnquenched wrath thou arte opprest
    whoe keepes a Iem that all the woorlds admyres
    cannot set safe at home in his desyres

    And yet the soonnes of god coolde not forbeare
    but they forgott relygyon, god, and dvtye wyf
                            to ofte
[105] seeing the daughters of men rarely fayre lyfe
    each to his harts desyre did take a beautye
    by which theyre impps were Molach sacryfise
    and they the fathers of Idolatrise

    Choose thou for wealth thou takest a moth wth it
[110] that eates the oute lwith pryde and bravery
    be kinde or curst or vse thy strongest witt
    her wealth shall wed thee to her slaverye
    and if shee gyues, shee taunts, or doth deplore
    soe thou wert better begg from dore to dore

[115] If for the stock of honor thou doest wed
    her kinred will Iade thy backe and state
    and thou hast brought a mristrisse to thy bed
    vnto whoese eares there must noe woord escape
    least chalenges contempte and punishement
[120] vndoe thy state and gyue the banishment

Then fyrst of all returne to state of grace [49ᵛ]
then god him selfe to thee a wife shall gyue
whose angels shall conduct the to the place
that none shall dare to take from thee and liue
[125] but thou with holy fume that fish shall burne
and chace those sperits that maketh others moorne

Christ is the churches powerfull head you knowe
lyke tytle hath the man over his wife
you finde what loue christ to his spouse did showe
[130] that gaue for her his pretious blood and life
woolde you commande; then learne for to obey
woolde you bee payde your debt; youre owne debt paye?

Christ doth not curse, sweare, rayle, at spouses error
but with softe voyce, with humble woords and teares
[135] and his good life, becomes hir gratious myrror
his loue and patience with hir weakenesse beares
<as mothers tende towarde aguisht tears>
he fouldes hir in his armes and <lapp> in his lapp
and with rich courdialls cumforts now her hart [S]

[140] Nor <h>is his bountye like a flinty rock
or water gotten from a pomise stonne
which makes necessyty to cry and knock
so longg as that the guifte is woorse then none
but hee doth watch oure ˄wantes and gyves vs store
[145] and smyles for Ioy when we doe aske for more

<Nor doth hee sounde a trumpet of expence
that all the woorld may his great bountye knowe>
Nor will hee suffer every slaunderous breath
to wrongg her fame and whisper him with lyes
[150] but doth revenge her infamy with death
and tenders her renowne as his owne eyes
                                        fame
for this wise husband knowes that her ill <name> [S]
<detracts his honour and augments his shame>
doth much dishonor his most honorid name [S]

[155] Then see this coppy of a lovinge heade [50ʳ]
and if his fayre example thou neglect

LADY ANN SOTHWELL

wee cannot thinck oure bonds are forfeyted
though wee your yoake and felowshype reiect
whoe liues in sperit is dead vnto the lawe<s>
[160]   the flesh and sperit never Ioyntly draw

But when your loue and bownty doth appeere   .5.
like Elkenah your are better then tenn soonnes
Iacob for Rachell served foreteene yeeres
whose loue still cured her churlish fathers woondes
[165]   none but the cursed Iewes for each smale stryfe
sought gods advise to put away a wife

forbeare to slaunder them with Irefull toonggs
as Elie, Hannah when shee cam to praye
but god that knew her hart and saw her wronggs
[170]   graunts her request before she cam awaye
daughters of Israell slandered throgh grudge
had satisfaction gyven them by the Iudge

Scorne not the counsels of a wife thats good
as Pylate did whose wife bad him forbeare
[175]   to tootch the holy innosent sacred bloode
but see your natures, Putyfar gaue eare
vnto his seeminge chaste till shee had toulde
the lye that forst Iust Ioseph vpp in houlde

She is thy honour therfore houde her deere
[180]   she is thy flesh: Whoe will his owne flesh hate?
her fayth thy vnbeleeving hart shall cleer
she is the prop and <a>comforte of thy state
the wise man that doth know his good can say
curst bee the hande that takes this helpe awaye

[185]   flesh of my flesh bone of my bone he cryes   [50ᵛ]
for thy deere loue man shall his father leave   [S]
        is   the   opticke artire   to the ies
as <the> softe skin that <in an eggshell lyes>
our indevyduall lovinge <s>harts shall cleaue
and I more harde will beare the stormes of weather
[190]   nor will wee parte till death doe vs discever

Ile toyle abroade and thou shalt woorke withine   [S]
Ile plough for corne and thou shalt make the 'bread

Ile graze the sheepe and thou the wooll shalt spinne
oure chyldren shall by thee bee nurtered
[195] I with vnpartiall loue and honest care
will quitt thy paynes theyre portions to prepare

Ile make our soonnes to woorke and stand in feare
make thou our daughters huswiues <g> clenly nymble
Ile teach the <men> to vse the swoord and speare   [S]
    boyes
[200] teach thou the gyrles to vse theyr sheeres and thimble
and you for vs shall <sdye> ritch purple gownes
    spin
and weele adorne your honours with ritch crownes

This like a stronge batalia forth they goe
gaynst whome this coward base adulterye
[205] dares not presume his rascalls troopes to showe
but doth ly buryed in obscuryte
thus is this monster kild or put to flyght
and lyeth hidden in eternall night

Thus man and wife one wax and one impression
[210] one byrth one deathe one gloryous resurrection
to whome one god hath gyven one lawes prescryption
doth lyue in perfect life of loues perfection
soe that the yoake in which twoo harts doe meete
the boorden seemeth light the draught is sweete

[215] Now feamale be not you so madd to thincke   [51ʳ]
for sexes sake your faltes shall hydden lye
hee is noe frende that at oure follyes winck
nor must you looke for my connyvencye
fathers in theyr death beds first calls the <ayre> heyre
[220] and then the rest in order doe repayre

Then learne to know your station and your duty
    lord
both to your lord in heaven and ʌ on earth
and thinck what pryvelege you gayne by beauty
men giues it you, tis none of yours by byrth
[225] for you are seconde borne the weaker creture
your soules pertycypating with your nature

LADY ANN SOTHWELL

for proofe goe bid the infant at your brest
make sillagismes in barbara or selarent
tell him by you he never shall be blest
[230] vnlesse he presently goe kill a gyant
what thinck you then <or what> woold you not this obiect
where god doth barr, the meanes, he barrs the effect

Yet see what honour god to you doth gyve
an Image of his owne to bee your head
[235] bounde not to parte with you whilest hee doth liue
by whome youre bodyes and your soules are fedd
by whose socyety your comforts springgs
and fills the heaven wth saynts the earth wth kinggs

Then for his sake whose Image hee doth weare
[240] for frendships sake that benefits you <this> thus
for natures sake which mothers ought to beare
be not vngratefull brutish impyous
nay for your owne sakes gy'ue these lords deew dewty
since vertue only is trew reall beuteye

[245] But if you will your god and head dispyse   [51ʳ]
like desolation you shall sitt and moorne
and from your odours shall infection ryse
your curled fronts shall vnto baldnesse turne
your fall shall bee like hers of Babylon
[250] that filde the woorld with loude confusion

And since your strength is sknow agaynst the soonn
or wax that yeelds to every slyte impression
know heere your Ioy or sorrow is begoonne
youre foule deformyty or rare perfection
[255] tis to be matcht to one that is vpright
for your camelyon hew turnes as your sight

for maydens choyce I haue not much to saye
for they are bounde vnto theyre fathers will
and yet they ought with dyligence to praye
[260] that god will gyve theyre father care and skill
                       honest   wight   [S]
to choose for them a wise and <sober> mate
           thow mayst still find fauor in his sight   [S]
that <may not wrongg that honorable state>

THE WORKS OF THE

If god doe blesse thee with <thee> a vertuous mate
tis as a crowne of honoure to thy heade
[265]   a sylent ignorance in thee seemes state
thy verteues fly, thy faults are covered
thou shalt haue hygh reguard in coorte and cytty
plenty at home, chyldren and servants dutye

But if thou haste a husband that is nought
[270]   thinck tis thy fathers faults on thee are layde
and it ther may a remidy be <f----->   [S]
<in him and thee that were not godly> taught   [S]
_{then let thy reson neuor}
and yett dispayre thou <not or> bee dismayde
poyson yeelds antidotes let his vexation
bee as thy crosse to bringe thee to salvation

Thou shalt not steale   [52^r]

Harken you potentates and mighty kinggs
is not this presept all to base for you
the osean fludgates, and the fowntayn springgs
2   are in your hands, you need not be vntrew,
[5]   and yet you are, the greatest theeves of all
that haue a beeinge<vp>on this massy ball.

for your ambytious covetous desyre
leads troopes of men like deere into the toyle
2   churches and cyttyes, fey'ldes of corne you fyre
[10]   like land Lavyathans you robb and spoyle
in which you say gods quarrell' you doe trye
and yet like Achabs prophets you doe lye

_{since would yoor}   [S]
And with you<r> wicked pouder policyes
<you> seeke to insnare the holy ones of god   [S]
[15]   beshur oure <greate> captayne will so blinde your eyes   [S]
that your owne swoorde shalbe made your owne rod
for hee will bringg a woonder in youre dayes
and your destruction shall advance his prayse

LADY ANN SOTHWELL

You make the fruitfull wombe to bee noe mother; [S]
rackell vepes for her
[20] and take away the helplesse infants syre
  you robb the frend of frend brother of brother
  you rend<s> gods glorye and the earths attyre
  youre sumpteous trayns and feasts breeds publike wrack
  and many a hungrye mawe, and naked back

<----> 10 [S]

he is a thefe that iustis
[25] <A wise man knowes there is noe trust in goulde
  and that a place of state hath littell' rest
  how often hath that soonne of David toulde
  that all was vanytye that man poscest
  witt, beauty, strength, pompe, place, rewle, parentage,
[30] gaynst fate and death, can haue noe pryvelege>

11 [52ʳ]

  <<Deiected Nabuchadneser coold tell'
  how littell <p> helpe did lye in pompe or place
  ritch purple sande not Dyves oute of hell',
  nor yet coold mony purchase Symon grace
[35] Iudas did beare the purse; and yet that trust
  did not importune, that the man was iust.>>

12

  <<And Iobe was ritch and yet not freed from payne
  Saule was a kingg, and yet he was afflycted
  and Absolon was fayre, and yet was slayne,
[40] the Iudges oulde in craft, the chylde convycted,
  Roboams soonne was <st>yoongg and yett hee dyed
  Samson was strongg and yett his armes were tyed>>

9.

& Goolde hurteth much and yet it cannot heale
  what is it then the covetous man woold haue
[45] or what avayles it him to robb or steale
  that carryes nothinge with him to the grauee
  vnlesse it bee the curse of Achans theft
  that neyther life, nor fame, or tresor left

THE WORKS OF THE

86

52 <--> [S]

1
[50]
Ritches are vnto men as is theyre foode
dyseased stomaks makes it fleame or gale
the strongg and sounde converts it to pure blood
then let vs not lyke kytes on carryon fall
but fyrst aske counsell of the grave physitian
what ritches best befitteth oure condition

<11> 53 [S]

[55]
2
Wee see oure yoonglings covet frute to eate
which breeds them full of woormes and rotten humor
doe wee those fondlings wrongg if wee them beate
from what wee know will bee theyre lyues consumor
and shall wee then assume more witt more care
[60] more love to ours, then god to vs doth beare

<--> 5<>7 [S][53ʳ]

who had
<Man hath> a selfe conserving inclynation [S]
gyven him by heaven to which there is anexed
pleasure to that wᶜʰ 'tends to preservation
and hurtful things with paynes are ever myxed
[65] And for his lyfe must be with lyfe supplyed
he is armd wᵗʰ witt and hands for to provide

<-->58

<hath sol her gide>
But now this faculty <is turnd awry> [S]
with thes wings fly [S]
self loue hath gott the roome of preservation
coveting and invading to supply
[70] the cense and appetyte with delectation
for< > wᶜʰ the <pa>reason passions and the will
ar seruill
Inᵗᵒ censualyty are <woorkmen> still [S]
aclsicll [S]
this god <for ----> and natur bonde [S]
thru [S]
hence spring the cuk of rapid ---- [S]

[53ᵛ is blank]

<--> 54 [S][54ʳ]

[75] for what wee hold not that wee shoold not <have>hold [S]

LADY ANN SOTHWELL   87

3   vnlesse wee woold deny gods loue and skill'
      and want of memory which makes vs <craue>bold   [S]
           or
      <has> power to gyve and take agaynst his will'
      <<whoe sayes his grace <so> suffycyent is for all
[80] vnder which gyft all others bountyes fall>>
      presuming mor on that one strencke or polisi   [S]
      then on gods prouidence or lebaraliti   [S]

                    <54> 5<4>5

      so that a theefe's an infidell whose trust
4   is not in god but in his owne intrution
[85] and hopes to buylde a babell out of dust
      with oute a care or feare of its confusyon
      and rushing in <t>gods seate there proudly stands
      to take the<s> power from oute his sacred hands

5   <5--> 56

      The lawe of nature gave a light to all
[90] <w>how comes it that one haulds a thousands portion
      those evills that did ryse in Adams fall
      monsters in nature nurcese of extortion
      haue wth there sorseryes and gileful treason
      made man <quite> starke mad and quite defast his reas[on]

                    <> 45

[95] And now he ravens like a frantick brute
      and makes his will the servant to his sence
      whose soule doth never with his god dispute
      but blyndely seates her in concupysence
      his dayes are few and evill; yet this wretch
                                <munny>   [S]
[100] doth with his dying Iawes at <silver> snatch
                                ˄mammon   [S]

8   _____   [S]

                    7   [S]

      <Hee is a theefe that Iustice doth delaye
5   hee is a theefe that crafty bargaynes maketh
      hee is a theefe that spends his owne deere daye

88 THE WORKS OF THE

with sinfull fooles that wisdomes lore forsaketh
[105]   hee is a theefe whose harte is full of stryfe
and robs him selfe of peace, the blisse of lyfe.>

<8> [S][54ᵛ]

<Hee is a theefe that <h>walloweth in treasure
and lets the poore lye fayntinge att his dore.
for want of that which overflowes his measure
[110]   his Iudgement is with Sathan to deplore
and begg for water for his cortched loonggs
that wrongde his savyoure in his brethrens wronggs
a prodygall is an vnnaturall thefe
A best y^t dothe preferre his owne desyre   [S]
[115]   before his childerens welfare or relefe   9
This pecocke treades his owne egges in ye myre
this canker to posteritie (was borne)
to be a firebrand in a stacke of corne.>

<<A gamester is a theefe and if not woorse
[120]   for lyes and oathes belongeth to this trade   10
and if he loose <then> hee is his owne cutpurse
his neybours if he win, to whome is made
noe promyse by oure god to blesse such gayne
that springs fro<u>m</u> noe good <greate> ∧ cause or honest payne>>

[125]   <<That huntsman is a theefe whose lyfe is ledd,
mongst brutes on whome he doth his wealth bestowe   11
such gyve vnto theyre doggs theyre childrens bread
and robs them selfes of tyme them selues to<e> knowe
<theyre> harts thus turnde coold love transforme <ouʳ>their shapes   [S]
[130]   such woolde be beasts and lyve amongg the brakes
this pruvith wee <th> a simpathy discouore   [S]
be twene the things beloueid and the louors   [S]

A myser is a selfe consuming theefe
this hyde bounde wretch is ritch potentially
[135]   immagynation houlds him by the teeth
and feeds the foole fatt most fantastically

LADY ANN SOTHWELL

his body and his purse houlds simpathye
as a consumption and a timponye>>

12

<Whoe steales a man and seles him ought to dye
[140]   a flatterer is a theefe that steales a harte
this sycofant doth into secrets prye
and then makes havock of mans better parte
which is his fame, that being once defaced
can never more agayne be fully graced>

[55ʳ]

[55ᵛ is blank]

40

[S][56ʳ]

[145]   A theefe although hee robb with swoord and fyer
his cravin harte is cowerdly and base
his thoughts lyes in the moodd and mounts noe hyer
that dares not looke afflyction yn the face
whoe <eale> countes him valyant that ne're mett a foe
<most>
[150]   he is ∧ myserable that was never soe

41

[S]

<<To fyght with beastes at Ephesus sayth Paull
avayleth littell if wee have not love
this love he speakes of is that brasen wall
which lame affliction seeks in vayne to move
[155]   and doth confyrme gods chyldren, but the badd
turne coward theeves, and desperately <t> runn madd>>

42

[S]

<This love in darkesome doongeon doth condole
not for in boults are boonnde both leggs and handes
but for the flesh close prysone to the soule
[160]   barrs her from god with much more Ircksom bands
for reason knowes, the goute, or a smale flye
may cryple all the Ioynts or blynde the eye>

43

[S]

Lynck chaunce and vyolence both in one chayne
say that a reame fales downe and breakes oure back
[165]   yst not all one if equall bee the payne

as if a prince did put us to the rack
thinck still on death so chaunce is but a fabell
opyinyon onely makes men myserable

44
[S]

Mee thincks my neyghbours dogg that barks at mee
[170] and (his owne) toongg that doggedly doth rayle
is all a like, I can noe difference see
both with confused noyses my eares assayle
perhapps in sinn^{man} thou didst for reason looke
opyinyon makes thee greeve that soe mistooke
[S]

4<5>5
[S][56ᵛ]

[175] A frend deseyve vs being put in trust;
wee knowe oure enemy woold doe the same
tis oure opynyon heere that proues vniust
in crowninge of a foe with a frends name
thys Metamorphoser of truth and reason
[180] with tastelesse toongg the mes'se of lyfe doth season

46
[S]

Agaynst which monster if wee coold prevayle
this chaunce and destenye which men calls fortune
shoold have noe power to make us laugh or wayle
nor with deepe sighs shoold wee oure fates importune
[185] but with gladd harte enioy the good thats present
and like a coonning cooke make sower meate pleasant

4<>7
[S]

for if a sparrow fall not withoute leave
to whome shall wee oure myseryes impute
to him whome <cra> strength or craft cannot deceyve
[190] with whom it is not lawfull to dispute
from whome the foe of David fled <am> ᴀ ayne
was by a smalle heare stayde till hee was sleyne

48
[S]

The surgeon that doth cure soome deepe deseaze
doth seare the flesh and scarrefy the bone

LADY ANN SOTHWELL

[195] his deepe insytions doe noe whitt displease
or sharpe iniections makes the patient mone
those corsives which vnto the wound is layde
brings hope of health; so wee are not dismayde

<48> 49 [S]

And wherfore are wee more impatyent
[200] to' beare those crosses which our god doth send
when all oure care cannot one payne prevent
nor all oure knowlege, know gods pryvate end
soe that impatience proves vs most vniust
< >
that doubts gods loue, and gyves his woord noe trust

5<4>0<9> [S][57^r]
                      much grast in cort [S]
[205] Admyte a sycophant <that stands in place>
vnto thy king and quene thoroug'h hate bely the
Sathan had power to vex Iobe in woorse <ca>sort [S]
thinck this affliction sent from god to trye the
what doest thou know but that thy princes grace
[210] may in thy harte gods image quite deface

51 [S]

If wicked men doe take away thy wealth
plenty may make thee wanton kick at god
thinck this impostune lancht for thy soules health
doe not repyne att the allmightyes rodd
[215] perhapps thy store of treasure may soe dull thee
                  s
a<nd> from this lyturgy tis want must pull thee

[Southwell's drafts, #2]

riches ar unto men as ar thar foode [S, to l. 64]
ar h
_____
            nis
tis weacke to repine at altorasion
sinsce he that can do all can doo no euell
                  ing
[5] aproue, eigh[ay] <nothing but> goods deprauasion
which nothingnis proseedith from the deuell
then let our wills conioyned be to his
that [which] can do all it cannot do amis

<----->
[10] what thow we see sum rise and othors fall

        men call
as whar this rise <mistes ga-----> I can not tell
for wealth land titels Is no rise attall
which breath and death doth make times carryi<n>ng ball
it[that] lets us thinke what euor doth betide us
[15] <woudste thow not haft to se-- truist>
tis good and beste to which gods grase doth guide us
<what sends a katt[cat] to acibytrate the case>

it[that] since all men to[do] labor to a<d>ttayn
to hygh fylisite how falls it out
[20] that most do spend thar labors but in vayne
and striue for that they euor goo with ovt
because they dig for fruit in barron sands
and spret thar nets to fish in highest lands

but If whe knwow whar happinis did dwell   [57ᵛ]
      not   thate
[25] we would thinke thise could giue soplys
wherfor <let> the law as a lone passing pell[bell]
                      crouns the toplis scies
from that gread iudge that <teror t--- to men>
            playnely tost   in
<-t>hath <he which cums to> to hyer honors soull
<shall know a thefe to be a harbraynd fooll>
[30] a thife thises[this is] a harbrayned courard and a fooll

---

now if a druncord may be called a man
which in to by consent can hardly fall
that he which hath his soull drouned in a pan
should it redayne[retain] the name of vnsiuall[uncivill]
[35] his theft mey well deserue the seill of treason
which unto lickecor hath betrayed his reason

that man hath a soull   [58ʳ]

nor is mens soules one uniuersall beame

                           all
eveneli spread throuth out [throughout] <the> flesh of man
[40] for sum sinke stantding pools whence flowse no streame
deseerue nor cckee[seek?] the halfe that othors can

LADY ANN SOTHWELL

<for if one soull ar coude unto all>
<for so all arts by repitesion meght>
sike [such] thinges forgot cuncur against sight

         all
[45]   whar if <on> souls war one of one condesion
               would neede but
all arts in all <ned only> repitesion

all corporal things with mattor is sustanid   [58ᵛ]
and each materiall [thing] holds and giues corrupsion
the soull of man py[by] mattor not mentaynid
[50]   what cannot touch can neuor [experience] eruption
so that this sperit of ours that feeds on truth
<from>our degayed[decayed] ageing gayns pouer and youth
    by

and that it is immortoll let us try
unto what end this soull of ours was made
[55]   what war all obgicktes if thar war no Ie
           war
or what <for> Iis if darknis all inuade
<shince ech supstance>
<what contenplasion of al>
who grantes esterrs[Esthers] the case must not denie
                    sperits
[60]   if all haue sperituall <souls the> cannot dye

let us make man O crasius trenitye
dud then to preach in heaven a gui-ding soull
his bodi this greate worlds epetome
all undon standing thar should all controll
[65]   all in age like thyselfe that neuor dies
             with him
but shall remayen <for age> aboue the scies

      An Inventorye of the Lady Anne Southwells goods   [59ʳ]
      sent from hir dwellinge at Clerkenwell to hir
      howse at Acton, inventoried by me Iohn
      Bowker. & Wittnessed by Margaret
      Mitton. & Mary Musgraue.

1631 sent
23 Aprill

A feather bead & bolster
A matt

94   THE WORKS OF THE

A payre of new canvas sheetes

[5] A white Rugg.

A Tapestrye Cauerlidd

A garden line

A spade.

A shouell

[10] A mattock

A rake.

sent.
26. Aprill

a high Chayre and 4 high stooles of scarlett fringed wth
yellow silke & studded wth brasse nayles

[15] 6 lowe stooles of scarlett studded not fring'd.

a chayre. 3 stooles & a longe Cushion of crimson veluett
garnished wth yellow silke.

A Carpett of Scarlett fring'd wth yellow silke.

2 Tapestry Couerled to couer ye stoole
A chayre & 2 stooles of Crimson Damaske garnisht wth yellow silke.ᴧ

[20] 5 longe Cushions & 5 short ones of black veluet imbrodered wth
coloured silke.

a rounde Table wth a Drawer

2 new Canvas sheetes to wrapp ye Chayres in

a payre of brasse Andyrons, tonngs, fyre shouell<s>, bellowes,

[25] & a Cappan of brasse suitable & a Course Sheete to wrapp them in.

X

A Trunck packt, wth 5 Curtaines, a Topp of a bedd, & vallance wth
the head of crimson & siluer sattin, and lacte & fring'd wth
siluer, and a peach coloured Taffata counterpoynt wth 3 breadths
of Taffata 3 els longe.

[30] A needle worke bedd wrought upon holland wth grapes & leaues in
blacke.

4 small Curtaines. 2 greate Curtaines, The bed tester. The
Beds head, The vallance fringd, 2 Cupboard cloths. all theise
of the forsaid black worke.

X

[35] One Bedstedd wth a corde & matt, one woll bedd, one fether bedd,
& bolster, one new blankett wth a China wrought quilt. 5 peeces
of busking tapestry containeinge 123 fl' ells.

One payre of Andyrons, wth toungs, shouell, payre of bellowes, &
a Cappan sutable. One close stoole wth a pan & Chamberpott, One

LADY ANN SOTHWELL

95

[40]   Trunck wth furniture for two bedds. One peece of ould tapestrye
to wrapp the other 5 in.   12 dos of glasse bottles in ye close
stoole & a greene say Curtaine. 3 bed tike pillowes, a cradle
to sweate in, a brush   2 Curtaines for windowes.

[59^v is blank]

you Gyannts, or Hyennas that doe dwell,   [60^r]
here proudly trampling o're your owne bredd hell *
Behould a Captaine, whose last Gloriouse ffight
Was to Subdue, the Prince of endless night
[5]   And in this conflict, he such honor wonn
As ffrom a Seruant he became a sonn
At fiue times fiue yeeres he exchanged the liffe
And went as bridgegroomes vse to meete a wife
Cheerfully, smileing, and at either hand
[10]   As bride mates, faith, and hope, did ffirmly stand
And bidds him tell each Libertine, vnstable
That hould both God and Heauen and ould wiues fable
They liue like beasts, ∧<and they like> beasts shall dye
And parteing Soules, doe offten prophesye
[15]   O' lett those teares his reuerend Parents shedd
Bee turn'd a Christoll Tombe and o're him laide
That ∧<beinge> transparant, euery eye may see
The truest Mapp, of mans ffelicitie
So will the fond world leaue this foolish trick
[20]   Of writeinge Epi<taffsms> vpon the dead
But rather write them one the Quick
Whose Soules, Ingraues of fflesh ly buried
ffor in this graue, you only see
But his Soules graue twoe graues well turnd to one
[25]   Now doth he liue, ffrom fflesh made ffree
Trust mee good ffreinds he is not dead but gone

*   And think that death, and Iudgment, is so farre
That with the Heauens, your ympiouse handes make warre

[The inventory of fol. 59^r, continued]   [60^v]

May .10.

2 payre of pott hangers for the Chimney
2 payre of pott hookes

a payre of Racks.

2 spitts:

[5] 1 pott to boyle meate in

26 pewter dishes

6 sawsers

a fyre forke, a pere of tongs.

12 May

2 Truncks of bookes

[10] a Couch couered wth gilt lether, bed, matt.

a bowle & pale

a skreene frame

a Rundlett of Aquavite

14 May.

2 Truncks one of bookes. 1 of linnen: 6 pere of fine

[15] sheetes 6 pere of course 3 pere of

pillow beeres 2 dos napkins 6 of damask 6 of <-->Canvas

12 of diaper 6 tabell cloths 2 of damask 4 of diaper

3 Towells. 3 night gownes, a skarlet wastcoate.

Harnes for 4 horses

[20] sweateinge Cradle

The weeke before whitsonday

a Table of Cedar 6 foote longe.

4 hutches for pidgeons

a spininge wheele

[25] 7 Iune   2 Court Cupbords

1 chayre table

a round table

an Iron drippinge pan

an Iron pott

[30] a spitt

2 pere of bellowes

a skellett

6 porringers—6 spoones

2 fyre shouells

[35] 2 payre of toungs

2 bedd coards

2 payre of Andyrons

2 Truckle bedds

<1 ould cupboard>

[40] 2 matts.

LADY ANN SOTHWELL

Apparell of my Ladyes sent the 14 of Iune to Acton   [61ʳ]
in a Trunke.

Imprimis a cloke, hood, & safegard of scarlett Kersye laced wth siluer

a Rose coloured veluet peticoate trimd wth gould lace

a watchet Saten peticoate trimd wth gould lace

a black satten peticoate & doublet imbrodered wth gould flowers

[5]   a black Calamintha gowne, peticoate & 2 stomachers <w>& bodyes

a black saten gowne kirtle & stomacher lined wth watchet

a payre of swatchett satten hustles laced wth gould lace & stomacher.

a black veluett gowne laced wth gould & lined wth crimson; & a

stomacher.

[10]   a black grograne gowne stript wth gould & lined wth changeable

taffata wth Kirtle & Stomach^r.

& bodyes to it

a black plush gowne Kirtle & 2 stomachers

a payre of veluet pantafles.

[15]   a black Taffata mantle

a payre of black brancht veluet bodyes

<a> 2 beuers

25 Iune   1 baskett of Candles 1 pott of meale 3 barrells of salt,

1 barrell of sope, 1 of vinegor 2 choppinge kniues, 1 hand

[20]   saw. 2 morters, 1 pestell, 2 tinder boxes, 1 sute of gilt

hangings 1 payre of virginmales, two Chaynes—one Iack,

fower pullies, 1 lyne, 1 skymmer 1 greene Rugg 4 Cushens

27 Iune.   1 greate Kettle, 1 greate pott 1 buckinge tubb, 1

pondringe tubb, 1 peele, 1 pere of fyre Irons, 1 grate

[25]   shouell 1 forke 2 pewter candlsticks. 2 brasse ones

3 potts, 1 pottle, pinte. quarte, 1 grid Iron, one

broyler of laten 1 Cullinder 1 Chaffing dish, 1 fryeinge

pan, 2 dos' of trenchers, 2 drippinge panns 1 brancht

brasse Candlestick, 5 pewter dishes 1 choppinge board.

[30] 30 Iune   2 fether bedds one flock bedd 4 white Ruggs. 2 bolsters 1

truckle bedd 2 matts. 2 large pillowes, 1 warmeinge

pan, 4 Canes 2 rodds---- 4 fowleinge peeces, 2 firkins

of butter. 2 cheeses. 2 matts, 2 bed cords 1 pere of

tables, 1 halbard. 1 heryet

[35] 2 Iuly   5 Truncks. 2 bottles of oyle. bootes & shooes of the

Captaines

[61ᵛ is blank]

[Receipts of the 1580s, numbers 10 and 11]

[62ʳ]

I   The Porter entred in to paye
The xvjᵗʰ of Dec' and ys to have per diem viijᵈ } viijᵈ

II   Dischardged the 14ᵗʰ Daye of Ianuarye
And thear is paid vnto him for 27 Dayes } xviijˢ /
[5]   at viijᵈ per Diem_____

[62ᵛ is blank]

[A receipt of the 1580s, number 12]

[63ʳ]

Phillipe Iones entred in to paye
the 24 of Dece' and ys to have per diem viijᵈ } viijᵈ

[63ᵛ is blank]

[Receipts of the 1580s, numbers 13 and 14]

[64ʳ]

Iohn Hogge entred into Paye the
10ᵗʰ Daye of Ianuarye and is to } vjᵈ /
have per diem_____

Imprest to Iohn hogge the 28ᵗʰ daye
[5]   of Ianuarij 1588 _____ } vˢ /

These are Likewise bookes belonginge to me

[64ᵛ]

99. Priuate deuotions in duodecimo
100. The Crummes of Cumforte in duodecimo
101. Meditations and Vowes in octauo.
102. A new & admirable Inuention &ᶜ ᵃ' in duodecimo.
[5]   103. The truth of our Tymes in octauo.
104. Select Cases of Conscience &ᶜ ᵃ' in octauo.
105 The Temple in Sacred Poems in octauo.
106. The Practice of Pietie in Octauo.
107. The English Dictionarie in Octauo.
[10]   108. The Christian Warrfare in quarto.
109. The Dippers dipt by Doctor ffeatley in quarto.
110. A Great Bible in folio.

LADY ANN SOTHWELL

[A receipt of the 1580s, number 15]   [65ʳ]

Iohn Oynion entred into Paye the 10ᵗʰ of ⎫
Ianuarye, and is to have per diem _____ ⎭   vjᵈ

A List of my Bookes

1. Caluins Institutions. in ffolio.
2. Caluins Sermons vpon Iob: in folio
3. Synopsis Papismi. or a generall veiw of
    Papistry by And: Willett. in Quarto.
[5]   4. Hookers Ecclesiasticall Politie. in folio.
5. Plinies Naturall History. in folio.
6. Generall History of the Netherlands. in folio.
7. History of the Romane Emperors. in folio.
8. Camerarius Historicall Meditations. in folio.
[10]   9. Triumph of God's Reuenge agᵗ Murther. in folio.
10. Orlando ffurioso. in folio.
11. Salust his history in English: in folio.
12. Eusebius Ecclesiasticall History in folio.
13. Spensers ffayrie Queene in ffolio.
[15]   14. Purchas his Pilgrimage. in folio
15. Gerard's Herball in folio.
16. An old Dictionary in folio.
17. Markhams Booke of Honour. in folio.
18. Mountaigne Essayes. in. folio.
[20]   19. Morrisons Trauells. in folio.
20. The Seidge of Breda. in folio.
21. Suctonius, of the 12 Cæsars, in folio.
22. Sʳ Chr: Sybthorps booke agᵗ Popery. in Quarto.
23. Dʳ Donnes Poems. in Quarto.
[25]   24. Matchiauels Art of warre. in Quarto.
25. Felthams Resolues. in Quarto.
26. Dʳ Kings Lectures. in Quarto.
27. Mornay, of the truenesse of Christian Religion. in Quarto.
28. The Treasury of Times. in folio.
[30]   29. Elian's Tactickes. in ffolio.
30. A Bible in Quarto.

100 THE WORKS OF THE

	31. The falls of vnfortunate Princes. in Quarto	[65ᵛ]
	32. The Art of Riding. in Quarto.	
	33. Blundeuil's Horsemanship. in Quarto.	
[35]	34 A french Testament. in. Octauo.	
	35 Barry's Discourse of Warr. in folio /	
	36 Barret's Theorike, & Practike, in folio. /	
	37 A Iournall, by Hexham, & others exc. in folio /	
	38 The Souldiers Grammer, in Quarto /	
[40]	39 The Politicke, & Militarie discourses of yᵉ Loᵈ De La Nowe, in Quarto	

40 Lawes & Ordinances of Warr. in Quarto
41 Garnet, a Iesuite, & his Confederat's: in Quarto /
42 An Apologie by Kᵍ Iames, for yᵉ oath of Allegiance in Quarto
[45] 43 Sʳ Walter Raleigh, of yᵉ Prerogatiue of Parliamᵗ. in Quarto

	44 Richard Crompton's Mansion of Magnanimitie	in Quarto.
	45. Hitchcok's Newyeres gift.	in Quarto.
	46 Atcheson's Militarie Garden;	in Quarto
	47 Richard Remnant, touching bees;	in Quarto
[50]	48 Lucius Annæus Seneca, exc.'	in Quarto
	49 Considerations touching a Warr wᵗʰ Spaine.	in Quarto
	50 Kᵍ. Iames his Entertainemᵗ, through London.	in Quarto

L. Elizabeth.-

	51 A sermon preached by the B: of London,	in Quarto
[55]	52 An Answer, to an Invectiue agˢᵗ. R. C:	in Quarto
	53 Lex Palionis exc. Challener;	in Quarto.
	54 Regis, Reginæ, Nobiles etc.	in Quarto
	55 directions for yᵉ cure of yᵉ Plague.	in Quarto
	56 Ordinances for Sequestringe Estates.	in Quarto
[60]	57 Kᵍ. Charles declaration, touching Scotland.	in Quarto
	58 Michael Dalton's Iustice of Peace.	in folio.
	59 Poulton<'s>, de pace Regis.	in folio.
	60– Daniell, of yᵉ history of England.	in folio
	61 Batman, vppon Bartholome,	in folio.
[65]	62 The Tryall of witts.	in Quarto
	63 Britannia's Pastorals.	in folio
	64 The Goulden ffleece.	in folio [66ʳ]
	65 Nosce teipsum.	in Quarto
	66 Seneca, his ten Tragedies	in Quarto
[70]	67 A service booke.	in Quarto

LADY ANN SOTHWELL 101

68 Great Brittans little Calendar.   in Quarto.

69 Robt. Bruce, his 16 sermons.   in Quarto

70 Conspiracie for pretended Reformation—   in Quarto

71 Iohn Copley a Seminary Prest,   in Quarto

[75]   touching Religion.

72 The Triumph of faith exc'.   in Quarto

73 A Sermon, called great Britains Salomon.   in Quarto

74 The Teares of peece.   in Quarto

75 The Bee hiue, of ye Romish Church.   in Octavo

[80] 76 The Confession of S^t. Augustine.   in Octauo

77. Aduancement of Learning by S^r fran: Bacon in quarto.

78. S^r francis Bacons Apologie in certaine Imputacions concerning the late Earle of Essex. in octauo.

79 The Magazine of Honour in quarto.

[85] 80 The Christians mourninge Garment in octauo.

81. Shadowes without Substance in quarto.

82. Articles agreed vpon by y^e Archbishops &c$^{ra'}$ in quarto.

83. Ierusalem's Peace in a Sermon in octauo. /

84. Warlike directions or y^e souldiers Practice in octauo.

[90] 85 A discourse of Valour in octauo.

86. The funeralls of Henry Prince of Wales in quarto.

87. Animaduersions vpon those notes &c$^{ra'}$ in quarto.

88. A Dialogue betweene a Parliam^t. man & a Roman Catholick. in quarto.

[95] 89. The Catholick Moderator &c$^{ra'}$ in quarto.

90. The Swaggering Damsell a Comedie. in quarto.

91. Eugenia or True nobillities Trance in quarto.

92. The Martyrdome of King Charles &c$^{ra'}$ in quarto.

93. Andromeda Liberata, or y^e Nuptialls &c$^{ra'}$ in quarto.

[100] 94. An Abstract out of y^e Records of y^e Tower &c$^{ra'}$ in quarto

95. An Apologie for y^e Armie by Dauid Ienkins in quarto.

96. A Post with a Packquet of mad Letters in quarto. /

97. Saint Peters Plaint in quarto. /

98. Doctor Ridley vpon y^e Lords supper in octauo.

---

the 3th of ffebruary   maister C   Preacher of acton   [66^v]
1632   In y^e 11th of Mathew.16 and 17. verses

I haue pyped vnto you and you haue not danced

I haue mourned vnto you and you haue not wept

102   THE WORKS OF THE

This shewes the hardness of our hartes that neither the musick of saluation
nor thretnings of Iudgment will drawe vs into sorowe for our sines, Rachell
5 wept ffor her Children bycause they wear not, this shewes owre Imodarate
sorowe for worldly thinges, but fewe with ye Virgin Marie seek Christ
Sorowinge for where sine is Christ is not and our sorowe and teares must
recale him, for our sines are writen in the booke of gods memorie, and our
teares is as the Spundge that blotteth them out <-r> our teares are that
10 preciouse pearle that the Merchant sould all his guades to purchase and theis
are the teares y^t shall be put into Christs bottle repent and amend <I>and
the kingdom of heauen is at hand. the lord graunt vs true repentence, and
aboundence of teares for our sines; but to worldly afflictions let our eyes be
drye, and bundle them vp as stubble in the hope that wee haue in Christ
15 Iesus,
But to Carnall man a pyper is more acceptable then a preacher and a min-
strill more then a minister, their hartes are hardened against the daye of
wrath

St. Augustine Ca. 8 of his booke. the Citie of god   [67^r]

Aduerse and prosperouse fortune are both assistants in a good mans Saluation: and there is nothing befalleth them but he can conuert it vnto an aug-
mentation of his vertues The cause why good men perish in this world with
the bad is that the Coniue or flatter at there vice, feeringe to loose there
5 liues, honor, or welth the prouoke gods anger to cutt them of hear though
not here after
Cha: the 1th
The Church warreth daily, but the end of on warre is the begininge of another, That shall be the last and most perfect victorie, when the Church
10 shall' be translated into heauen to remaine for euer in peace with the king
and peace maker, (Iesus Christ.
The tyrants subiects are his slaues, and himselfe slaue to his lusts, and pleasures
Cha: ye 9th.
15 No man saueth his gould but by denying of it nor his god but by Confes-
sing him, so the one is Couerd by lyes, the other enioyed by truth
St. Augustine. Cha: 11th:
Sumptuouse funeralls are rather solaces to the liuinge then furtherance to
the dead, for whether o^r bodyes be throwne to fish ffowles or bests god is
20 able to asume euerye atome or hear

LADY ANN SOTHWELL   103

The Eternall spheres his gloriouse Spirit do holde.
To which come few that lye embalmd in golde

[67ᵛ is blank]

[68ʳ]

A booke of the nature of foure footted bests written by C[onradvs] Ges[ner]
in lattin, and translated into English by Edward Topsell wherin these to
shew the glorye of God in his Creation, and the nature of bestes how far
they are profittable seruicable, and medicinable, poysonable hurtful and
5 pernitiouse to man, I haueing survayed the booke haue for my ow[ne]
memorye sett downe some perticulers that I best affect;

And ffirst of the <u>Manticora</u> that hath a face like a ma[n] and a bodie
like a Lyon haueing three dubble rowes of teeth like a sawe, and a
tayle like A Scorpion armed with a sting he is swifft of foote as a
Hare, greedie of appetite after the flesh of men, he is called Antropo-
5 phagi that is to say ma[n] eaters, it is also called Hyænna;

There is an other kynd of Hyæna called Crocuta bred in Ethiapiæ gotten
betwixt a Lyoness and an Hyæna, their fatt is good against yᵉ go[ut] their
bloud against leaprosie, many other cures the haue for the dissease[s] in
man; but bycause they are not to be had it is to no purpose to discrib[e]
10 them. /

of the Lamia:

The Lamia hath a face and brests like a woeman, with long heire on the
head, the pawes like a Beare, and tayle like a horse, the bodie of it is like a
Panther, with Scales all ouer like a ffish, and the hinder feet like an oxx,
15 Aristottle calleth them in greek Impusæ changing themselue[s] ffrom one
shape into another; some suppose them to be Pharises and thos[e] that vse
to change Chilldren, the Poet reporteth that this Lamia wa[s] a beutifull
woeman and daughter to Bellus who Iupiter being in lo[ue] with stole her
out of Lybia and brought her into Itelye where he got many Children of
20 her, but Iuno killd her Children as soone as they we[re] borne, and vexed
her with a restless estate, that shee could neuer b[e] able to sleepe, wher-
upon shee stole awaye and killed other Children Iupiter in compassion of
the wrong which Iuno had donn her, giue her exemptile eyes that might be
taken in and out at her owne pleasure, and gaue her power to transforme
25 herselfe into what shap[e] shee would, this may pass for a fable. and may
beare a good morrall

of the land Tortiss or Turtle:

This beast carieth allwayes his shell vpon his back; it is reported by the Poet
that Iupiter bidding all the foure footted beasts to dinn[er] all assembled but
30 the Tortiss at last when dinner was donn the Tortiss came in, Iupiter asking
him why he stayed so long, he reply[ed] his owne house gaue him most
honnor, Iupiter being angrie a'iudged him that he should still carrie his
house vpon his back

of the Rhinoceros:

35 The Rhinoceros is of a monstrouse shape and of a beawtifull coulle[r] for he
is yellowe speccled with purple his feet are like an Elaphants so is the shape
of his bodie, his eares like a Swine his bodie is all ouer as if he weare in
compleat armour, his head is like a horsses and o[ut] of his nose their comes
a horne which is longe, strong, and sharpe with which he fights, his naturall
40 enuye is against an Elaphant he is taken only by virgins, and vpon a virgins
lapp he will fale asleepe, and so is taken./

of the Beauer:

The Beuer is called canis Ponticus he is about the bigness of an Otter is vsefull vnto man, his heire and his skine makes cloathing and hat. of his stones
45 their is made a gumme called Castoreum good against epolepticall and
parolepticall disseases, thus much of the Beaue[r]

of the Ape.   [68ᵛ]

The Ape as the Auther saith was Created for nothing but to be laught at or
to make men laugh, and yet he reporteth his harte being dryed and grated
50 into powder and drunk in white wine doth reviue the Spiritts of the harte
their is many kyndes of Apes, but vnder this Ienus is contained Munkies
Baboones Satyres and all that deformed crue whose Quallities are but
knauish and rediculouse /

of the Bison or wilde Bull.

55 I finde no other propertye in him but an extream heat in his fflesh and
bloud and that whersoeuer he lickes he killes. /

of the Buffe.

The Buffe is <a> bodied like an Ox, and headed like an Hart, and will
change couller like a Camelion the make targetts of his skinne against the
60 shott of arrowes. /

of the Dromedary

The Dromedary is a kinde of a Cammell of fifteene Cubitts hye, and six
cubitts long, he will trauell one hundred miles a daye and carye twoe thousand waight, when they com to bucking time they are full of maliciouse

65 furye, and will remember them that haue donn them iniurie and kill them
if the can surprise them. /

of the Catt.

A Catt is the Epitomie of a shee Lyon, the Egiptians doe obserue in the
eyes of a catt the increase of the Moonelight for with the Moone the shine
70 more fully at the full, and more dimly in the change and waine and the male
catt doth also vary his eyes with the sunne; for when the sunne ariseth, the
apple of his eye is longe; towardes noone it is round and at the euening it
cannot bee seen at all, but the whole eye sheweth alike. /

of the Colus.

75 The beast Colus is hunted and taken by mysicke his bigness is betwixt a
Ramme and a Hart he hath twoe hornes which are little vsefull but for
Spectacles or haffts for kniues. /

The Poets fame, and Gesner reporteth, that neere Mayanona a fountain
there grue a Plaintain vnder which was bredd a Hydra that had seaun heads,
80 wherof one of the heads was said to bee Immortall, this Hydra Herculus
fought withall and slue and in the head which was immortall he dippt his
dartes which gaue them that strength of poyson, that immediatly it killed,
all that he wounded with those darttes; it is said that Iuno helped him to
kill it, bycause he called to her for ayde, so that malice is to be intreated if
85 it be either worshiped or implored

<Epothegmes> Apothegmes [69ʳ]

	1	He that knowes not where to finde the Sea, let him take a riuer for his guide:
Bushop Kinge	2–	It is a happie necessitie, that makes a man better, then he would be./
Fox	3–	<He that buildes vpp vertue in wordes and destroyes it in action is an audaciouse hippocritt one yᵗ builds vp fame wᵗʰ one hand, & hell wᵗʰ an other>
	4	Preuention, is the harte of pollicye
	5	He that must depend vppon god for his saluation, and dare not trust him for a Morcell of bread, is a laboriouse Athist
	6	He that makes a<n oath> vowe which is not consonant to the word of god is a foole in the makeing of it, and a knaue in the keeping of it
	7	The Romains affirme that all the saints departed this life are in

porgitorye, where the ^are^ barred ffrom the presence of God; then
to what end doe they praye to them that are debarrd the presence of God, this is absurditye, therfore let them ether put
awaye Porgetorye or leaue praying to Saints:

8   Guilt of sinne, and feare of punishment, keeps the Consience
still wakeinge, and the harte still akeinge the way to Quiet
them both, is to be reconsiled to God in Christ Iesus for thear
is no other remedye neither in heauen, nor Earth, <Tambarlin
would be an Emp^r^our the Angels as god>. /

9   Sinne faintly repulssed inuites Sathan to ffurther assaults

10   There is no man so misserable, that hath not something to reioyce him nor no man so happie that hath not something to
torment him

11   Desires is like an exolation that neuer leaues assending till it
fale into hell, for Tomberlin would bee an Emporour the
Angels as god

12   A Glutton diggs his owne graue with his owne teeth

13   He that is so kinde harted as to be drunke to entertaine his
ffriend, makes the Diuell Maister of the ffeast and himselff
foole to the Compeny, I had rather bee suspected for a miser
then knowne to bee a beast

14   The Spainricks affirme that gould, and the harte of Man, doe
Simpothise in nature, hearin they hould their best annalasies
both brought to best vse by stronge necessities, the Hermeticks
say the harte in the bodie ^of man^ resembles the sunn in the firma-
ment- the one inlighten's the great world the other viuivies the
less; hearin the moste agree as th[e] sunnes beams driues all-
ways downe to the Center, so the affections of our harte lyes
euer groueling their. your Doggmaticks saye the harte is made
of Harmonie but he y[t] sees what siuill warrs thear is betwixts
thoughte and thoug[hte] would supose it to bee made of discorde

14   Hee yt builds vp virtue in wordes, and destroyes it in action,
putts a Torch into ffames hand to light himselff into hell. /

15   he that hath good motions, and soone letts them pass tells ye
Diuell yt god hath looked in at his windowere

16— It is more happiness to be borne dumm, then to haue a [69ᵛ]
tongue of blasphamie

17– There are three deaths that pursue man, ffirst the death of
grace while hee is in the world, the death of Saints is in the
graue, and the death of the soule' in hell; lett vs bee carefull to
preuent the first, and the other twoe are preuented for vs.

18– A fflatterer and a hyenna are synonimices, and both are antra-
pophagie that is men killers;

19– Hee that takes glorye in repeatinge his owne vices, carries the
pestilence still in his mouth. /

20– As Russticitye befitts not a gentleman, so Inckpott tearmes best
become a Pettagogg.

21– Hee that referrs repentence till the Intresse surmount ye princi-
pall, neuer cares for freedome.

22– Hee that desires the acquintence of great personages, pursues
his owne slauarie, I had rather ly at ease vpon my owne Palett
then kneele by anothers

23– As Custorium drawes blood at the nose by smelling, so a blas-
phemar drawes blood from the harte of a Christian by hearing
of him.

24. I had rather be a toad then a fflatterar, but I had rather be
nothing then either of them.

25. Afflictions ar the schoole of god

26 In the risurection of Christ the earth presented a naturall bodie
into heauen, in the decendinge of the holye ghoste the heauens
                    bestowed
<presented> a quickeninge Spirit to the earth /

27 Man is of a Middle Creation, betwixt the Angells and the
bestes his knowledge aught to be answerable to his Creation,
not so presumptuouse as to prye into the secretts of God, nor
so <stupifyed> stupid as not to knowe his reueilled will

28 He that sleepes in the Cradle of Carnall securitie the Deuill
hath put out both his eyes, but he that is awake by the stinge
of consience may caste awaye his spectacles.

29 Hee that hath to much, or to little of this worlds wealth dyes,
the former killeth the soule, the second the bodie

30 That perplexed Concience that thinks god cannot forgiue him,
denyes his omnipotencye, and he that thinks he will not forgiue
him accuses him of falsehoode, for he hath sworne by himselff./

108   THE WORKS OF THE

How that the Law of the Gospell is   [70ʳ]
more perfect then all other lawes.

As there is but one o'nely god, one onely christ, one onely faith, one onely church, and one onely gospell: so likewise vnto the world is but one onely diuine lawe, imprinted alreadye by god in the minde of man, darkened by sinne, expressed somewhat by morall Philosaphy, but much better by Moses,

5 and most perfectlye by Christ, and a new by Christ, the spirit of god being the guyde, powred in, imprinted, and written in the bowels, and in the hearts of the regenerate, as god aforetime promised by his prophet—They call notwithstanding the naturall law, those Cannons, rules, and truth practised, of that which is right, and of that which is not right, imprinted in

10 the booke of the minde, in the which euery one reading, when he commeth to the yeares of discretion, without any other master and booke, he discerneth by himselfe good from euill, And the truth it self, inasmuch as by Moses it was expressed in tables, is called the law written: Wheras afterward by Christ, the holy Ghost being the guide, it was in a more perfect manner

15 imprinted in the heartes of the regenerate, that is <a> called the Euengelicall law, of grace and of the spirit. where is to be noted, that allthough a philosopher hath for example, imprinted in his minde this truth, that god ought not to be dishonoured, but honoured, and knew that this thing is most right, yet notwithstanding he obserued not this most iust lawe, yea, the

20 Iewes, albeit they had this same truth, not onely imprinted in the minds but also expressed in the tables of Moses, and discerned the righteouss from the vnrighteous, and that with greater light then they Philosophers, they could in nowise obserue that iust and honest law, because they were letted by theire concupisences. but in a Christian already by faith regenerated, the

25 goodnesse of god through Christ is in such sort imprinted in his heart, that by the liuely, spirituall tast and feeling which he hath in Christ of god, he cannot dishonor him, yea, by the spirit which he hath, the which prevayleth agaynt <all> his carnall concupisences, he is constrayned to honor him, yea, by the spirit which he hath; and according to the measure of faith which he

30 hath, the philosopher then albeit he knew in part his bounden dutie, he did not therfore fulfill it bicause the flesh resisted him, and in like case also the Iew, albeit he knew, and that better then all the philosophers, what the will of god is, neuerthelesse being without Christ and without gra[ce] he obeied it not, wherefore he shall be punished the more grieuously, as hee had

35 greater knowledge of the lawe of god. The naturall lawe therefore, and much more the written law, is the minister of death and damnation, whereas the

Euengelicall law, of spiri[t] and of grace, is the minister of lyfe and saluation: wherefore Paule speaking of it, sayd, the lawe of the spirit of lyfe in Christ Iesu, hath deliuered mee from the law of death and of sinne. The writen law, therfore is vnperfect,

                    although.

Although the naturall lawe be much more vnperfect, seeing [70ᵛ] that albeit they shew those things which ought to bee done, they doe not therefore giue the grace to bee able to obserue them, The lawe naturall, then was as it were in darknesse, The lawe of Moses in shadowes, and the Euangelicall law in light, the law naturall came at midnight, Moses lawe at the morning, and the Euangelicall lawe at noone daye, The naturall lawe came with a little candle burning, Moses lawe with a great torch, but couered, and the Euangelicall lawe with the cleere light of the Sun. The naturall law saw god in his creatures, Moses law in the scriptures, and the Euengelicall law in Christ, the naturall law seeth not christ, Moses law saw him and shewed him afarre off, and the Euangelicall law hath seene him openly, and imbraced him for his owne, the naturall law hath embraced noe man, Moses law hath painted him out, with giuing him coulours, the euengelicall law hath giuen him spirit. The naturall lawe made him serue by reasons, Moses lawe for feare, and the euengelicall law for loue; The naturall lawe deliuereth vs from worldly infamy, Moses lawe from the tyranny of Pharao, and the euangelicall lawe from the tyranny of the world of the flesh, <and> of sinne, and of the diuell; The naturall lawe hath for the guide vnderstandinge, Moses lawe a piller of fire, and the euangelicall lawe the holie Ghost. The naturall lawe is the lawe of philosophers, Moses lawe hath him for the author, and the euangelicall lawe is of Christ. The naturall lawe feedeth men with woorldly things, Moses lawe with Manna, and the euangelicall lawe with god. The naturall lawe buildeth vp a worldly common wealth, Moses lawe the holy citie of Hierusalem, and the euangelicall lawe the holye Countrey. By the naturall lawe we were straungers, by Moses lawe seruants, and by the euangelicall lawe free and the sonnes of god. The naturall lawe guided vs to a certaine humaine felicity, Moses lawe into the land of promise, and the euangelicall lawe vnto heauen. The naturall lawe is a burthen fit for humaine strength, Moses law is a burthen sharp and grieuous, and the euangelicall lawe is pleasant and delectable. The naturall lawe hath a respect to the comlines of vertues, Moses lawe vnto felicitie, and the euangelicall lawe vnto the glory of god. The naturall conducteth thee into Aegipt, and there leaueth thee, Moses lawe deliuereth thee from thence, maketh thee

110   THE WORKS OF THE

75 walk thorough the desert, and the euangelicall lawe bringeth thee into the
land of promise. The naturall lawe begetteth thee vnto the world, Moses
lawe killeth thee vnto god, and the euangelicall lawe raiseth thee againe. The
naturall lawe accuseth thee, Moses lawe condemneth thee, and the euangelicall lawe saueth thee: The naturall <----> lawe awaketh man when hee
80 sleepeth, Moses lawe maketh him to tremble, and the euangelicall lawe
setteth him at rest; The naturall lawe maketh men righteous in their owne
sight, Moses lawe in the sight of the world, and the euangelicall lawe
maketh them righteouse in the sight of god. The naturall lawe promiseth
not any thing that is supernaturall, Moses lawe maketh promises of most
85 rich diuine things, and the euangelicall lawe obserueth them. The naturall
lawe maketh vs men, Moses lawe maketh vs angells, and the euangelicall
lawe euen as gods. wherfore the naturall lawe is good, Moses law better, and
the euangelicall lawe best and most perfect; let vs pray therfore vnto the
lord, that hee would imprint it in our heartes, to the intent that wee may
90 render to him all prayse, honour, and glory, thorough Iesus christ our lord,
Amen. /

[Acton receipts of 1632 and 1633]   [71ʳ]

esquire
Memoranduum that I Robert Iohnson ˄ doe
accknowledg my selfe to be fully sattisfied and paid
foʳ. the Tennements
for. the whole yeares Rent,˄held by the Lady Anne
Souththey wittn<>es my hand. 1632

[5]   Robert Iohnsoun
                                       An Iohnson

In the presents of
Tho: Warburton.

September 1632

[10]   Memorandum that I Robert Iohnson Esqʳ doe
accknowledg my selfe, to bee fully sattisfied and
paide for the <w>halfe yeares Rent for the   [S]
Tennements held by the Lady Anne Southwell
wittness my hand; this present Michelmas daye
[15]   1632
Wittness
Sam: Rawson: Robert Iohnsoun
                                       An Iohnson

Memorandum that I Robert Iohnson Esqʳ doe accknowled my selfe
[20]   to be fully sattisfyed and paid for the <hal>halph years Rent for the
Tennements held by the Ladie Anne Southwell wittnes my hand
the 25th of Aprill 1633

Wittnes   Robert Iohnsoun
Samuell Rowson   An Iohnson

[Acton receipts of 1633 and 1634]   [71ᵛ]

Memorandum that I Robert Iohnson Esqʳ doe acknowledge my
selff to be fullye satisfyed and paid for the halph years rent for the
tennament held by Captaine Henry Sibthorp, and the ladie Anne
Southwell his wife, wittness my hand the 10th daye of Nouember
[5]   1633. I saye receiued the some of ffiftie shillings which is the halph
years rent. due at Michelmas last

Witness
Samuell Rowson   Robert Iohnsoun
                                                 Ann Iohnson

Receiued by mee Anne Iohnson Executress <and sole heire> ⎱ lⁱ s d
[10]   vnto Robert Iohnson Esqʳ deceased the somme of ffiftie
shillings for one halph years rent for the Tennaments
held by Captaine Henrye Sibthorp, and the Ladie   -02 -10 00
Anne Southwell his wife, Scituated vpon the Stean in
Acton I say receiued the some of ffiftie shillings the
[15]   25th of March 1634   Ann Iohnson
Witness
Samuell Rowson

                                                 Widdow of
Receiued by mee Anne Iohnson Executress and ₐ<sole heire vnto>
Robert Iohnson Esqʳ deceassed, the some of ffiftye shillinges
                                                              liⁱ s d
[20]   for one halph yeares rent for the tennaments held by Captaine
                                                              -02–10–00
Henry Sibthorp and the Ladie Anne Southwell his wife
scituated vpon the steane in Acton I saye receiued ffiftye
shillinges the 29th of September 1634
                                                 Ann Iohnson
[25]   Wittnes
Samuell' Rowson
Mary Phillips

112   THE WORKS OF THE

[72ʳ]

Mʳ. Iohnson dyed the 18ᵗʰ daye of Nouember 1633 and was burieed the one
and twentith of the same Month, the text that Mʳ. Roger Cocks Ministe[r]
of Acton tooke vpon the funerall was out of the words theise; Now is the ax
put to the roote of the tree, therfore euery tree which bringeth not forth
5   good fruite is hewen downe and cast into the fyere;
his Comendations vpon the deceassed partie were foure, first his humilitye
for though by the exelencye of his qualitye which was Musick, in which hee
excelled most men his Compeny was desired both of princes and great
personages yet he did ascociate the poorest of the parish both with his
10 compenye, his coumforte, and his Councell;   he was   and earnest
his second Comendacone was his Charritye, for ∧<a well> willinge∧ to sett
peace amongst allmen, and readye to forgiue an Iniurye offored to himselff,
and to assist <any man In> aduersitie, his third was his patience which was
expresst both in his life and death, And the fourth was his penitencye;
15 And thus much off my owne knowledge, I haue knowne many men liue like
Philosophers and dye like ffooles, but he liued like a lamme and dyed like
a Champion, fullye conqueringe his owne affections and passions, and at his
last gaspe tooke his leaue of his ffrends, as if he had bine to goe a Iorney
Intreated them to sett him vpright in his bed and to leaue him that they
20 might not hinder him of his passage

[Acton receipts of 1635 and 1636]   [72ᵛ]

Rec'. by mee Anne Iohnson Executrix <and sole heire> ⎫
vnto Robert Iohnson of Acton Esqʳe deceased the somme ⎬ li' s d
of ffiftye shillings, for one halph yeare; rent, for the ⎪ 02–10–00
Tenaments held by Captaine Henry Sibthorp, and the   ⎪
[5]   Ladie Anne Southwell his wife Scituate vpon the Stean ⎭
in Acton, I saye receiued the 25th of March 1635
Wittness   Ann Iohnson
Samuell Rowson

I vnder written acknowledg, to haue rec': the sum   ⎫
[10] of fiftye shillings, beinge all that is due to me for   ⎬ li' s [d]
rent of the dwellinge howse that Captaine   ⎬ –02–10–0[0]
Sibthorp <now liueth in> & his wyfe the Lady   ⎪
Southwell now liueth in, & heare with to be fully   ⎪
satisfied, I say receiued the 29 of September   ⎭

LADY ANN SOTHWELL 113

[15] <u>1635</u> witnes my hand
     witnes   Ann Iohnson
     Ioseph Hopton

     <memorandum that I Anne Iohnson widdo do acknol[edge]   [S]
     to haue re seued the sum of 2 1 >   [S]

[20] Receiued, by me Anne Iohnson, y^e ∧ widdow of Robert ⎞
     Iohnson esq^r deceased, the sum of tow pounds ten ⎟
     shillings, beinge the full halfe yeares rent, due ⎟
     now att o^r lady, ∧^{day} for the tenniment <>now in ye occu- ⎟
     pation of Cap: Sibthorp, & the lady Anne^{ten} ⎟ 02–10–[00]
[25] Southwell his wyfe; beinge vppon the steane ⎟
     in Acton, and doe acknowledg my selfe fully ⎟
     satisfied, from the beginninge of ye world ⎟
     to this day, beinge the 25th of March, <u>1636</u> ⎟
     I say rece': the sum a boue said, wittnes my ⎠
[30] Wittnes / hand   Ann Iohnson
     Ioseph Hopton

     To the never dyeing memorye of that   [73^r]
     Ladye every way worthie the Lady
     Anne Southwell whoe vpon the
     second of October in the yeare
[5]   of Grace 1636: & of her age 63
     Slept Sweetly in the lord theis
     few lyne<u>es</u> are dedicated by—
     Roger Cock<u>es</u>: a true louer
     & admirer of her vertue<u>es</u>.

[10] The South winde blew vpon a springing Well:
     Whose waters flowed & the Sweete streame<u>es</u> did_∧^{swell}
     To such a height of goodne<u>es</u> that they lent
     the lower playne<u>es</u> a feedinge Nourishm^t
     Vntill at last (like envious Phillistine<u>es</u>)
[15] Remorselesse death wth restlesse time combine<u>es</u>
     to stopp the current, but Victorious fame
     Triumph<u>es</u> o're death & time, & strike<u>es</u> aflame
     Out of her Ashe<u>es</u> wch doth burne soe bright
     That it may giue the world per<u>p</u>etuall light

[20] Consecrated to the memory of the Hono.r &
Ornam.t of her sex, the Ladye Ann Southwell
of Corneworthie in the Countie of Devon:
eldest dawghter of Sr Thomas Harris, Kt and
Sarjant at law Married first to Sr Tho:
Southwell<s> of Spixworth in ye Countie
[25] of Norfolke, Kt. afterwardes to Henry:
Sibthorpe Sarjeant Major & Privye
Councellor of the province of Munster
in the Kingdome of Irland wth whome
she liued tenn yearees. /
[30]   The Paterne of
                      Conjugall loue
                      and obedience
Shee was a Ladye by the Generall verdict of all that knew her
reputed the liueing treasury of grace & nature Ioyntly conspireing
[35]   by her
Zealous constancye in religion liberall Charitye in Almees
Exemplary Vertue in life discreet affabillitye in behaviour
Pious frequency in devotion profound knowledge in learning
              Permanient Exactnees in beautye
[40] To make her vp the compleate' character of female perfection
                      Shee liued
            Publicklye honered by her Soveraigne
            passionately affected by her Equalles
            observantly respected by her inferioures
[45]   worthiely admired by all
                      and dyed

      In Christian peace and resolucion the second day of
      October in the yeare of or Lord <G>1636 being the 63 and
climactericall yeare of her age and doth here rest
[50] Expecting the second & glorious Epiphanye of or Saviour
till when her precious name will prserve that Happie
memorye of her worth wch is but weakely Expressed
in this sadd monument of an Endlesse affection
dedicated to her by her said deare & sorrowfull husband
[55]   Henry Sibthorpe

LADY ANN SOTHWELL
115

An Epitaph composed to the Eternall memory
of the Vertuous & well qualifyed Lady the Lady
Anne Southwell deceased the second of
October 1636:

[60] Seekeing for choycest attribut<u>ees</u> to Rayse
A Piramid to Lady Southwell<u>es</u> Prayse
I found invention of soe low a flight
Her worth was still aboue my fancy<u>ees</u> height
At last com<u>ees</u> fame & whisper<u>es</u> in myne Eare
[65] If thou a worthie Monument wouldest reare
Call her Rare peece of Nature soule of art
learninges
Nurse of religion <natur<u>ees</u>> better parte
Mirour of Lady<u>ees</u> vertu<u>ees</u> goulden mind
The Grac<u>ees</u> Temple Darlinge of the Nine
[70] Heavens Ioy Earth<u>ees</u> wounder truth<u>ees</u> faire patronesse
Thou mayest giue more but she deseru<u>ees</u> noe lesse
H S

[Fragments]   [73ᵛ]

angrie
angry

and
n
the
at the Res
[5] t intʳ in
and the
Lord

Consecrated to the Memory of ~   [74ʳ]
The Honour and ornamᵗ of her sexe ~. /

The Lady Anne Southwell.

Eldest daughter of Sʳ Thomas Harris of Corneworthy in the Countie of
Devon Kᵗ and Seargeant at Lawe. Maried first to Sʳ Thomas Southwell
of Spixworth in the Countie of Norff Kᵗ. Afterwardes to Henry Sybthorpe Sergeant Maior and Privy Councellour of the Province of Mun
          the kingdome of   whome
[5] ster in ∧   Ireland, with ∧<wᶜʰ last> she lived tenne yeares /

116

The patterne of coniugall love & obedience.

She was a Lady by the generall verdict of all that knew her
Reputed the living Treasury of Grace and Nature Ioyntly Conspiring

[10]

By Her

Zealous constancy in Religion,

Exemplary vertue in life,

Pious frequency in devotion,

Liberall Charity in Almes.

[15]

Discreet affibility in behaviour.

Profound knowledge in learning.

Permanient exactnesse in beautie.

To make her $\wedge^{\text{vppe}}$ the <exact>^{compleate} Character of ffemale perfection.

She Lived

[20]

Publiquely honoured by her soveraigne

Passionately affected by her equalles

Observantly reuerenced by her inferiours

Worthyly Admired by all.

And dyed

[25]

In Christian peace and resolution

The second day of Octob in the yeare of our Lord 1636, $\wedge^{\text{being y}^{e}\text{ 63 & Climatericall yeare of her age}}$ and doth
here rest expecting the second and Glorious Epiphany of our Saviour.
Till when her p^{r}cious name will <u>pre</u>serve that happy memory of her
worth, wch is but weakly exp^{r}ssed in this sad monum^{t} of an Endlesse
[30] affection dedicated to her by her sayd deare and sorrowfull husbande

Henry Sybthorpe

wyfes   [74^{v}]
inscription

Appendix I: Southwell as a Compiler and Composer

[See the Introduction, pp. 23–28, for a brief discussion of this appendix.]

Sigla

S   Lady Anne Southwell

HS   Captain Henry Sibthorpe, who signed and dated his hand in 1636 on fols. 73 and 74

HS-2   possible variations of Henry Sibthorpe's hand

JB   John Bowker (although this may also be a variation of Sibthorpe's hand), in charge of the inventory, fol. 59^r

SR   Samuel Rowson, who signed his name as a witness six times on fols. 71 and 72

JH   Joseph Hopton, who signed his name as a witness twice on fol. 72^v

TW   Thomas Warburton, who signed as a witness once on fol. 71

X-80   an unidentified secretary hand writing the receipts of the 1580s

X   unidentified scribes

F   Folio bound into volume

T   Folio tipped onto a guard

Watermarks: Nicholas Lebe

  NL^1 —with "Ɛ" in shield

  NL^2 —with "B" in shield

Folio No.	Content	Scribe	S's Name & Hand	Hand	
1r	sonnets	JB	1		F no watermark
v	blank				
2r	["Lie"]	JH	1	S	F no w/m
v	blank				
3r	letter to L. R.				T pot w/m
v	"		1		

4r	Falkland / note	JB / HS	1		T (pasted flat on folio)
v	blank				F NL[1]
5r	receipts / "Hym"	X-80 / HS			F NL[1]
v	"predicables"	SR		S	
6r	receipts	X-80			F no w/m
v	"	X-80			
7r	"Castle hauen"	SR			F NL[1]
v	blank				
stub					
8r	"Seneca"	JB			F NL[1]
v	" & 2 poems	JB			
9r	2 poems	JB			F NL[1]
v	2 sonnets	JB			
10r	"ffrayle love"	X: first 7 lines; JB: lines 8–36			F C Denise
v	blank				
11r	"Nature"	SR			F NL[1]
v	blank				
12r	Honor father	X			F NL[2]
v	"	X			
13r	"	X		S	F no w/m
v	blank				
14r	blank				F NL[2]
v	blank				
15r	blank				F no w/m

APPENDIX I

v	blank				
16r	"wifes"	X–same as first 7 lines, f.10			F no w/m
v	blank				
17r	F. Quarles	JB			F no w/m
v	blank				
18r	"to Doctor Adam"	HS-2	1		F no w/m
v	"	HS-2			
19r	"	HS-2			F no w/m
v	L. R. elegy	HS-2	1		
20r	"	HS-2			F dog
v	"	HS-2	1		
21r	L. R. / Cocks	HS-2 / HS	3		F dog
v	["Exequy"]	HS			
22r	4 poems	SR	2		F dog
v	"Envie"	SR		S	
23r	"Sommersett"	SR			F dog
v	"eight soules"	SR			
24r	[Elegy, G.A.]	SR			F no w/m
v	"	SR			
25r	"loue"	SR			F no w/m
v	blank				
26r	"Vnless him-selfe"	SR			T horn & baldric
v	"Grandams cause"	SR			F no w/m

27r	"frayle worlde"	X			T no w/m
v	"	X			F NL[1]
28r	1st "Com-mandement"	SR			T unidentified pillars
v	"	SR			F no w/m
29r	"	SR			T no w/m
v	"	SR	1		F NL[1]
30r	blank				F NL[1]
v	"Empourers"	SR			
31r	"Who euer sawe"	X		S	T NL[2]
v	"	X		S	F no w/m
32r	"	X			T NL[2]
v	"	X		S	
33r	"	X		S	T NL[2]
v	"	X		S	
34r	vs. images	X		S	T NL[2]
v	"	X		S	
35r	" / god's "name"	X		S	T no w/m
v	" [Prec. 3]	X			
36r	"	X			T no w/m
v	"	X		S	
37r	" / "saboth"	X		S	T no w/m
v	" [Prec. 4]	X		S	
38r	"	X			T no w/m
v	"	X			
39r	"	X		S	T no w/m

v	"	X			
40r	"	X		S	T no w/m
v	"	X			
41r	"	X			T NL^2
v	"	X			
42r	"	X			T NL^2
v		X		S	
43r	"	X		S	T no w/m
v	"	X		S	
44r	"	X		S	T no w/m
v	S. drafts #1	S		S	
45r	"	S	1	S	T NL^2
v	"	S		S	
46r	"	S		S	T no w/m
v	blank				
47r	blank				T NL^2
v	"Adooltery"	X		S	
48r	"	X		S	T NL^2
v	"	X		S	
49₁	"	X			T no w/m
v	"	X		S	
50r	"	X			T NL^2
v	"	X		S	
51r	"	X			T NL^2
v	"	X		S	
52r	"not steale"	X		S	T NL^2
v	"	X		S	

53r	"	X		S	T 2 stanzas pasted flat
v	blank				F no w/m
54r	"steale" con't.	X		S	T no w/m
v	"	X		S	
55r	"	X			T NL^2
v	blank				
56r	"steale" con't.	X		S	T no w/m
v	"	X			
57r	" / S. drafts, 2	X / S		S	T no w/m
v	"	S		S	
58r	"	S		S	T no w/m
v	"	S		S	
59r	Inventory	JB & HS	1		F no w/m
v	blank				
60r	"Gyannts"	SR			F no w/m
v	Inventory, con't.	HS			
61r	"Apparell"	HS			F NL^1
v	blank				
62r	receipts	X-80			F no w/m
v	blank				
63r	receipt	X-80			F NL^1
v	blank				
64r	receipts	X-80			F NL^1
v	booklist: #99–110	HS			

APPENDIX I

65r	receipts / books	X-80 / HS			F no w/m
v	books	HS			
66r	books	HS			F no w/m
v	scriptural com.	SR			
67r	"St. Augus- tine"	SR			F NL[1]
v	blank				
68r	mini-bestiary	SR	"I"		F no w/m
v	"	SR			
69r	"Apothegmes"	SR			F no w/m
v	"	SR			
70r	"Law"-theo- logy	SR			F NL[1]
v	"	SR			
71r	Acton receipts	TW / SR	3	S	F no w/m
v	"	SR	3		
72r	obituary, R. J.	SR			F no w/m
v	Acton receipts	SR / HS	3	S	
73r	draft for f. 74	HS	3		T Rose over -M
v	[Fragments]	HS			F "Claude Denise"
74r	memorial	HS	1		T two pillars
v	2 words	HS			F no w/m

Totals: Southwell's name occurs 28 times and her hand 43 times, plus 2 references to her in titles: "my Ladyes" & "I"

Appendix II

British Library Lansdowne MS. 740, fols. 142–67.

To the kinges most excellent Ma^tye.   [142^r <143.>]
Darest thou my muse present thy Battlike winge,
before the eyes of Brittanes mighty kinge.
Hee that all other states exceedes as farre
as doth the sunne a litle glimmering starre
[5]   <The only touchstone of great natures storye.
in whome all artes reside, & hold theyr glorye.>
To whose blest birth the Cherubins did tender,
all the endowments for a princely splendor
<whose sacred lippes doe neuer part asunder
[10]   but as the Heralds of all grace & wonder>
You lines, excuse my boldnes in this matter
& tell the truth, my hart's to bigg to flatter.
Yf in the search of this world I could find
one to exceed the vertues of thy minde
[15]   the height of my ambition would aspire
to offer vp these sparckles to that fire.
since all fall shorte of thy soules qualitye
more short<e> then of thy states abilitye.
Tis thy attractiue goodnes giues mee scope
[20]   to come (dread Soueraigne) on the -n-es of hope.
& offer vp this tribute to thy meritt
this sacrifice to thy deuinest spiritt.
I know in God there doth no<e> ill abide
nor in his true Epitome, no<e> pride.
[25]   Thou art the nursing father of all pietye,

LANSDOWNE MS. 740

the mightye champion for the Deitye.
Tis of the high Iehouah I doe singe.
to whome doth this belonge but to the kinge.
great God of heauen, thankes for thy gracious fauours
[30]   great king on earth, accept the poore endeauors,
                 of your ma^{tyes} most humble
                       & faythfull subiect.

               Anne Southwell

             [written upside down]
wth feet of clay to enter the most hollye   [142^v]
or watrye balles to stare against ye Sunne
alas it is but blinde presumptuous follie
a parchase sought, by wch wee are vndonne
[5]   if off thy court I am, there will I rest
             secret
leaue<ing> <sacred> councell to thy sacred brest

Precept.3.   [143^r <144.>]

         Thou shalt not take the name of the Lorde
           thy god in vayne; for the Lorde will
              not hold him guiltlesse that
              taketh his name in vayne.

1.   Heere is our hartes corruption most exprest
        & spreds it self more then in any other
        those faultes that are by temporall lawes deprest
        euen for afliction sake wee seeke to smother.
[5]   but to blaspheme or take gods name in vayne,
          is held a sport, because tis freed from payne.

2.   Poore birdlime batt, whome Sathan hath in hold,
        think<e>'st thou that god will lett this treason dye?
        gaynst his owne honor is his care soe cold, /
[10]   because hee doth not thunder sodainlye?
          This waightye busines is of soe much trust,
         as hee will not committ it vnto dust.

3. Noe hee himself will take this cause in hand
    & to himself will satisfaction make,
[15] with spreading leprosye heel plague your land
            shall take
    & giue you spotts that none <shall take> away‸
        This precept standes before, Thou shalt not kill.
                dread
    is it of lesse regard <then> in his ‸ will?

4. Looke but at home into thy priuate hart<e>,
[20] Yf men doe slander, or abuse thy name,
    wilt thou in patience take it in good part<e>
    count him thy frend that doth thy creditt shame?
        to saue thine honor thine owne vaynes shall bleed,
        this sparckle comes fro̲m god, therefore take heede.

[25] 5. Hee is as ielous of his name as you   [143ᵛ]
    what though to right a wronge, hee bidd you sweare
    take heede the cause you pawne him for, bee true
    or els, twere better that you did forbeare.
                        sacred
        Nor for ech trifle, <doe not> vse his ‸ name,
[30]   such custom will gett power to make truth lame.

6. I haue confined my penne to, to few lines
    they cannott limitt out this precepts boundes,
    in these exorbitant & wicked times
    although to sweare a lye might seeme the boundes
                        of vaine oathes tane,
[35]   yett there are thousands more, <whose badd effect>
        'gainst   which doe gods name prophane
        <in> this comma̲und, <gods name doth much detect.>

7. For wᶜʰ of all our actions can stand free
    that slides away from any of the rest,
    whose eyes are in his soule may playnly see,
[40] these grapes for one sweete wine togither prest.
        & all togither in one current runne,
        yf one bee broken all are straight vndone.

8. Man is the vessell for this sacred drinke
    yf hee like old sower cask doe make it mustye
[45] or by some vnspidd crannye lett it sinke
    hee must bee held as lothsome & vntrustye,
        such filthy vessells, wee unhead & burne,

LANSDOWNE MS. 740   127

Because they Cannot vnto
<before they can to any> sweetnes turne.

9.   Nor is there other hope to keepe them stanch   [144ʳ <145.>]
[50]   to serue for any purpose that is good,
          they are like rustye almondes, wee must blanch
          theyr tawnye huskes of in the lambes deere blood
              for only that hath power to make them able
              to sett out banketts at gods <reall> royall table.

[55] 10.   Why sayth the Drunkard, murderer, & theefe,
          the saynts in this haue noe more share then wee,
          that phisick came to giue sick men releefe;
          stay naked bird, gett fethers, & then flee.
              Hee came to call all sinners to repentance
[60]   then stay not there, but take out all the sentence.

      11.   When in our consortes wee leaue partes vnstroken
          as eights, fifts, thirdes, that echo one another.
          Yf but a semiquauer time bee broken
          in theyr resultanses you cannott smother
[65]   the players fault soe is it wᵗʰ gods worde.
              wee must leaue fumbling, & all partes affoord.

      12.   The deepe ground base of this graue harmonye,
          is called Repent. the high stretchd spirituall treble
          is to Amend, that nimbly doth replye
[70]   & to ech sembrief doth eight quauers double.
              The last conclusiue stroake doth touch all partes.
              gods kingdome is at hand. Reioyce all hartes.

      13.   Christ dyed for all offenders, is it true   [144ᵛ]
          but did hee dye for Iudas, can you tell?
[75]   Hee dyed for all that will bee borne anew
          & not for those that wilfully rebell.
              You will repent, but can you point the time
              or thinke yt wilbe Easy as your Crime.
              <or haue you caught repentance vp in lime.>

      14.   Perhaps you will, when you can sinne noe more,
[80]   must none but beautyes stand in Pharaohs court
          & only gods house hold impostum'd gore
          where help is to bee had, sick men resort,

Tis happy truth, but doe not come to late,
there is a time to shutt this glorious gate,

[85] 15. For hee comes quickly, that reward doth bringe
when heauens bright lampe shall not exhall a vapor
or shedd one christall dropp vppon the springe
& now mee thinkes the fire doth catch my paper
waking & sleeping to my thoughts doth come
[90] the dreadfull terror of the day of doome.

16. Awake my soule, my conscience knockes, awake
cast of this stupid lethargie of sense
goe to gods house, & there advisement take,
& bee noe longer bogg<e>'d in diffidence.
[95] sublime thy facultyes, seeke sacred springes
take only comfort in the kinge of kinges.

17 Bee bold to tell, to threaten, & advise   [145ʳ <146.>]
all these proud rebells in my frighted brest,
they are hells denizens, that doe surprise
[100] a trauailling prince, that fayne would bee at rest.
& for thy honors sake to heauens kinge call
that theyr owne fabricke on theyr heads may fall.

18. Tell them thou hat'<e>st them as the iawes of hell
Lord lett thy loue lend fewell to this hate,
[105] & say what my distraction cannott tell
what power thou hast theyr furyes to rebate.
& make fierce death (that takes vs in the toyle)
to drinke as sweete & smooth as milke & oyle.

19. You litle brattes that hange about my knees,
[110] your beautyes shall no<e> more enthrall mine eye,
my brestes are drye, my Iewells are your fees,
weare them for her sake that shall neuer dye.
when I am gone, skorne not your first warme bedd
whome dying makes to liue, & life makes dead.

[115] 20. Yett ere I goe, this charge on you I lay
to keepe gods precepts euer in your harte,
your white & redd will quickly fade away

LANSDOWNE MS. 740

129

 are permanent & will not part
but they<r sound beautye neuer will departe.>
they'l guide you heere, & carry you aloft
[120] & keepe you euer fayre in face, & thought.

21. To you I lend these poore fruites of my studye, [145ᵛ]
wch to my shame tast not of the lampes oyle.
the fault is yours, they are soe dull & muddy
they haue bene to much toss'<e>d in your fond toyle.
[125] for at your gamballs yf I hold not place,
you looke as yf I did you some disgrace.

22. Now must I make you garlands for your heades,
to imitate<s> the peacocks of the court
& then goe furnish out your childing beddes,
[130] where troopes of parachitoes must resort.
& what welth cannott, paynes must needes effect,
or els my loue is turned to cold neglect.

23. & thus like bees you hange about my browes,
skarce one but half hower out of fower & twentye
[135] your hunting, feasting, reuelling allowes
 queasy
my <surfett> stomack that is growen to dayntye
for this wild stuff. Thus hurryed yett I send
these forced lines in all your hoobubles< > penned.

24. Who takes god in his mouth, not in his harte,
[140] although his tongue bee eloquent & free,
yett wth those knowing Diuills hee holdes this parte
O Iesus what haue wee to due wth thee.
These tinkling Cymballs take gods name in vayne.
Only to worke the barme from of theyr brayne.

[145] 25. Hee doth not honor god, that his worde knowes. [146ʳ <147.>]
(the diuell vnto Christ could cite the lawe.)
but hee whose holy conuersation showes
how gods precepts doe keepe his harte in awe:
for wicked fooles; a pyed cote better fittes
 wisedomes
[150] theyr backes, then ∧ prouerbes doe theyr wittes.

130 APPENDIX II

26. Such as from tauernes come to heare a preaching
& driuell out a text when they come back.
condemne his method, & reiect his teaching
say they haue better stuff in theyr owne pack.
[155]   Theyr fayth & workes are iust togither borne
like Samsons foxetayles in a field of corne.

27. They speake not to instruct, nor read to learne,
but are like fencers making a brauadoe
that neuer could true martiall deedes discerne
                                            Scaladoe
[160]   yett in a shopp will prate of a <Parradoe.>
      These vse gods worde as wolues doe vse theyr holes.
dawbe on fayre text to colour theyr fowle soules.

28. They say that Abraham loued his mayd & wife,
& Lott & Noe both were drownd in wine,
[165]   & why should they liue such a sober life
since these were men in birth almost deuine.
foolehardye flyes to play about this candle
                                        should
& want the touch that<e> sacred thinges <doe> handle.

29. For Saraes handmayd signifyes the law,   [146']
        is
[170]   & <m> a mountayne stretching into bondage,
wch is a yoake in wch all men must drawe
though some doe slipp the coller in theyr fond age,
for till the promised freedome bee attayned
wee must plowe out the feeld how euer payned.

[175] 30. Then leaue this idle chatt, it goes for sinne,
& fall to worke ther's nothing gott by sloth,
a lazye hand doth make the bodye thinne,
this vice doth wronge gods name more then an oth
                                    his
They wronge theyr knowledge & <theyr> giftes abuse
                            u
[180]   that in theyr soles good knowledge did infuse.

31. Such knowers must bee whipp<e>'d wth double stripes,
that knowe theyr fathers will & doe it not.
the stinge of conscience giues theyr soules such gripes
                                    haue
that for vayne glorye sake this skill <hath> gott

LANSDOWNE MS. 740

131

[185]
> vnlesse theyr hartes bee seared, I cannott tell
> how they should chuse but beare about a hell.

32.
> Such as haue bene traynd vp in christian lore
> & fall away to blinded papistrye,
> are more blasphemers then those boyes that rore,
[190]
> who when othes fayle, sweare out the letanye.
>> These Iudasses the brethren more doe slander
>> then many legions that in desartes wander.

33.
> These putt theyr candle vnderneath theyr bedd,　　　[147ʳ <148.>]
> theyr light shines not for men to giue god glorye
[195]
> may these gett Purgatorye, they are spedd
> they studye noe booke but the Legendarye.
>> Theyr fayth is weake, they thinke gods mercy spent
>> & seeke to purchase pardon at a rent.

34.
> & now on pilgrimages they must runne,
[200]
> & stripp & whipp & fast & goe to masse,
> & fee ech saynt till they bee quite undone,
> heere the blind Prophett kickes the silly asse.
>> Rome holdes not vpp more fopperyes then this land
>> yett as I hide mine eyes, I stay my hande.

[205] 35.
> For I haue not to doe wᵗʰ others actions
> how this gettes <land,> or that doth wronge his place　　*(wealth written above land,)*
> I hate to bee th' Appendant vnto factions,
> nor will I euer seeke a bad mans grace
>> Or call him sweete whose breath is as a fogge,
[210]
>> or prayse his shape, <whose> belly ∧ <is> a hogge.　　*(that's above whose; ed like above is)*

36.
> Ile rather eate drye bread & drinke cleere water,
> then bee that flye that feedes on filthy sores,
> or stoope my soule a peece of dirrt to flatter,
> or ioy in what comes in at these back doores
[215]
>> who hath prides itch ∧<take> fortunes curry combe.　　*(lackes above take)*
>> I will not <clapp> the waues to produce fome.　　*(beate above clapp)*

37.
> I haue enough, because I am content,　　　[147ᵛ]
> Were I the worldes sole darling, I must dye;

^{It}
<w^{ch}> holdes but shadowes, & those are but lent

[220] wch ech day Death layes leuell at mine eye.

               ^{to}
But I will watch him <now> & pare his nayle,
& putt his best plea to the Ieo fay'le.

38.   Tis sixteene hundred since his darte was broken;
Who for an vnarm'd enemye takes care?

[225] Oh but hard fortune, how may that bee token?
for fortunes teeth, this bullett I prepare.
That Prouidence wch from the wombe did take mee,
his louing bounty neuer did forsake mee.

39.   If I bee gone, the world will not need mee

[230] & I shall haue as litle need of it
             ^{hath euer yet}
Hee that ∧<fedd Eue> will euer<more> feede mee
           ^{sawce}
shall I for ∧<feare> goe pine away my witt
since all is well by whome all thinges are done,
Ile neuer care how fast the glasse doth runne.

[235] 40.   You leeches hence, & pack away your drugges,
your cataplasmes & your fomentations,
                       ^{trash}
you are deathes harbengers, your ∧<thirst> his dugges
you giue noe life, but lengthen out vexations
for all your cement is not worth two strawes

[240] to hold out death, though it may botch some flawes.

41.   Yf in Hibernia god will haue mee dye,   [148^r <149.>]
I cannott haue your capon eaters knell,
yett for a pound Ile haue a hundred crye,
& teare theyr hayres like furyes sent from hell
                             ^{madd}
[245] poore wretched soules, they'r <are> full of such ∧ fittes,
the Pope doth cozen them of wealth & wittes.

42.   Lord yf it bee thy will, giue them more light
& cutt of theyr seducer from his throane
that the tenne hornes may worke him that despite

[250] told to St Iohn by reuelation
for whilst this Hidrae holdes his head aloft
ther's litle hope to haue them better taught.

LANSDOWNE MS. 740

133

43.   As litle hope Christes flock should liue in peace.
or theyr defender free from envyous treason,
[255]   for day by day wee see these goates increase,
        & yett my hopes doe lead mee <from> the<> reason
           why Sathans rage growes dayly more & more,
           his lease hath almost worne him out of doore.

44.   Some call god to the barre, to haue him tryed
[260]   why this is chosen, & that is reiected
& more <all>
   <but more> like flames of the first angells pride,
   whereby theyr fond ambition is detected.
        wretch, what wert thou y^t seekest thus high to mount
        when god made all, to call him to account.

[265] 45.   Yf of thy councell hee had stood in neede   [148^v]
hee would haue cald thee, but yf thou intrude,
the place is holy, therefore take good heede
least angry Iustice doe thy pride exclude,
        of his hye secretts, had hee thought thee fitt
[270]   hee would haue giuen a correspondent witt.

46.   But giue him thankes thou wert not made a dogg,
& being made throwne straightway into hell,
lett reuerent feare bee made ambitions clogg
behold thy father Adam, how hee fell,
[275]   Hee would bee as god, & then wretched creature
        hee straight became the vnderling in nature.

47.   When thou wert sprawling in thy sanguine clowtes
scrambling wth both thy fistes to hide thine eyes,
his louing pittye did not giue thee floutes,
[280]   although those balles durst not approch his skyes
        to close thy skull hee gaue thy mother thumbes
        & milk to moisten thy soft toothlesse gummes.

48.   when first thou breath'dst this ayre, ech plannett takes
thy constitution & doe make a brall
[285]   filling thy litle world wth sad earthquakes;
yett god that will not haue thy fabrick fall
        till the due time, his prouidence appointe<th>d
        wth serpents oyle the serpents stinge bee noynted.

	49.	Thy numberlesse dizeases doe excell	[149^r <150.>]
[290]		all other creatures. nor bee discontent
		thy numberlesse affections did rebell
		& faultes & paynes must bee equiualent.
		aboue all creatures thou thy god didst braue,
		& to all creatures thou must bee a slaue.

[295] 50. Of curious inquisition stand in feare
wch was the diuells & old Adames itch
since thy reward is Midas asses eare
though knowledge doest the mind of man bewitch
      wee'r
<wth> midle creatures lett vs keepe the meane,
[300]   who mounts to hye doth take gods name in vayne.

51. I speake not of vayne swearers all this while,
wch seeme the nurses of this high offence,
because such pitch doth wth the touch defile,
men giuen vp to a reprobate sense.
[305]   for these doe beare about ye plague will greeue the<u>m</u>
    wch is, that noe wise man will ere beleeue them.

52. Othes are the com<u>m</u>aes, colons, period,
of theyr discours, at wch they make but sporte,
these houndes feare not to teare the life of god
[310] Ioseph gott this disease in Pharaoes court.
    The marke of blasphemye stickes in his face
    Whose tongue is tipp'd to doe his god disgrace.

53. Should Pope, Turke, Moore or Saracen doe this   [149^v]
it could not doe the god of gods a shame,
[315] this chaffe & stuble is not counted his
but those that take on them his sacred name
    yf they doe soe, how is theyr father sham'd
    & how much more are such sonnes to bee blamed.

54. For more then yea & nay is counted euill,
[320] & othes are to the soule as dartes & swordes,
the voyce of truth sayth, they come from the diuell
then neuer sweare to make men trust your wordes.
    twere better that thy kinge thought thee a lyar,
    then that thy mouth should harbor this wild fire.

LANSDOWNE MS. 740   135

[325] 55. For Truth is stronger then the strongest king
        & God will haue it knowen how ere depressed,
        ^{besides a}   ^{will}
        <soe euery> wise man ‸<can> discerne the thinge,
        then chayne thy tongue & thou mayest bee reblessed
            for Sathan like a cunning bulldogg creepes
[330]   wayting to catch a christian by the lippes.

      56. Wth reuerend feare cast of this vice & then
        thy self mayst iudge wch is the happiest creature,
        a mastife madd, or a blaspheming man;
        the dogg hurtes man, man hurtes the god of nature.
            to quitt our harmes, wee knock him on the poll
[335]   to quitt gods honour, hee doth damne our soule.

      57. & such liue dogges are better then dead lyons,   [150^r <151.>]
        yf kinges & princes goe to condemnation
        twere better sitt wth dogges at Lazarus viandes
        then beare a scepter wth such reseruation
[340]   though good poore men doe want a marble chest
            Angells will reare theyr tombes in Abrahams brest.

      58. Who makes a vow to wedd a second wife
        before his first bee dead, doth wronge gods name
        presumtion stickes a canker on his life
[345]   & a detect of murder to his fame
            besides the diuell will asist his vow
            to make an end of her hee cares not how.

      59. These Herods othes, where they bee kept or broken
        seeme to preiudicate gods prouidence,
[350]   besides they doe a naughtie life betoken,
        & is indeed the nurse of all offence
            they doe disioyne what god had ioyn'd before.
            filled wth neglect they euer shalbee poore.

      60. Who vow to bee reuenged for wronges begunne
[355]   doe proudly wrest gods weapon from his hand,
        & mock him when they pray his will bee done,
        these not on god but on theyr owne power stand.
            ^{to be bleest}
        Hee wrastles not as Iacob <for a blessing>

[360]

That tempts gods wrath by his owne ire exprest
<but tempts gods wrath & soe acquires a cursing>.

61.　Vengeance is Gods & doth to him belong　　　　　[150ʳ]
　　　then ought wee lay these foolish vowes aside,
　　　should hee but vse due iustice for ech wronge,
　　　wee doe him, out of ignorance & pride.
[365]　　　　would wee not thinke vs happye in this case,
　　　　　yf swelling earth would hide vs from his face.

62.　Who makes a vow into a good profession,
　　　hee enters league wᵗʰ god to bee his frend,
　　　　　　boue all　　　　　　　of
　　　lett him ∧ beware <of all> this transgression
[370]　　of looking back, & hold out to the end.
　　　　　for a perfidious frend hath this hard fate,
　　　　　hee turnes loues needle to the point of hate.

63.　When kinges make vowes to keepe theyr kingdomes lawes
　　　yf they proue cruell, gripple or vnkind,
[375]　they throwe theyr state into the commons iawes
　　　who euer were found turbulent & blind
　　　　　as Dauid's grandsonne did, whose childish pride
　　　　　tooke yonge wild parasites to bee his guide.

64.　When subiects vow truth to the Lordes anoynted;
[380]　wᶜʰ are selected & deere to his loue;
　　　men by his gratious prouidence appointed
　　　to rule on earth as hee in heauen aboue,
　　　　　when such proue false, these most accursed elues
　　　　　wᵗʰ Achitophell are forced to hange themselues.

[385] 65.　Is it the kind aspect of maiestye　　　　　[151ʳ <152.>]
　　　begettes contempt wᵗʰin theyr dunghill hartes
　　　much rather should theyr happy dignitye
　　　like the warme sunne rayse vp theyr vertuous parts.
　　　　　least when theyr hatefull eyes leaue of this light
[390]　　　　theyr horrid soules wayle in eternall night.

66.　These Iudasses in wᶜʰ the diuell doth enter
　　　can not perceaue when a good king is gone,
　　　on what tempestuous seas the world doth venter
　　　how many thousand soules is drown'd in one.

LANSDOWNE MS. 740

137

[395]
 Death thou doest well these monsters to confine
 wch had they life would skale the christaline\<line>.

      smile
67. I cannott chuse but ∧\<swell> to see these bladders
 grow only bigg wth a pestiferous wind,
 like naked Iackdawes tumbling from theyr ladders,
  leauing theyr fames for antidotes
[400] \<striuing to flye to soone, leaue life> behind
  & yett my smiles & teares togither striue
  to thinke though some bee dead some are aliue.

68. Well god is good & prouident & stronge,
 hee that keepes Israell neyther sleepes nor slumbers
[405] hee is the iust reuenger of ech wronge
 a good man shalbee safe from all theyr cumbers.
  though thousand bulles of Rasan rayse theyr hornes
  theyr furye shall begett but theyr owne skornes.

69. For mee, I haue of all but litle reason   [151^v]
[410] to flatter gaynst my harte that happy land
 where I was borne, who like fruit out of season
 hath layd on mee an envious stepdames hand
  yett doe I pray all Catelines may perish
  & our Augustus happily may florish.

[415] 70. Thou most almightye, powerfull & immense
 thou that makest kinges, & rulest on sea & land
 bee thou his tower, his fortresse, & defence
 & euer keepe him wth thy gratious hand.
  & blesse that christall orbe wherin did lye
[420] th' vnvallued gemmes of his posteritye.

 \<80.> Who for his owne sake seekes his cuntryes good,
 71. doth beare a face but like a painted drabb
 such doe I wish were choked in her mudd,
 whose smoothed faces haue a harte all skabb
[425] but for christes spouse sake wish her happy grace
  who noe where els dares shew her frighted face.

 \<81.> For I by booke haue trauelld all the world
 72. to find out the religions of all landes
 ech where I see how ignorance hath hurld

138 APPENDIX II

[430] her foggye mantle vppon all theyr strandes
I will not dare to iudge theyr misteryes
yett I will euer fly theyr villanyes.

                                        & light,

73.   My witt & Iudgment is as poor \<as any\>   [152ʳ \<153.\>]
      my lines are on the oceans brow a buble
                                        mite

[435] yett the poore widdowe did present\<e\> her \<penny\>
      hee helpes the building that doth bring but stuble
                  ech   all
        God filles \<all\> soule\<s\> & polisheth \<ech\> braynes
      Then   atheists   flout at   \<humble\>
        \<&\> none but \<asses then\> will \<flout\> ₐmy paynes.

              \<\>flouting

74.   This \<flattering\>   is a colt that euer winches
[440] whome I haue longe since tyed vnto the racke
      when first I backed this iade hee dashed at princes
      & almost broke my neck from of his back.
        his sire is pride, a sanguin witt his damme
        to hell hee must, for out of hell hee came.

[445] 75. Wᵗʰ skorners & deriders lett him passe
      for what can man flout but hee wronges gods glorye,
      I rather chuse to ride a sluggish asse
                          snorting
      then this wild hott proud \<spirited\> Dromedarye
        that runnes his rider out of sight & brayne
[450]   yet tires at noonetide in the fayrest playne.

76.   This bird eyed beast will start at euery straw
      his flaxen mane is thick, his head is small,
      hee will not brooke a bridle in his iawe
      hee hath the staggers & doth often fall.
               shallow   \<solid\>
[455]   yett at his prancing \<should\> wittes make \<them\> sporte
      hee fittes best for a footcloth nagg at court.

77.   Take of his trapping & hee is vndone   [152ᵛ]
      hee is the raggedst iade that ere you spide
      hee's restye, yett a whipp will make him \<ride\> runne
                 frights
[460] the colick thunder \<rores\> not like his pride
        & yett a wise man that knowes how to vse him
      before
      \<or for\> a fidler or a foole will chuse him.

LANSDOWNE MS. 740

78.   A poore man richly clad belyes his state
this butterflye doth catterpillers breed,

[465]   that alwayes hange about a strangers gate
& in his vineyards on his fruits doe feed
    the flame of pride doth burne him in the budd
    & keepes his ofspring choaked in the mudd.

79.   A rich man basely' arrayed slanders gods guiftes
                 badge
[470]   this drunken seruant layes his \<bagges\> to pawne
to couetousnes, yett these must bee his shiftes,
hee cares not for himself but for his spawne
    hee blisters sound skinne wth cantharides,
    to bee a licence for his beggeryes.

[475] 80.   A couetous man misdoubtes gods prouidence,
a pro\<u\>digall is to full of presumption.
a ragefull man doth mock christes patience
a sott to his owne honor giues consumption
    an idle man is like a tedious dreame
[480]   a busye man is as a toyling streame.

81.   But I am almost past my hundreds bound: [153ʳ \<154.\>]
I must goe back & fetch more fooles alonge
such as in this precept may challenge ground
as men that doe gods name the greatest wronge,
[485]   These are in'chanters, witches, figure 'flingers
    that putt gods weapons in the diuells fingers.

82.   Theyr Demonologye I must orepasse
           De occulti
& let Agrippaes \<di oculta\> damne
what face sees hee that maketh hell his glasse
[490]   & leaues the sacred springes from whence hee came
                           e
    the worde'\<e\>s vnborne that must portray these findes
    that invocate\<s\> gods name to wicked endes.

83.   But litle better is that man that sayes
I would to god this house or land were mine,
[495]   how can hee thinke god heares him when hee prayes
that lettes the sunne of righteousnes decline
    the foe is readye at this\<e\> sacrifice\<s\>

$$\text{his black flyes.}$$
to make it carion fitt for ‸<hells black sises.>

84. The tongu's a world of wickednes wee see
[500] & yett it is the herald of the harte
$$\text{naughtye}$$
a crabbed fruit descryes a <nastye> tree,
though some haue witt to couer it by art
yett when the bookes of conscienses are redd
the spring will lead vs to the fountaynes head.

[505] 85. And now from them I passe to lawfull swearers   [153ʳ]
Gods peacemakers, the shields of guiltlesse blood
$$\text{in vayne}$$
they<> take gods name ‸ that are forbearers
to doe theyr neyghbour or theyr cuntrye good
They doe mistake this precept & gods lawes
[510] that flye the widdowes, or the orphans cause.

86. Yf god haue putt a secrett in thy brest
it is a talent that must bee employed
thou must not thinke t'enioy thy masters rest
when by thy fault a good man is destroyed.
[515] Then sweare, yett sweare by nothing but his name.
Who is thy god & biddes thee doe the same.

87. Sweare not by Saturne, Ops, by Ioue or Iuno
for soe thou honorest Idolls in this euill
such swearers are the brainsick sonnes of Luna
[520] for these <s>we<a>re, men made Idolls by the diuell
His depositions noe wise man may trust
that calles hells Iurors to approue him iust.

88. A lawfull oth doth good, & tis a merritt
but not to him whose harte is full of euills
[525] hee gaynes by it that serues the Lord in spiritt
for Iudas by Christes name could cast out deuills.
To the vnholy all thinges are vnholye
& theyr best workes shall beare the crowne of folly.

89. A magistrate may quickly make him sweare   [154ʳ <155.>]
[530] whose harte is seard wᵗʰ hells vnhappy flame,
hee will nor frend nor king nor cuntry spare

LANSDOWNE MS. 740

that for ech trifle pawnes ∧<his> sacred name. [gods above "his"]
    These boyes at blow point call theyr king for iudge
    that for ech nothing make gods name to trudge.

[535] 90.   Some bragg they'l not sweare for a thousand pound
    but lett such pray to keepe temptation back,
    for yf the deuill gett an inch of ground
    hee'l put our resolutions all to wrack.
        & bind a thousand cyphers to ech pound
[540]   till hee haue brought our conscience in a swound.

91.   Lett's watch our tongues our thoughts, & watch yᵉ <time> [diuell above "time"]
    for hee standes watching vs both night & day
    let's pray to god to free vs from <all crime> his euill
    there is noe other helpe or hope or way
[545]   Hee'l make the litle ringewormes skarlett coate
        proclayme reuenge to the proud bulles deepe throat.

92.   Hee is a ielous god & cannott brooke
    the enemye should snatch away his loue,
    but yf our owne base hartes doe make vs stoope
[550]   hee cares not for such crowes, heel chose the doue
        the gotes vppon his left hand hee doth keepe
        but on his right do<th> stand the chosen sheepe. [e above "th"]

93.   Hee'l visitt vs, but not as hee did Sara,   [155ᵛ]
    but as hee did the old world in a floud
[555]   & meete <proue like> Ahimilech & Pharaoh [wᵗʰ proud above "proue like"]
    yett not as our vayne hopes haue vnderstood
        wᵗʰ a consuming fire hee'l vex our soules
        & burne vs up like litle paper ∧rowles. [sk above "rowles"]

94.   O would men make good vse of pretious time
[560]   wᶜʰ is the handle of felicitye,
    then would not these lye snoring in the slime
    of <stupid base> & darke philosophye. [idle vayne above "stupid base"]
        like taylors needles whipping vp & downe
        to leaue a white stitch in a sable gowne.

142   APPENDIX II

[565] 95. from earth wee rose & to the earth wee sinke
            & in the midle way wee doe noe good
                         only
            but ∧ <howrely> flesh past, wch all workemen thinke
            would but disgrace the garment yf it stood
                   our foolish actes like footstepps sett in snow
[570]   serue but to track a theefe where ere hee goe.

       96. the<n> Dagon<s> image brake but at the knees
            that<e>at the armes, that fell before the arke
            gods Image hath a worser fall then these
            his head fell of & tumbled in the darke
[575]   & euer since the obiect & his eyes
                   could neuer hold true correspondencyes.

                          ges
       97. The wa<y> of our <fore>fathers sinne was death,   · [155^r <156.>]
            yett God in mercy mindfull to releeue vs
            sealed a religion wth vs in our breath
[580]   wch giues a balsam to those woundes that greeue vs
                        lendes
                   & <giues> vs nimble winges that mount the skyes
                   to carye vp our dayly sacrifice.

       98. W^th Iudgment hee hath alwayes mercy mingled
                                           sunnlike
            & to our ayd sent downe his <only>∧ sonne
[585]   yett in the brakes wth Adam wee are tangled
            like trewant schollers wee a sporting runne
                   that when the repetition day drawes neere
                   in stead of knowledge, wee are filled wth feare.

       99. When kinges cast garrisons in time of treason
[590]   wee doe this policy of state misdoubt
            yett by a new supply, wee see his reason
                                  captaines
            was but to putt old lazye <soldiers> out
                   whose griple handes the soldiers belly skarres
                   & stratagems procrastinate badd warres.

[595] 100. Soe when the Lord shall burne this earth wth fire
             hee will bee worship<e>'d & still magnifyed
                                     whose
             but wth a new conception; <our> desire
             shall alwayes by his will bee ratifyed.

LANSDOWNE MS. 740

& when the old world sees the new worldes glorye

[600] theyr portion is to ∧<sitt> & to bee sorrye.
see

101. Had I the most mellifluous tongue of angells
& did the spheares lend <tuning> to my songe
cadence
to draw the<s> <foule trangression> from these wrangles
brattes of Adam
like strawes in streames they'l beare this <noyse> alonge,
<---------vice>
[605] <O> goe & learne in great Iehouaes schoole
Then *vice*
who takes gods name in vayne is but a foole.

[one blank folio follows: <157.>]

Precept.4. [156ʳ <158.>]

Remember the Sabbath day to keepe it holy, six
dayes shalt thou labour & doe all thy worke.
but the seuenth day is the sabaoth of the
[5] lorde thy god, in it, thou shalt not doe
any worke, thou nor thy sonne, nor thy
daughter, thy manseruant nor thy
mayd, nor thy beast, nor thy stran-
ger that is within thy gates.
[10] For in six dayes the Lord made yᵉ heauens & the earth
the sea & all that in them is, & rested the seuenth
day; therefore the Lord blessed the Sabbath day & hallowed it .
/.

1. In six dayes God made this admired ball,
this verdant couch wᵗʰ lillyes ouerspred
engrayl'd it wᵗʰ a liquid christall wall,
& hunge a double vallence ouer head
[5] of fire & ayre, fring'd round wᵗʰ starrye lights
vnder whose fabrick walke<s> all liuing wights.

2. There this immortall mortall prince hee pl<>ac'<e>d
who had free will & high commaund of all.
thus all compleat & wᵗʰ all graces grac'd
[10] the voyce of voyces to his type doth call

Labour six dayes, but keepe the seuenth ∧ holy
day
when hee biddes rest, all labour is but folly.

144 APPENDIX II

3.   In this day sum<u>m</u>on vp thy weekes expence   [156ʳ]
       that from thy lord thou mayst acquittance haue
[15]   & heape not vp offence vppon offence
       ingraue thy sinnes before they thee engraue
           Mercy is for the liuing not the dead
           when life is gone, Iustice in power doth spredd.

4.   In this day rest from all thy worldly paynes
[20]   take out the harrow fro<u>m</u> the plowmans handes
       refresh his faynting lim<u>m</u>es & tired braynes.
       & from thy oxen take theyr yoaked bandes
           tis six to one, then hauing soe much oddes,
           twere badly done to steale that day that's gods.

[25]   5.   This sacriledgeous thef<f> drawes on a curse
       & doth defile what god did sanctifye,
       knitting vpp fire & flax both in one purse
       this stollen time eates downe times treasurye
           & robbes vs of that holy saba<o>th rest
[30]   wᶜʰ Christ the Lord of saba<o>th hath exprest.

6.   Six dayes thou art to labour sayth the Lord,
       heer's Adams curse chayned to necessitye
       but then thy labours plentye shall affoord
       wᶜʰ doth agayne sweeten calamitye
[35]   All thyne owne worke in six dayes thou mayst doe
           though not soe much as sinne invites thee to.

7.   For yf thy worke in those six dayes bee bad   [157ʳ <159.>]
       or left vndon, the seuenth is defaced,
       for worldly cares will make thy visage sad
[40]   & guilt of ill will in thy harte bee placed
           Then to keepe holy this high day of rest
           thou must worke faithfully in all the rest.

8.   Nor art thou bid to sleepe out this high day
       to singe, daunce, game or guzzell out thy time.
[45]   but in gods vineyard thou art willed to stay
       & cutt downe thornes that ouertoppe<s> his vine
           for thou must neuer rest whilest thou art heere
           yett in this day thy future rests appeare.

LANSDOWNE MS. 740

145

9.   Nor art thou bidd to labour heere alone
[50]   but thou art bound to bring thy familye
thy wife & thee, two louing hartes make one
Christ & his church explane that simpathye
      thy children & thy seruants are exprest
      by thee & them gods vineyard must bee drest.

[55] 10.   Besides the honor due to the creator
how beneficiall is this time to all
where wee may learne to knowe both god & nature
& what by sinne or grace to vs doth fall
      & by our knowledge like to mortall gods
[60]   resolue & reconcile what is at ods.

11.   Where yf there were noe time giuen vs by grace
but still like swine to grouell in the mire
how should the soule her facultyes deface
or how would man to higher state aspire.
[65]   O gratious god thou forcest vs to this
      not soe much for thy glorye as our blisse.

12.   Thou hast noe need of vs to fill thy skyes   [157$^\mathrm{v}$]
for Cherubines & Thrones ador$\overset{\text{n}}{\wedge}$e that place,
Where all doe stand w$^\mathrm{th}$ louing watchfull eyes
[70]   & ioy to see the glorye of thy face.
      still singing Haleluiahs to thy name
      & w$^\mathrm{th}$ due reuerence aye extoll the same.

13.   Thou hast noe need of vs to fill thine earth
or to <a$\overset{\text{dresse vp}}{\text{dresse}}$> thine altars w$^\mathrm{th}$ perfumes
[75]   Thou canst replenish it with Angells birth
whose heauenly formes noe humane stuffe assumes.
      where noe rebellious thoughts, or heedlesse sloth
      shall rowse thy iustice or prouoke thy wroth.

14.   Only thy loue mou<e>'d in those sacred springes
[80]   then darke, now cleere & blessed element,
the very soule & nurse of growing thinges
w$^\mathrm{th}$ whome thy gratious spiritt did frequent
      & mouing there, sett all the world in order
      & made her flowing armes earthes fruitfull border.

146   APPENDIX II

[85]   15. & from the light the darke did seperate
              deuiding cold & moyst the hott & drye,
              yett ech with others to participate
              & propagate by a sweete simpathye.
                  Soe that, not men, but Angells, starres & spheares
[90]   ech one the elementall liuery weares.

     16. Gods first weekes worke doth as a symbole stand
              of all the time that is to come & past
              by milliarious ∧ prophetick handes   *peeres,*
              hath drawen earthes longitude, times reckoning cast.
[95]   A thousand yeeres are one day wth the Lord,
                six dayes of worke, the seuenth day rest affoord.

     17. The first day voyd & emptye doth present   [158^r <160.>]
              Adams apostasye, voyd of all grace.
              raigning a thousand yeeres in Cains descent
[100]   in Seth the promised seed, the light takes place
                  God <seperateh> the darkenes from the light   *seperates*
                  good men are day, the wicked men are night.

     18. The second day god made the firmament
              & partes the moist deepe counsells of the proud
[105]   Babells confusion wth the deluge went
              the blessed seede & spouse an <-->ark doth shrowd
                  & her fresh springes a christaline doe make
                  the rest theyr place in sulpharous channell take.

     19. The third day when the waters were deuided
[110]   the virgin earth presents all store of treasure,
               Abraham, & moses by gods word <were> ayded   *now*
              in a Satrapick dance keepe sacred measures
                  as ∧<true fields> solid ground, in them god graues   *fruitfull*
                  his drad commandes, the rest are giddye waues.

[115]   20. The fourth day god did make the sunne & moone
              In the fourth thousand yeere came Christ that sonne
              his church the<-> moone, Apostles starlike shone
              <souccoring> the gentiles wth cloudes ouerrunne   *lightening*

LANSDOWNE MS. 740   147

Thou Alpha & omega, thou blest light
[120]   thy sacred beames be<e> euer in our sight.

21.   The fift dayes worke was fish & fowle that flyes
           Hydraes
  & now those monstrous Heresyes did crall
the Dragons & the Locustes did arise
                 seas of
that on heauens childing wombe throwe ∧<s out> gall
[125]   who to the wildernes afrighted runnes
to ease her throes, & beare her groning sonnes.

22.   The sixt day all the beastes & beastly natures   [158ᵛ]
of Turks & Pope & other brutish factions,
at euen the Lord & soueraigne of those creatures
[130]   gods image commes to keepe them in subiection
When all the heresyes must fade away
& then drawes on the holy Sabbath day.

23.   Yett first god calles his Image to the barre
those that of the forbidden tree haue eaten
[135]   a fierye sword from Paradise doth scar<r>e
& from the tree of life theyr boldnes threaten
Thus goeing hand in hand wᵗʰ the creation
                 out
it pointes <out> the worldes end∧, mans perturbation.

           wizzard <gazeling>
24.   <<& now mee thinkes I heare some ∧ <gallant>> say
[140]   how dares this foolish woman bee soe bold.
ask Iahells nayle yᵗ Siseraes head did stay
            that   her
& Iudiths sword <soone> made ∧ <a> hott loue cold
Hee that enabled them, enables mee.
               hee'l
yf thou seeke knowledge <will> enable thee.>>

          soule that
[145] 25.   <<How cloudye is that ∧ will not seeke
to know as farre as finite dust may knowe
who <->made him & the world, & both doth keepe,
Angells & men & the darke hell belowe
in whose breath all thinges bee & liue & moue
[150]   whose prouidence doth gouerne all wᵗʰ loue.>>

26.   <<Mans mind a mirror is of heauenly formes
& though created, yett hee can create

148 APPENDIX II

his polish'd thoughts the quill & booke adorne
wch clouds of ignorance doth captiuate.
[155]   <If thou> If thou
<A> All the.>>

26. The life & soule of soules is contemplation   [159^r <161.>]
It makes a man to differ from a beast
& brings him to the god of his creation
[160] & shewes, how first hee tumbled from his nest
           how both
& by his fall ∧ his wings fell <all soe> lame
   & how   hee may impe
<noe> fethers <can bee imped in>to the same.

27. Vnto that god of order & of time
wee owe the time that his word hath sett downe
      <i>   stayre
[165] Religion is the <Cedar> by wch wee clime
the gole wee seeke is an immortal crowne.
All worldly pleasures are expired by death
that hanges in the incertaynty of breath.

28. & who, to play a kinges parte for a day
[170] would spend these pretious minutes in attiring,
who are more traytors to theyr state then they
that peacocklike stand still themselues admiring
who can enioy themselues or what they haue
that seeke not god till they haue found theyr graue.

[175] 29. Seuen hundred twenty names the Rabbines found
to expresse god to theyr capacityes
who sayles to farre, may sett his shipp on ground
& gazing on the sunne, dazell his eyes
for what hee is, noe man hath euer told
[180] nor none shall knowe whilst hee is wrap'd in mold.

30. The Cherubins wth six winges are portrayed
two, for gods errands still attend on him
two ouer theyr heads are euermore displayed
two stand betweene gods glorious face & them
[185] two for mans weakenes theyr fayre feete doe hide
because they knowe him frayle yett full of pride.

LANSDOWNE MS. 740

149

31.   Yett some that seeme to search heauens azure skye   [159ᵛ]
                      is a threefold
doe say there ‸<are three seuerall> hierarchye<s>
where threefold three degrees of angells flye
[190]   that still attend gods sacred maiestye.
        & hand in hand doe from gods hand come downe
        till the last hand the heads of mortalls crowne.

32.   For mee that am but a poore peece of durt
to weake to looke an angell in the face,
[195]   Ambition shall not doe my soule that hurte
to mount soe high I humbly begg gods grace.
        but from his back or feete to bee instructed
        wch is the Christ, & his twelue deere selected.

33.   Hee knowes god best that first himself doth knowe
[200]   to bee but wretched, poore, though proud & vayne.
how like a shadowe hee doth come & goe,
that all his labours heere are greefe & payne
        that all his sences beare deathes fearefull skarres
        & all his thoughts are still at ciuill warres.

[205] 34.   & when poore wretched man beholdes his weakenes
who cannott make a flye with all his skill
hee may behold the all creators greatnes
& stand the more obedient to his will
        beyond his chayne poore ape hee cannott skipp
[210]   yett naught can tame this bedlame but a whipp.

35.   Spend not your time in cobwebbes like a spinner
but wth the publicane confesse & say
O god bee mercifull to mee a sinner
to come to god there is noe other way
[215]   for faythfull prayers pierce the christall skyes
        & is the best accepted sacrifice.

36.   The Preacher in the middest of all his store   [160ʳ <162.>]
wch by succession or his labour wonne
doth in his contemplation explore
[220]   that all is vanitye beneath the sunne.
        yf there bee ought that can contentment bring,
        wee may bee bold to reprehend this king.

150 APPENDIX II

37. Ther's noe true frendship left amongst acquaintance
noe stedfast comfort in a worldly state,
[225] noe peace of mind w^{th}out a sound repentance,
noe life saue fayth's but death doth violate
True ioyes descend like cristall dew on flowers
the earth sends fogges euen to her darlings bowers.

38. To weare rich robes, to laugh & sleepe at ease,
[230] to gourmandise & haue mens cappes & knees,
alas what poore base, triuiall thinges are these
monkeis haue cheeftaines, ther's a king mongst bees
Should angells Iuniors looke for nought but this
Th' Assyrian
<the Chaldeen> tirant fared not much amisse.

[235] 39. But hee in middest of all his glorious crew
& consecrated full crownd cuppes of gold
when deaths defiance at his proud head flew
see how his ioynts did shake & harte grewe cold,
& that proud hand against the lord soe rear'd
be
[240] had noe power left to drye his eyes <all> blear'd.

40. Could noe fayre minion wth her iuory arme,
noe parasite wth an inchanting tale
nor noe great Sophist wth a powerfull charme
rowse vp those drowsye spiritts & face soe pale
[245] Is death soe bold to looke kinges in the face
& wth his lead, beate downe theyr golden mace.

41. Beleeue it not, hee dares not bee soe bold   [160ᵛ]
theyr
for euen that thought would check <your> proud ambitions
yett   theyr
<but> yf you seeke for all <your> sires of old
[250] they'r past like vapors, they & theyr phisitians
O cruell death, how bitter are thy stinges
to those that to much ioy in worldly thinges.

42. Gods children in the fierye furnace singe,
Paule in the stockes, th' Apostles at the stake,
[255] they skorne at death, asking where is thy stinge
or wher's the conquest of that dreadfull lake?
while Belialls brattes doe hide theyr fearfull heades
& thunder makes them crawle vnder theyr beddes.

LANSDOWNE MS. 740

151

43.　Nor maruell I to see them soe distressed,
[260]　　for where's theyr hope, on what doe they depend
　　theyr crooked course by heauen cannott bee blessed
　　& heere theyr leprous stewardship must end.
　　　　The Iustice of the Lord will not acquitt them
　　　　　　　　　　　　fowle
　　　　when as theyr owne, ∧<full> conscience doth endite them.

[265]　44.　& lett them minse theyr sinnes as small as cinders
　　theyr soules shall find them when the corps is dead
　　gods fire will trye the mettaill out of imbers
　　yf it bee gold, or brasse, or drossye lead.
　　　　O would men looke vnto that dreadfull day
[270]　　　　they would not thus theyr better part betray.

45.　That in the flesh like panting pulse doth lye
　　strangled in sinne, scarse hauing any motion
　　on wch the carelesse wretch ne're throwes his eye
　　but letts it sinke like pearle throwen in the ocean
[275]　　　　forgetting that the dreadfull day of doome
　　　　must yeeld vp all from out of all thinges wombe.

　　　　　　　　　　　　　　the truth decides
46.　W^{ch} time is neere at hand <by all surmise>　　　[161^r <163.>]
　　& yett the angells pride did ne're more florish
　　Adams rebellion, Cains fratricides.
[280]　Sodomes black lust the seedes of mortalls nourish
　　　　the theft of Achan, drunkennes of Lott
　　　　& all the worst of all doth most men spott.

47.　To lay fayre colours on a wrinckled hide
　　or smooth vp vice wth eloquent discource
[285]　Who writes for pence, be<e> he<c> soc turpified
　　& lett those nine Chima'raes bee his nurse.
　　　　to teach him crawle the Heliconian hill
　　　　& in Pernassus dipp his iuorye quill.

48.　for mee, I write but to my self & mee
[290]　what gods good grace doth in my soule imprint
　　I bought it not for pelf, none buyes of thee
　　nor will I lett it at soe base a rent
　　　　as wealth or fame, wch is but drosse & vapor
　　　　& scarce deserues the blotting of a paper.

152 APPENDIX II

[295] 49.   Nor am I soe affected vnto rime
      but as it is a help to memorye
      because it doth commaund a larger time
      to wrapp vp sence in measures quantitye,
          nor marres it truth, but giues wittes fire more fuell

[300]   & from an Ingott formes a curious Iewell.

    50.   & though some amorous Idiotts doe disgrace it
      in making verse the packhorse of theyr passion
      such cloudes may dimme the sunne but not deface it
      nor maruell I that loue doth loue this fashion

[305]   To speak in verse, yf sweet & smoothly carryed
          to true proportions loue is euer maryed.

    51.   Tis loue hath woue this rugged twine of mine   [161^v]
      quickening my harte wth such a sprightly flame
      that frozen death can neuer make it pine

[310]   nor sad affliction hath the power to lame
          for loue & fire ech other best resemble
          both hott & bright, both vigilant & nimble.

    52.   Away base world, hence shadowes, hence away.
      you shalbee noe corriualls to my loue

[315]   for hee is fresh as is the flo$_{\wedge}$rye may
      & truly constant as the turtle doue
          his breth like beddes of roses cheere the morne,
          his hayres reflex the sunne beames doth adorne.

    53.   From his fayre eyes, the world hath all her light
[320]   & till hee look'd on her, shee lay as dead
      sh'ad <had> eyes before   se
    <It had an eye> but tho<yt> eyes had noe sight
     They
    <w^{ch}> now are in her soule, then in her head
          shee spake before, but knew not what shee sayd
          like pratling babes, or doting age decayed.

[325] 54.   Some few could see & speake wth triple sence
      & what were these, but harolds of thy comming
              point
      thou gauest the<yr> eyes, the <payne> of future tense
     Coles
    <bowles> from thine altar tipp'<e>d theyr tongues wth cunning

LANSDOWNE MS. 740

153

[330]

to tell great Dauids ofspring they should see
a new Ierusalem raysed vp in thee.

55. A holy temple & a holy people
that should noe more bee bondslaues vnto sinne
whose basis should oretopp the towring steeple
of that fayre type, & yett this must beginne
[335] from lowest dunghill, to advance his horne
who wth sweet vnguent shall his spouse adorne.

56. In midst of earth, euen where the hart doth lye   [162^{r} <164.>]
there shall the first stone of this fabrick stand
the cunning builder will most firmely tye
[340] ech peece from out of time or ruines hand
for what hee reares, noe envye may confound
who can consolidate ech bleeding wound.

57. & now my Loue wth hope doth gather winge
leauing this dunghill & her bed of clay
[345] & wth the mounting larke beginnes to singe
in ioy & honour of this Halcion day.
when men & Angells all at once shall moue
rays'd by the flame of sweete bright feruent loue.

58. Ile not manure, weede, water, digg or dresse
[350] this earth noe more, vnlesse the vine spring vp
wth full charg'd grapes fitt for my deere loues presse
yeelding forth licquor for his sacred cupp
Lett mosse & cancker ouertopp the rinde
& I will hate to thinke that it was mine.

[355] 59. That vine wch his most sacred hand hath planted
yf it proue barren, in soe good a soyle
to w^{ch}, nor sunne nor rayne, nor season wanted
what keeper settes by such a fruitless toyle
who when hee visites it, & shall acquire
[360] nothing but stalke, that stalke must to ye fire.

60. Can Loue bee barren, noe, it cannott bee
the active sunne may sooner loose his heate,

154 APPENDIX II

& passiue earth well labourd, yeeld noe fee
& mortalls liue that haue but stones to eate.

[365] Tis male & female, & both sex is full
absence inflames, & neerenes cannott dull.

61. Hence Loathsome ground baytes, I am sick wth loue, [162^v]
& growen to queasye for such fussome dyett,
on payne of curses doe not seeke to moue
[370] my thoughts awry that now are all at quiett
& fill<e>'d wth admiration of his beautye
to whome all true perfection oweth dutye.

bee
62. Mine eares <are> deafe against the clamorous world
yee
& <though> mine eyes see not her fluttering pride
[375] lightening & thunder that abroad is hurld
wth wch my hart to longe was stupifyed.
yett now I see twas but a dunghill smoke,
the more wee pudder in't, wee sooner choke.

63. you witty wantons, leaue your foolish loues,
[380] though pearle & currall ouerspredd your skinne
making you looke like swannes & siluer doues
& loue that loue wch makes you fayre wthin.
Colour's an accident that will decay
a superficies spred but ouer clay.

[385] 64. To boast of it I could as well as you
to whome kind nature hath noe stepdame bene,
but <may not> sinnes infection makes them more to rue
that beare a leprous soule in a fayr skinne.
To him that built vs wee doe giue abuse
[390] & turne best mettaill to the basest vse.

65. But bee as louing Dames as you are Louely,
not to your flattering seruants, formes or glasses,
to place or trappings; these thinges are but follye
& will approue the louers of them asses.
doe
[395] your loues soe layed ∧ make <wise> men thinke you moles
<smooth> but <me>devoyd
fayre soft & wittye <blind for want> of soule<s>.
< >

LANSDOWNE MS. 740

155

66. Are you denyed soules then, you shelles of men, [163ʳ <165.>]
  are they but hatched in you & flye away
  noe maruell though theyr wisedomes doe contemne
[400] your sex, since you are only formall clay.
    <Goe search the sacred writt, where you shall find>
    but trust them not that would perswade you soe
    such serpents but advise you to more woe.

67. Goe search the sacred writt, where you shall find
  what your creation was & to what end
[405] Lett not theyr envious folly make you blind
  who pittyes him that is not his owne frend.
    Adam did sleepe whilst <hee> built your fayre frame:
            god
    & hee still sleepes that would haue you thus lame.

68. & yf you thinke yourselues to weake to looke
[410] into the depth of those hid misteryes
  goe to the Lambe, hee will vnclaspe the booke
       hee
  nor will ‸ skorne at your simplicityes
    hee is the best proficient whose life showes
             what ere
    yᵗ of god <&> from god comes ‸<all> kee knowes.

[415] 69. Yf eyther men or angells thinke they'r wise
  that very thought proclaymes them fooles & simple,
  it throwes a cloud of dust <of> ouer theyr eyes
  they cannott see the way to gods hye temple
    Lett vs ioyne Land to Land & towers to towers
[420]   how like a snowball standes this worke of ours.

70. But would you trust to these vociferations
  how fowly would you sink in all base sinne
  wᶜʰ nought could stay but hope of your saluations
  nor would you feare for theyr stout menacing
[425]   theyr liues, theyr states & theyr posterityes
    would bee the subiects of your treacheryes.

71. But lett not these fooles boltes beate downe your houses [163ᵛ]
  & make you wound your soules wᵗʰ foule neglect,
  yf you bee pure in hart you are Christes spouses,
[430] whose loue will honor you wᵗʰ true respect
    then bee you good, yf they will cleaue to euills
    you shalbee saints when such men must bee diuells.

156   APPENDIX II

72.   Custome hath giuen them that liberty
     wch you in noe sort must presume to take,

[435]   nor doe not venter on such ieapardye
     as will but sett you in a fierye lake
         worke your saluation out wth feare & trembling
         & care not though men call your truth dissembling.

73.   Rayse you the superciliums of your eyes

[440]   though but to see theyr fellow spheare, the sunne,
     they say from thence a shower of arrowes flyes
     to wound theyr hartes by wch they are vndonne.
         Natures free dowrye they call ∧<a> temptation
         to quitt theyr faultes they'l challenge great creation.

[445] 74.   Dare you but write, you are Mineruaes bird
     the owle at wch these battes & crowes must wonder,
     they'l crittickize vppon the smallest word
     this wanteth number case, that tense & gender
         then must you frame a pittifull epistle
[450]   to pray him bee a rose was borne a thistle.

75.   Could you, as did those Sybells, prophecye
     men will but count you witches for your skill
     or bee endowed wth any <facultye> qualitye
     they'l poyson it wth some deprauing ill
[455]   Envye is barren & yeeldes nought but weedes
         & feares least better ground haue better seedes.

76.   Nay should a wise & honest harted man   [164^r <166.>]
     commend a virtuous woman for her life
     would they not say the worst of him they can
[460]   & cutt his good names throat wth envyes knife.
         call him your bedesman, parasite or minnion
         what sanctitye can scape from bad opinion.

77.   & where liues hee dares row against this tide
     noe not while that admired virgin Queene
             who sometimes raignd
[465]   <that lately raigned> & your sex stellifyed
     who like stout Debora, did skorne the teene

LANSDOWNE MS. 740

of Romes proud bulles <her> ^whose^ euer watchfull eye<s>
the church <like cannon strongly> ^and state did truely <be>^ fortifie<s>.

78. A sanguin woman is of all accurst
[470]   although that constitution bee the best
shee must bee merry though her neck were burst
& mirth setts all these spanniells vp in quest.
to hunt on drye foot, for it cannott bee
goodnes & mirth should hold a simpathye.

[475] 79. A melancholly woman that is sadd
although her deedes bee good & thoughts bee holy
yett shall shee beare the censure to bee mad,
& all her actions must bee skornd as folly
yf shee bee great in place, her grauitye
[480]   must bee the nurse of some foule prodegye.

80. But what neede I speake further of complexion
on wch none but your sophiest spend theyr <mouthes> ^dotes^
the landskip witt can find a fitt detection
for all your gestures wordes, & for your <clothes> ^coates^
[485]   But good men will not doe thus that are wise
for they will tender you as theyr owne eyes.

81. Then for theyr<s> sakes pardon the others errors   [164^v]
lett not theyr euill harden you in euill
but chuse the wise for fathers frends & mirrors
[490]   & knowe hell was not made but for a Deuill
The wise will stay you yf your weakenes fall
& rayse you w^thout envye pride or gall.

82. Bee wise as serpents, innocent as Doues
you are borne subiects & you must obey
[495]   <till> ^that^ death, wch all you<rs> feare<s ^all^ &> clogges remoues
tis god you honour in it <& not they> ^lett them bray^
hee will reward you <in it>, at theyr bountyes spurne
naked they came, & naked shall returne.

83. & when you both are stript out of this clay
[500]   there will not bee a difference in your sex

you haue one Iudge & must goe both one way
the good wth good & bad wth bad soules mix
    twill bee to late when you in hell shall grone
      to curse those soles that taught you, you had none.

[505]   84.   Virgines bee wise, & keepe your lampes still burning
          wiues to your head<s> bee full of constant truth,
          widowes reioyce in him that cheeres all mourning
          turnes black to white & wrinckled age to youth
              giues you new names, new honours, hyer places
[510]   whose pompe queene Sabaes siluer throne disgraces.

    85.   And would you hold this state, enioy these ioyes
          then in the mire lett not your spiritts fall
          reiect not god, nor count his iudgments toyes
          nor wth the foole, say, ther's noe god at all
[515]   but that there is a god you must consent
              then are you bound to keepe his testament.

    86.   had you noe soules & were but morrall beastes   [165^r <167.>]
          yett were you bound to the creators law
          should earth, ayer, water, fire breake his behestes
[520]   & slipp the yoake or seeke aside to drawe
              how would the ∧<brauen> fedd world fall full <her> crestes
              like starued infantes at <her> withered brestes.

    87.   Or should the Lord himself breake the decree
          wch by his owne drad name hee sware to keepe
[525]   how many worldes in this great <-bowle> might bee
          as many monsters <heere> as flockes of sheepe.
              as many plagues to worke proud mans decay
              as there are animals that now obey.

    88.   To all his labours hee a law hath giuen
[530]   & spake but once, yett all doe still obey
          as well to nature as the host of heauen
          & none but only mankind falles away.
              whome hee still calles by Angells, wonders, dreames
              & by his deere sonnes sacred bloud in streames.

LANSDOWNE MS. 740 159

[535] 89. & haue not all these powres the power to drawe
your hartes to loue, but you will still bee cruell
will you wth Trochilus pick the serpents iaw
wth Esopes cock spurne back the pretious iewell
  could not the woundes & gall you gaue him then
[540] sweeten your hartes, you bitter harted men.

90. \<There is a family called loue, that glorye
to stripp the text as naked as they please
& turne gods booke into an Allegorye
on wch theyr sick devotions only seaze
[545] They would seeme singular, \<t^{but}hey\> know not why
  to flye the church & her com<u>mu</u>nitye.\>

These verses & those that follow though crossed out are fitt to stand

91. \<This loue is worse then hate, & full of ire   [165ᵛ]
searing theyr hartes that theyr owne bosomes smothers,
[550] flax may haue better safetye in the fire
then can the brattes of these distempred mothers.
  see how the deuill deales wth blind Devotion
  to make the lame runne on wth swifter motion.\>

92. \<Some are soe pure that yf motes lye awrye
[555] of from theyr stalles they skipp to snatch the scepter
& it must licke the mote from out theyr eye

stet.

 or proue it may lye soe by text in scripture
  tis most pure pietye makes them moue all
  the corner stone, all though the fabrick fall.\>

[560] 93. \<Nor maruell I to see these netled hennes
flye into \<t^{thereis}histles\> & forsake theyr charge
burye theyr talent & reiect theyr frends
vnlesse theyr night shade poppy may enlarge
  since errors must arise in the last day
[565] to harme th'elect yf possibly they may.\>

94. \<But these deformd reformers of the word
scandale the church & hurte the publick peace
more then the popish bulles or Romane sword
by to much clemencye these flyes increase

160 APPENDIX II

[570]
> at home a surplesse makes them sitt & mourne
> but heere fiue churchmens s͜ates serues not one turne.>

95.
> <& can these waspes account the truth theyr guide
> is true zeale voyd of peace of loue or pittye
> doe not these angry prophetts seeme to chide

stet.
[575]
> the Lord for sparing the repentant cittye
>> call you these pastors, whose rude pastoralls
>> are nodes sett to the sacred springes downefall.>

96.
> To what an angle is the true church driuen   [166'<168.>]
> for pittye sake, looke downe Lord on her cares

[580]
> & send forth faithfull laborers from heauen
> to gleane thy wheate & cast away the tares
>> Least sectes & schismes & <fowell> heresyes
>> choake vp thy seed wth sad calamityes.

97.
> Thou bread of life, yf shee want thee shee starues

[585]
> thou liuing water, yf thou fayle shee dyes
> <they still repine although they still increase>
> <the> nought but thy sacred flesh & bloud will serue
>> to please the iudge, or cleere our clouded eyes
>> In thee wee only liue & moue & be<e>

[590]
>> & our dead soules are all rev<>iued in thee.

98.
> To th'vngodly, god sayes ther's noe peace
> like troubled waters they doe throw vp durt
> they still repine although they still increase
> they neuer speake but tis to some mans hurte

[595]
>> theyr soules nor bodyes can haue any rest
>> sinnes vlcer doth soe gnawe vppon theyr brest.

99.
> Such cannott keepe the peacefull sabbath day
> the tipe of rest in god cannott bee heere
> they may goe to the church & heare & pray

[600]
> theyr conscience stinge though wounds them euerywhere
>> they must haue peace in god that keepes it holy
>> to seeke it elsewhere is but painfull folly.

100.
> There is a conscience quiett, but not good
> steep'd in the deepe gulf of securitye

LANSDOWNE MS. 740   161

[605]   they sttrech at eas\<p>e, but tis, like swine in mudd
       theyr festered woundes they dare not mundifye
           such doe not keepe but sleepe the the sabbaths rest
           & dreames detayne them till all time bee past.

101. There is a conscience good, but voyd of rest   [166ᵛ]
[610]   that dares not take vnlawfull libertye
       these are like armyes in a good cause prest
       vnquiett till \<they gett> they gett the victorye
           they keepe but not enioy the sabbath rest
           nor can they till theyr fayth bee fully blest.

[615] 102. There is a conscience that is good & quiett
                       firmely stood
      such as by falling haue more ‸\<strength to stand>
       in middest of plentye they vse sparing dyett
                       gather food
      & from the barren rock can ‸\<presse some>
           These both enioy & keepe the sabbath rest
[620]   theyr full summd plumes sitt quiett in the nest.

103. And though they bee aflicted whilst they liue
       they are rich gummes that smell more sweete by bruising
       or diamonds cutt that doe more lustre giue
       or steele that lookes the brighter for the vsing
[625]   The rust of wealth doth not theyr soules besmeare
           they call not death nor yett his comming feare.

104. Nor are they like the dead sea voyd of motion
       but busye chimmickes turning lead to gold
       they lye at hull in the tempestuous ocean
[630]   & yett the tempest maker makes them bold
           to tred on serpents wᵗʰ theyr naked feete,
           & face to face the boldest
           \<to beard the beare & fellest> lyons meete.

105. These are not like the superstitious Iewes
       that sleepe the sabbath wᵗʰ theyr losse of blood
[635]   noe act of pietye will these refuse
       this day to doe theyr church or cuntrye good
           they know the saba\<->th was not made for play
           but for more worke then any other day.

162

APPENDIX II

106. [Beca]use it is gods day of   [167ʳ]
[640]   the Burgesses are Angell
        the prophetts & Apostles
        the bills that showe<s> the
                Christ is the speaker
                vp to bee ratifyed.

[645] 107. The subsidye that this
        wch out of his prerogati
        is that all men in true obedienc
        & not to change theyr soueraigne for a new
                nor alter his decrees in any parte
[650]   & that to him wee sacrifice our harte

108. The penaltye for breaking these decrees
                                    endlesse
        is that the soule must burne in ∧<lasting> fires
        heere are noe lawyers to bee had for fees
        the Advocate is Iudge, who payes ech hire
[655]   all pleadings or demurres come out of season
                when death comes to arrest vs of hygh treason.

109. Hee giues not vp a liuely sacrifice
        that stayes till withered age hath made him dead
        who letts the sunne sett ere hee doe arise
[660]   hee were almost as good still keepe his bedd
                O come & learne at great Iehouaes schoole
                a Sabaoth breaker is a busye foole.

                this divine poem.   [167ᵛ]
                <way of knowne pri
                ther her invention>
                this Ladyes facultye.

[5]   oe other qualitye
                en ouer all to rimes
                hese moderne times
                ight some witt expresse
                would herself scarce dresse.
[10]   qualityes <admired> acquir'd
                to bee admir'd ation liues in her behauior.

LANSDOWNE MS. 740

163

wch is as gracefull as shee full of fauour.
Ther's nothing art or nature doth descrye
but shee can draw it through her needles eye

[15]   when yf she chaunce to worke by imitation
shee goes beyond her patternes commendation
all to the life is soe exactly done
as nature doth by pencill of the sunne
What is't a Lady can or ought to doe

[20]   but shee both knowes & doth excell in to
yett shee well weighing all that may reside
in great place titles, & a braue outside
bedeckd wth Iewells, knowes true honours flowe
from wthin, not layd out to th'optick showe

[25]   Transcendent thus in all, her chiefest studye is
to know god though, herself, & that wch good is
as in this clearer mirror may appeare
to euery Readers eye & hearers eare
whose worth compared wth others of her sex

[30]   they'rs like the concaue are, hers the convex.
In this, these graue & holy meditations
were not her worke but<->> her sweet recreations
Hence other Ladyes neede not then despayre
to bee as easely wise, as fine & fayre.

[35]   H.

The workes of the Lady Ann Sothwell:
Decemb: 2° 1626:

Sonnett: 1.
Fly from the world, ò fly, thow poore distrest
where thy diseased sence infects thy Soule
And where thy thoughts doe multiply unrest
Troubling with wishes what they strayt controls
   O World betrayer of the mynd
   O Thoughts that guide us being blynd:.

Sonnett: 2. ^a
When J sitt reading all alone that secret booke
     Wherein J sigh to looke
how many blotts there be, J wish J could not see, or from my selfe might fly
       or from my selfe might flee,
Heauens J implore, that showes my Guilt
     To hell J dare not goe
The World first made me rue, my selfe my woes renue
     To whom then shall J sue.
Is there no hope in death? yes: Death ends all our woes.
Death me ~~will~~ ME ~~whose~~ will lose, myselfe ~~Am~~ all my foes:.

Somn: 3. ^a
Farewell fond world, the onely Schoole of Error,
The Chaos whence all stormes and tempests rise:
Mount thow my Soule unto that Sacred mirror,
That showes men are but fynite Sommer flyes:
   And there wth piety bewayle their Cares:
   Whose fond Laborious Webbs are their owne Snares:.

Sonnett 4. ^a
If in the flesh where thow indrench'd dost Ly
Poore Soule thow couldst lift upp thy lymed winges
Carry thy selfe upp to that azurd Sky
And wash them in those Sacred = Cristall springes
   where Joy and requiem the holy Angles singes
   And all Heauens Vault wth blessed Eccho Ringes:.

Sonnett. 5. ^a
shall J sublyme my soule to frame a letter
And to the Sisters proue a ready better
To Stritfull muse on Hieroghliphicks mount
And tell the World J skorne their base attempt
Fit scriueners feeke that ~~idly falls~~ fame that idly falls
   Upon the keper of Romes Capitall.

Folio 1^r: The title folio of the commonplace book

2

Goe sole the bodies guest   Tell those that braueth most
vpon a thankles arrand   They begg for more by spendinge
feare not to touch the best   And in their greatest cost
the truth shalbe thy warrand   Seeke nothinge but commendinge
And yf they doe reply,   And yf this doe deny
boldlie giue them the lye   then giue them all the lye

Goe tell the court yf glose   Tell schooles they want profundnes
And shines like rotten wood   And onelie liud by seeminge
Goe tell the church it shewes Tell artes they want true grounds
Whats good but doth noe good And but by esteeminge
Yf court or church reply,   Yf schooles or artes reply,
Giue court and church the lye Giue schooles and artes they lye

Tell potentates they liue   Tell phisicke of her boldnes
Actinge but others attion,   Tell nature of decay
Not loued unles they giue   Tell charitie of coldnes
Not strong but by their factions Tell iustice of delay
Yf potentates reply,   And yf they doe deny
Giue potentates the lye   then giue them all the lye

Tell men of high condition Tell beautie it is a flourish
That rules affayres of state Tell tyme it eldvils be neuy
Their purpose is ambition Tell they all must perish
Their practise onlie hate,   And fortune doth bewray
And yf they doe deny   And yf they this deny
then giue them all the lye then giue them all the lye

Now when thou hast as I — commaunded thee done blabbinge
All-though to giue the lye — deserues noe les then stabbinge
stabb at thee he that will — Noe stabb the sole can kill

Anne Southwell

Folio 2ʳ: Ralegh's "The Lie," with the signature "Ann Southwell"

Fol. 44ᵛ, of the Southwell drafts, #1, in her own hand

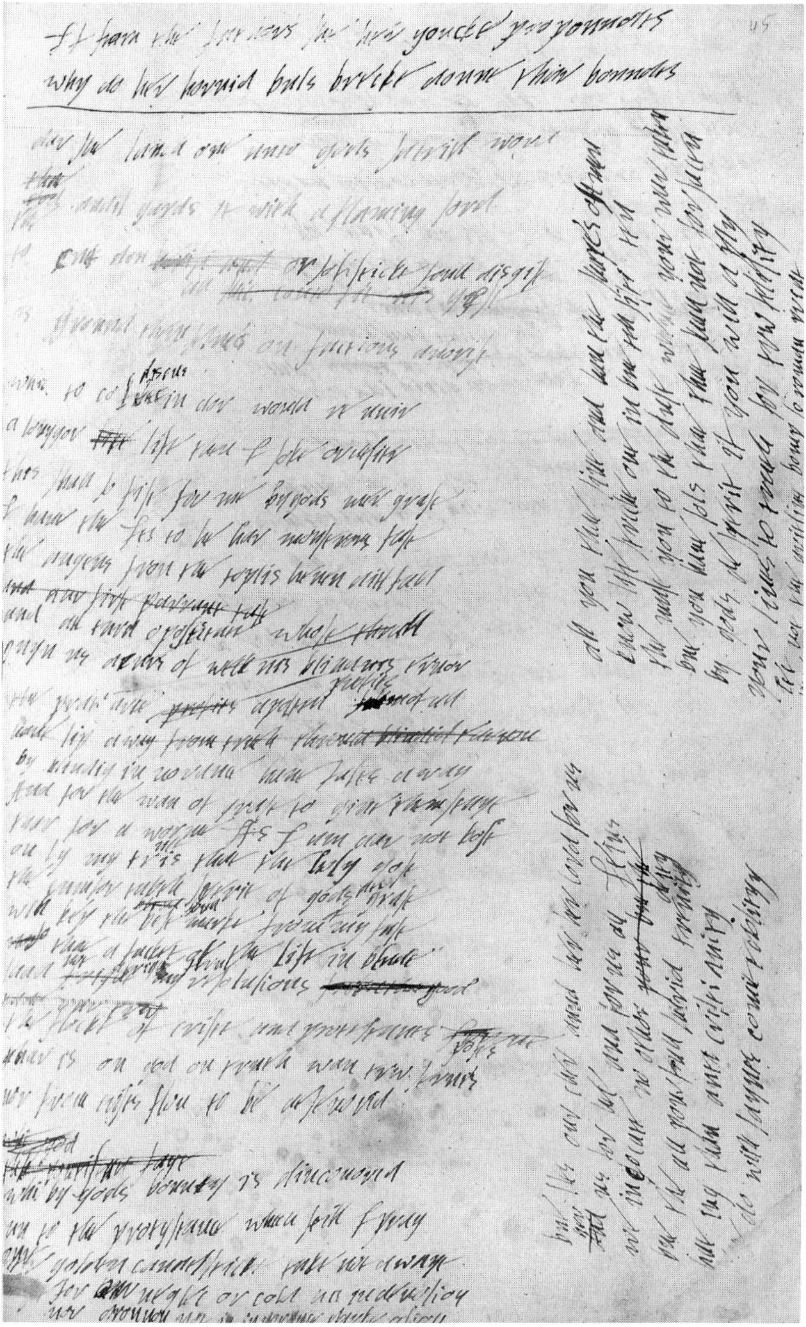

Fol. 45r: Southwell drafts, #1, continued

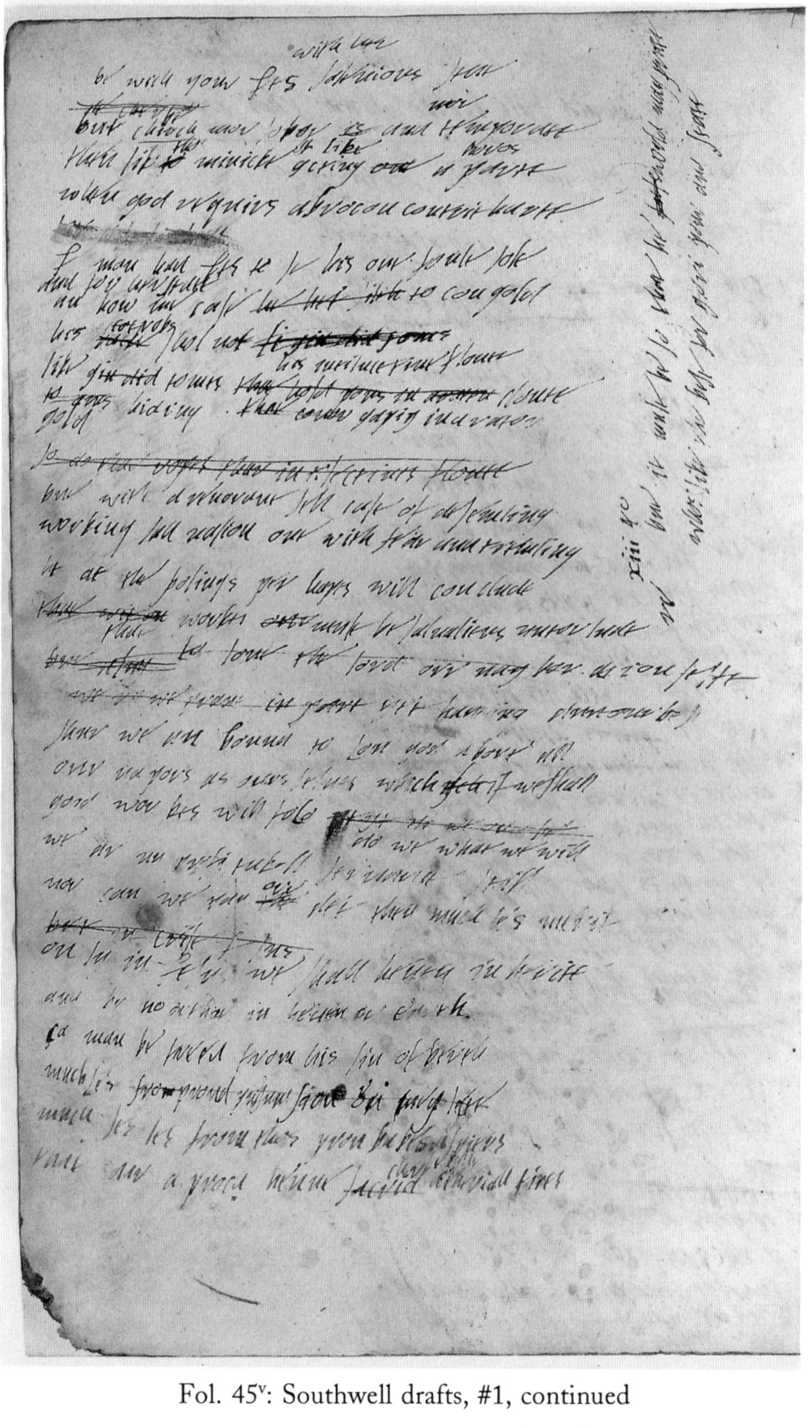

Fol. 45^{v}: Southwell drafts, #1, continued

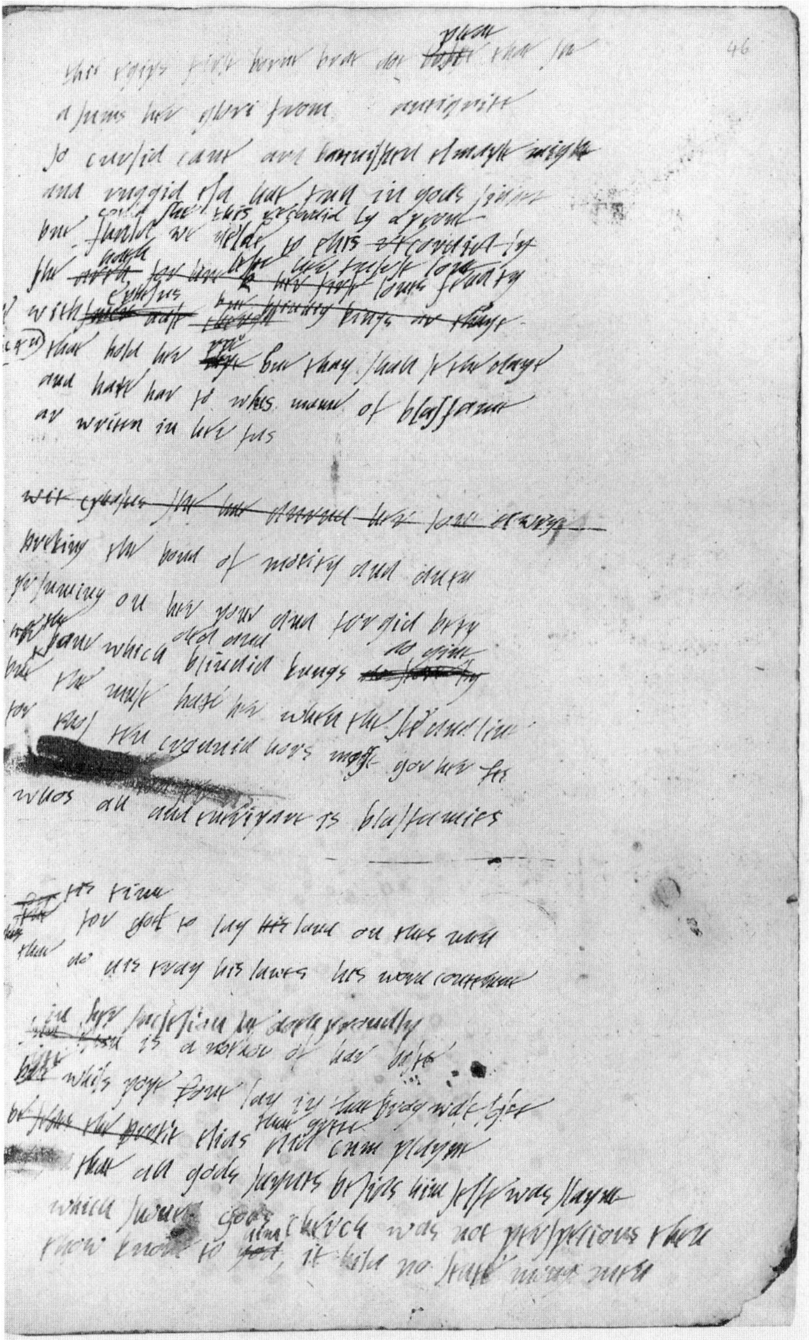

Fol 46r: Southwell drafts, #1, continued

5 is much grast in core
Admytt a sycophant that
vto thy king and quene thorough hate be by the
Sathan had power to vex Jobe in woorse sort
thinck this affliction sent from god to trye the
what doest thou know but that thy princes grace
may in thy harte gods image quite deface

§ 5?

If wicked men doe take away thy wealth
plenty may make thee wanton kick at god
thinck this imposture lancht for thy soules health
doe not repyne at the almighties rodd
perhapps thy store of treasure may soe dull thee
and from this lyberty tis want must pull thee

what thou we see sum vise and oythers fall
men can this vise f can not tell
for eth bad fules no vise atall
which breth any deth doth make tims carnyiong ball
tis good and best to which gods grast doth giues

Fol. 57ʳ, of the Southwell drafts, #2, in her own hand

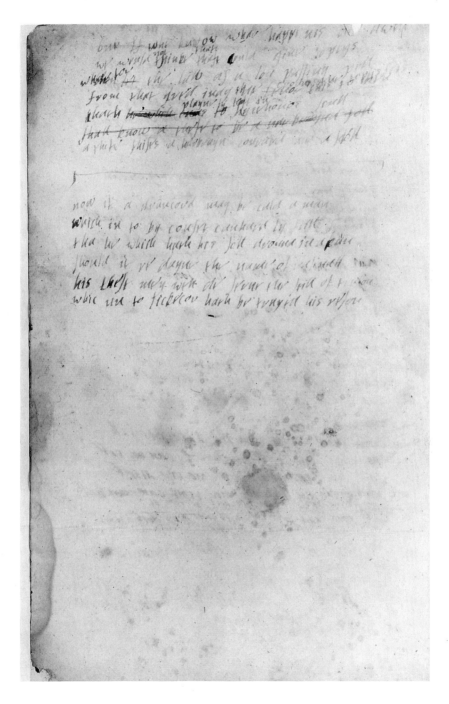

Fol. 57ᵛ: Southwell drafts, #2, continued

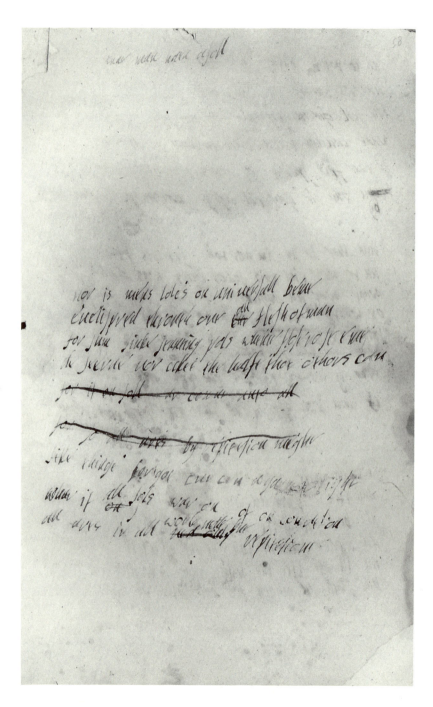

Fol. 58r: Southwell drafts, #2, continued

Fol. 58ᵛ: Southwell drafts, #2, continued

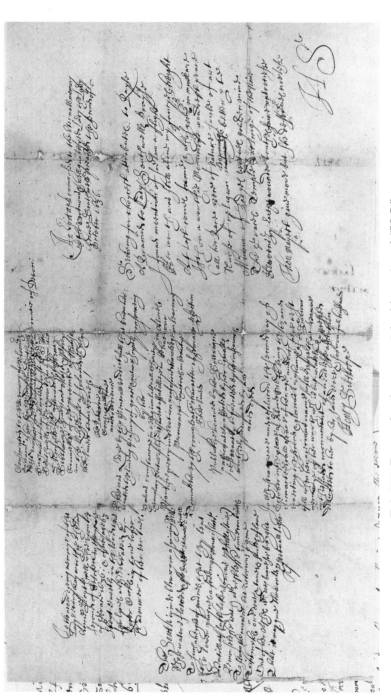

Fol. 73r: Poetry for the memorial tablets, signed "H.S."

Consecrated to the Memory of ~
The Honour and ornament of her sexe ~ /

The Lady Anne Southwell.

Eldest daughter of Sr Thomas Harris of Cornworthy in the Countie of Devon
Kt and Searigant at Law: married first to Sr Thomas Southwell of Spixworth in the Countie of Norf Kt. Afterwardes to Henry Sybthorpe Sergeant Maior and Privy Counsel-
lour of the Province of Munster in the kingdome of Ireland, with whome she lived teenn yeares;

The patterne of coniugall love & obedience.

She was a Lady by the generall verdict of all that knew her
Reputed the living treasury of Grace and Nature ioyntly Conspiring

By Her

Zealous Constancy in Religion.
Exemplary vertue in life,
Pious frequency in devotion,
Liberall Charity in Almes.
Discreet offability in behaviour.
Profound knowledge in learning.
Permanent exactnesse in beautie.
To make her the exact Character of female perfection.

She Lived
Publiquely honoured by her soveraigne
Passionately affected by her equalles
Observantly reverenced by her inferiours
Worthely Admired by all.
And dyed

In Christian peace and resolation
The second day of Octob in the yeare of our Lord 1626, and doth here rest expecting the second and Glorious Epiphany of our Saviour. Till when her pious name will
preserve that happy memory of her worth, wch is but weakly expressed in this sad monument
of an Endlesse affection dedicated to her by her said deare and sorrowfull husband

Henry Sybthorpe

Fol. 74ʳ: The memorial used for the black stone tablet still hanging in
St. Mary's Church in Acton, signed "Henry Sibthorpe"

Textual Notes

Where the letters which have been changed are ascertainable, the note indicates that one or more letters have been written *over* others; where they are not, the note says that a letter or letters have been *corr.* A number above a stanza in the meditations is referred to by the number of the line below the number.

The name of the scribe for most of a page is listed in Appendix I. Where a different hand appears, even for a few words, or an aspect of the physical appearance may have relevance, it is noted here. Occasionally two lines or whole stanzas are deleted by large *X*s, apparently made by Lady Anne's typically splayed pen (as illustrated especially by marginal notes like the "scratched" vertical lines 73 and 74 to the right of lines 61–72 on fol. 53ʳ): fols. 26ᵛ (25–28), 33ʳ (61–66 and 74–79), 35ᵛ (25–42), 36ʳ (43–54 and 61–72), 41ʳ (243–54), 49ᵛ (146–47, with small *x*s), 52ʳ⁻ᵛ (25–42), 54ʳ⁻ᵛ (101–38), 55ʳ (139–44), and 56ʳ (151–62). These are not listed in Appendix I as an indication of Southwell's hand, however, because they could also have been made by a scribe.

Abbreviations used in the Textual Notes and the Commentary:

L	Latin
S	Lady Anne Southwell
HS	Captain Henry Sibthorpe
SR	Samuel Rowson
X	the unidentified hands which write many folios
corr.	corrected
T	Title
over	written over

Letters written above or below the line have been omitted.

[1ʳ] The word "Sonnet," with its number, is always written in the left margin, slightly above the first line of the poem, here and on fols. 9ʳ and 9ᵛ.

"Sonnett: 1ᵃ". 4 they] *inserted and blurred;* Controle] e *over* d

"Sonnett: 2ᵃ". 3 How many blotts there be] *written in left margin*

[2ʳ] [Ralegh, "The Lie"]. The page of consistently clubbed ascenders and descenders,

178 NOTES

similar to the hand of Joseph Hopton on fol. 72ᵛ, is unique among the folios; the letters are predominantly italic with a few secretary letters, such as the upside-down "r," and reversed "C."

1–24 Goe . . . lie] *written in the left column* || 16 their] r *corr.* || 23 deny] e *corr.* || 25–48 Tell . . . lye] *written in the right column* || 50 Deserues] D *over* d

[3ʳ⁻ᵛ] "To . . . Ladye Ridgway" 4 worldes] *an ink blot follows* || 15 & Drye . . . Bloud] *a crease through the line partly obscures letters* || 26 Repletion. Therefore] *the paper has a mended tear from the left, above these words* || 32 your] you *faintly written* || 56–58 vera . . . An: o:/] *a large blot obscures legibility* || 57 prvto turi] *conjecture*

[4ʳ] [A letter to Falkland] A fine nib is being used. Flourishes, hyphens or tildes fill out ends of lines, following the words or syllables "in" in line 2, "Philo" in line 4, "as" in line 5, "of a" in line 6, "guift of" in line 7–8, "death" in line 12, "those" in line 13, and "your" in line 18. Their original purpose seems to have been to make a perfectly straight right-hand side of the letter, forming a rectangle 5 x 3 1/2 inches; they have been dropped. Even the cancellations are carefully and uniformly done with a rhythmic scroll. The page has a neater appearance than any other, probably because of the importance of the addressee. Creases show that the paper must have been folded into small rectangles for some time before being pasted down on fol. 4.

4–5 Omnia mea, mecum porto] *written with a heavier ink in an upright style—in contrast to the slant of the rest of the writing* || 19 plus vltra] *written as the Latin words in line 5 are* || 22–25 1628 . . . Ireland] *the hand of HS*

[5ʳ] "A Hym to Christ" 6 Natiue] N *corr.* || 11 Charity] the descender of the "y" sweeps to the right edge of the paper; it is the longest stroke of this kind in the poem, perhaps to emphasize the activity of "Christ'"

[5ᵛ] "5 predicables" 1 5 predicables] S *wrote* 5 pre || 11 Apparailing] ai *corr.*

[6ʳ] [Signed receipts of the 1580s, numbers 2, 3, and 4] 7 Debe] b *over* k || 30 solc-giars] *either a* c *or a part of a letter is between the* l *and* g

[6ᵛ] [Signed receipts of the 1580s, numbers 5, 6, 7, 8, and 9] 23 Pape] *possibly* Paxe || 31 Bargaine] *this could be transcribed as* Bargame, *but see fol. 6ʳ, 30, where it is spelled* bargayne.

[7ʳ] [Psalm 25, to the Earl of Castlehaven] 1 A[nne] B] *the line is trimmed, but the bottom of the next letters could be* lunt. *A descending loop in the next word shows enough space for the word* daughter, *if the descender is a* g. *The right-hand corner has been torn off, allowing space for the rest of the word* daughter. *See the commentary.*

[8ʳ] "A Paraphrase vppon Lucius Anneus Seneca" 18 <t>him] i *over* e || 36 <->or] *the word was probably* nor *before the crossout occurred*

[8ᵛ] "Blessed Life" 13 men<ds>] e *over* y

[9ʳ] "Dialouge: / Sonnet." T Dialouge:] u *over* v(?) || 15 are] e *over* t || 17 wold'st] o *corr.*

[9ᵛ] "Sonnet: / Like to a lampe wherein the light is dead" 14 thy] th *over* m

[10ʳ] "ffrayle Loue" Two styles, if not hands, appear here. Lines 1–7 show a careful and decorative mixed secretary and italic; lines 8–36 are written in a slightly smaller and more hurried style and the first letters of each line are less decorative. Some letters, however, are quite similar, like the *d*s in "vnder" (line 5) and "goddesse" (line 33), suggesting that line 8 and following may be only a change of style and the pace in which it was written. The first style or hand resembles the hand of John Bowker of fol. 1. The only drawings in the volume are the two fingers at lines 25 and 30.

11–12 Those . . . gall] *the lines are squeezed into the right margin between lines 10 and 13. The vertical line at the right of the refrain is drawn up to the "X" at the left of the lines to be inserted.* || 12 are] r *corr.* || 23 choke] c *corr.* || 35 thus] us *over* --e(?)

NOTES

179

[11ʳ] "Nature, Mistris off affection" Written in bold letters, on a page about 1/4 inch shorter than the preceding pages, the size of those until fol. 15.

[12ʳ–13ʳ] "Honor thy father and mother" *T* Honor ... the] *the line is trimmed* || 2 the] e *inserted* || 11 colored] d *corr.* || 15 witt] i *corr.*; tendes] d *over* t*(?)* || 17 dear] a *over* e || 31 siluer] u *corr.* || 34 stay] t *over* h || 51 them)]) *over* ; || 54 duteous] *second* u *over* o || 77 whome] *The scribe started to write another letter before the* w.

[16ʳ] "All.maried.men.desire.to.haue good wifes" The periods in lines 1 and 2 seem to be deliberate dots, which may suggest a hesitancy on the part of the scribe. Others may be ink flecks, but are included because of their position on the lines. The clear secretary letters, carefully written, resemble those of fol. 10, 1–7. The poem is written on a page of standard size, which has been folded twice vertically. A small hole, made by corrosive ink, is at the right of line 1.
3 wodd] o *corr.*

[16ᵛ] The page is blank, but in the bottom half are ink blots not from fol. 17ʳ.

[17ʳ] "F<w->ayne would I dye" The leaf has been folded twice vertically. The first letter of each line is written boldly to emphasize the name "FRAVNCIS QUARLES," as explained in the Commentary. The word "Hyperbolizeinge" (line 9) ends in a double flourish, which emphasizes its meaning. The word "Immortalitye" (line 4) and those at the end of lines 1, 2, 3, 10, and 11 conclude with smaller flourishes. The flamboyancy of the writing suggests the desire to honor the one being praised. Lines 6–14 are written with a finer nib than lines 1–4, but by the same hand.
T whil'st] il's *corr. and inserted* || 2 life<ht>] f *over* g; e *inserted*

[18ʳ–19ʳ] "A Letter to Doctor Adam" The following words are written in letters slightly larger than the letters of other words: "Man" (line 32), "Scala Cæli" (line 91), "Cælum Empiræum" (line 92), "Adam" (line 117), and "Halleluiah" (line 120).
T Letter to Doctor] *over indecipherable words* || 11 not] t *over* e || 21 diuine] *first* i *over* e || 24 fiuefould] fiue *over* g---- || 29 did] did *over* doth*(?)* || 60 curled] d *inserted* || 62 coabations] *first* o *corr.* || 86 But] B *over* b*(?)* || 87 euerlastinge] *third* e *over* s || 101 hope] h *over* e*(?)* || 102 breach] h *corr.* || 108 Orbes] O *corr.* || 119 expectinge] x *corr.* || 123 ffinis] *a flourishing line underscores the word*

[19ᵛ–20ᵛ] "An Elegie ... / to the Countesse of London Derrye" 17 on] o *corr.*; hirʳ bosome] h *corr.* || 25 <caret>] *the word is another inch to the left of line* 25 || 26 (whoe ... course)] *an inserted line* || 27 Alma] A *corr.* || 30 compos'd] d *over* e || 37 glideinge] *first* i *corr.* || 41 if] f *corr.* || 42 should] s *over* t*(?)* || 44 adore] d *corr.* || 51 Fayne] ay *corr.* || 57 thus] u *over* i || 69 eies] *first* e *corr.* || 70 downe] d *corr.* || 73 bitumeous] e *corr.* || 78 descent] *first* e *over* i || 83 Charon] C *over* A || 92 loue God] G *over* g || 94 likc] *a* v *started and discontinued after the* e || 100 but ... hold] *the line was inserted* || 115 kinge] e *over* s || 118 speakeinge] g *corr.*

[21ʳ] "An: Epitaph vppon Cassandra MackWilliams" *T* MackWilliams] c *inserted,* k *over* h || 6 not'] *the strongest accent mark in the manuscript underscores the denial and suggests that Lady Anne was dictating the poem*
9 starr gasears] *in the hand of an unknown scribe*
"Written in commendations of Mʳ Coxe" Written with a lighter black ink and a finer nib than used for the above poem.
T (the] *over* his || 11 strucgleinge] *first* g *over* l*(?)*

[21ᵛ] [Henry King, "The Exequy"] The 120 lines are written in a hurried and cramped way, to fit on the page.
1–58 Accept ... eies] *written in the left column* || 4 a] *ink is blurred* || 52 dome]

e *inserted* || 59–121 In ... Finis] *written in the right column* || 75 trust] *second* t
corr. || 76 atome] t *corr.* || 78 monument] second n *corr.* || 101 Thus] T *over* t
|| 103 nor] r *over* w || 104 swiftly] *corr. and blurred*
[22ʳ] "What if I wante the dross of Tagus Strann" 2 mvddie] v *corr.*
"An Epitaph vpon the king of Bohemia" 7 For] *corr.*
"An Epitaph vpon yᵉ king of Swede" 5 wee] *first* e *over* h || 18 Gusstauus] *first* s
is a long one over an italic s
[22ᵛ] "Come forth foule Monster" 6 O] *S(?) added* || 7 Mvrtherar] v *over* o || 14
Worss] *first long* s *over an italic one* || 16 breed>] S *corr. to* doth *before deleting and
added upside-down caret* || 20 -arb of>] S *seems to have deleted a letter with a
descending loop and written the* e *and a* *before deleting the word;* ‸Grace] S *added an
upside-down caret* || 27 ecquode] u *over* h || 34 would] o *over* h || 36 fflagidon]
over another word || 46 mudd] *conjecture; letters are trimmed below the word*
[23ʳ] "An Epitaph vpon the Countess of / Sommersett" 2 tis Deff] s Deff *corr.;* <-nes>]
conjecture || 7 a] *the ink blurs the letter* || 13 Well] ell *corr.* || 21 not] *either an
accent mark or another letter started before the word* || 27 Now] w *corr.* || 30 All]
over are
[23ᵛ] "Only eight soules, the waued tost Church did keepe" 3 awaik<t>ed] k *corr.* || 5
And] A *corr.* || 11 Michell] M *corr.* || 20 thakes] *the* h *a scribal error?* || 21
heauen] *second* e *over* r; h<ad>r] *reading uncertain*
[24ʳ⁻ᵛ] [Henry King, "An Elegy upon ... Gustavus Adolphus"] 19 Those] T *over* t ||
47 &] *conjecture; SR rarely uses* &. *Published editions read* or. || 53 thyne] y *over* i ||
66 fall] ll *corr.* || 67 Yet ... Sun] *tops of letters are trimmed;* liffes] ff *over* g(?) ||
123 thyne] y *corr.*
[25ʳ] "The more my soule doth shrinke from loue" After the first Latin phrase in line 2,
the following three (lines 4, 6, and 8) are written in letters slightly larger than those
in the preceding phrase.
3 may<ht>] ay *over* ig || 15 graue's] e *corr.* || 18 oʳ:] *inserted* || 19 And] A *corr.*
[26ʳ] "Vnless himselfe against himselfe weare bent" The inserted paper is brown and has
irregular edges; it is torn and mended on the horizontal crease across line 28. Biblical
citations are written in the left margin.
32 this] t *inserted* || 58 Chymæras] y *over* i
[26ᵛ] "Sʳ. giue mee leaue to plead my Grandams cause" The color of the ink in the
writing and the crossouts seems to be the same, suggesting that the deletions occurred
shortly after the writing.
4 <peruerse>] <peruerse> *corr.;* resolu'd] *conjecture* || 56 Monarck] k *corr.*
[27ʳ⁻ᵛ] "In this frayle worlde" An X hand, perhaps a highly restrained one of HS. Some
of his typical letter forms appear. The inserted page has been folded over twice, hence
the mended vertical tear.
6 Without] Warburton *corr.;* feare] e *corr.* || 30 bide] b *corr.* || 36 masters] a *is
obscured by a vertical tear* || 39 the] e *over* y || 43 voyage] vo *corr.*
[28ʳ⁻29ᵛ] "The ffirst Commandement" The meditation is written on very browned and
wrinkled paper, which has several strong creases. Folio 28 has one strong vertical
crease and three horizontal creases; fol. 29 has two prominent horizontal creases,
along with vertical ones.
2 to] *inserted in left margin* || 3 subblime] m *lacks a minim* || 20 carieers] i *over* r
|| 26 milke] k *corr.; ink fleck follows the word* || 68 pearc'd] ar *corr.* || 88
Empyreum] y *over* e || 91 esau] *conjecture* || 93 through,which] *comma used to
separate words?* || 107 B e] *reading is uncertain and blurred; probably extraneous* ||
121 contemne] t *corr.* || 122 S] *partly torn away*

NOTES   181

[31ʳ–32ᵛ] "Who euer sawe himself but in a myrrour" The very browned paper has many creases. The punctuation added in lines 21 and following and the scribal corrections are in black ink, in contrast to the brown ink of the writing.

5 her] *ink obscures the upper part of the word* || 12 steay] e *inserted* || 15 a woorme] *ink blot obscures* a || 16 h[ar]te] *the paper has been pealed off most of the* ar || 18 other lou[e]] *the paper has been pealed off most of the* e *of* loue || 37 obscvrytye] c *inserted* || 40 servind] *faintly written* || 44 mankind] d *over* g || 47 humble frends] *over erasure* || 49 serue ... pryvate] *over erasure* || 64–65 The ... Rome] *lines are written vertically in the left margin, between lines 41–54* || 68 will,] *comma uncertain* || 93 weight] e *over* i || 94 fame or] *over erasure*

[32ᵛ–33ᵛ] "I am thy god" 1 <I>] *S* wrote g *partially over* I || 5 <or ... > creasion] *S added* || 6 epitome] *over* Image || 8 [lot]] *blot obscures, conjecture* god || 9 <I>] *S wrote part of the* g *of* god *over the* I || 16–18 When ... trancelusantraye] *written vertically in left margin* || 16 inclaye] l *corr.* || 23 doth] d *over* t || 27 yet] e *over* i || 30 god] *S wrote* g *over* I; doth] *S wrote* th *over* e || 31 he] *S wrote over* I || 32 encountering] ing *inserted* || 37] the cumfrtor we] *although not deleted, the phrase probably should be, so that the line could read* his holy sperit of loue he forth did sende || 44 his] *S wrote;* him] *written by the hand of lines 80–82 below* || 45 hee] *S wrote;* th] *written by the hand of lines 80–82 below* || 57 feare] *ink blot underneath;* proceede] c *over* s || 71 flow] *S wrote* flow *over* top || 78 hatid] *S added* || 79 his] *S wrote* is *over* e || 80–82 A note ... Augusten] *written, with a finer nib than other lines, vertically in the left margin, between lines 74–85, by the X hand in lines 44 and 45 above* || 89 whose power<he>each place] *over erasure* || 90 can make] *extra minim of* n *deleted*

[34ʳ–35ʳ] "Thou shalt not make to thy self / any graven Image" The numbers in the left margin have been made by the same hand and pen that wrote the marginal note on fol. 33ᵛ, 80–82

2 <f>] *erasure* || 5 trembled] *S added* d || 6 non] non*(?) S corr. the second* n *which could also be a* w; resembled] *S added* d || 11 creature] *over erasure* || 12 feature] *over erasure* || 23 that] *second* t *was inserted;* Sall] S *over erasure* || 34 dun] un *over erasure* || 41 looke] *S corr.* || 46 <t>hym] y *over* e || 53 the] *S adds;* hygh] g *over erasure* || 54 theyre ... eares] *over erasure;* eares are] *the letters* ares a *are written over the partially erased* fild || 59 whome] *over erasure* || 71 affections] *over erasure* || 78 the] *S wrote* || 81 <fm>arues] *the entire word is written over multiple erasures: the* m *was partially over* f *or* s *and another letter; then the* m *was crossed out and a* c*(?) was written above* || 83 foole] oo *inserted over a letter;* e *corr.*

[35ʳ–37ʳ] "Thou shalt not take the / name of god in vayne" 1 exprest] *over erasure* || 4 seeme] *second* e *corr.* || 47–48 these ... heavye] *the first four words of both lines are written over an erasure* || 51 like agayne] like a *over erasure* || 73 100] *written in the upper left corner;* embassadore] b *corr.* || 74 provyde] y *corr.* || 75 warr] *first* r *corr.* || 79 stet] *conjecture* || 92 dew] d *corr.* || 93 <o>skinn] o *erased;* f *retained as* s || 97 barque] u *over* e || 99 hope<s> and feare<s>] *the* s *is erased in both words* || 100 foole] *has an accidental(?) stroke after the word;* <l>] *erased* || 113–114 and ... tyme] *lines in an X hand, which resembles the very careful one of S on fol. 39ʳ, line 119* || 117 doth] d *over* g; stab] b *over* f, *followed by a stroke* || 120 takes] ke *corr.*

[37ʳ–44ʳ] "Thou shalt keepe holy the / saboth daye" 17–18 t'is ... that's] *the apostrophes are formed like carets* || 20 acquittance] *the first* c *is corr.* || 24 her] *S wrote* er *over* is || 35 this] *is over* at; <from fighting had> ... <d>] *erased* || 62 game] g *over* d || 70 church] r *corr.* || 81 pray] ay *ink is blurred* || 83 lo] o *written over bowl of* b*(?), or possibly the word is* ho] h *over* b *but not deleted* || 85 Goe] *over erasure of*

182 NOTES

-hy(?) || 99 they] ey *over* is || 102 hy] *is actually* <t>h<e>y<re>] t *and* e *were erased and* re *was crossed out to read* hy || 104 Elysha] sha *blurred* || 112 dyd] *second* d *over* t || 115–18 Let ... fill] *heavier ink, forming clubs on ascenders* || 118 nor] r *corr.* || 119 so ... mistory] *probably a very careful hand of S, which became looser in the next line as she continued writing* || mistory] *or corr.* || 122 for shuch] *the bar of the* f *continues across until the* u || 128 hym] y *over* e || 132 walkes] k *corr.;* bore] r *corr.* || 146 dyd] y *corr.* || 153 Then] *over erased* B-- || 163 falles] *second* l *is a long* s *with the bottom erased* || 165 Idlenes] dle *corr.* || 174 homisite] homi *over* par- || 176 are] e *corr.* || 190 choose] c *over* s || 191 place] *over*---d || 201 <t>bordered] t *erased;* b *over* h || 207 makeing] k *corr.,* e *inserted* || 209 ropes,] p(?) *begun before the* r || 231–36 [A s]ouldyer ... multeply.] *written on a piece of paper pasted down the left edge, over lines 237–41. The upper left corner has been damaged and the surface is gone from the first three lines at the left. The paper was probably first put over lines 255–60, for* mount *(at the end of line 256) completes line 232, and* nt *(at line 258) completes line 234* || 231 reth <an>atitian] *first* t *over* c, <an> *is a conjecture* || 232 the<s>] t *inserted;* e *over* i || 235 equitye] i *over* y *or vice versa* || 256 mount] *see the note for lines 231–36* || 257<on>] *a piece of tissue paper is pasted over the word to delete it* || 258 nt] *see the note for lines 231–36* || 260 holy] *almost erased* || 267 Which Syon top] ich Syon top *corr.;* archytecture] *first* r *corr.* || 280 <e>] *erased* || 286 aboute] *over erasure* || 292 notions] *minim before the* n *was deleted* || 303 <s>] *erased* || 310 sweetly] t *inserted* || 316 polyticks] y *over* i || 319 these] se *inserted* || 329 bowe] *ink fleck follows* || 342 fowntayne] t *and* y *corr.* || 345–48 this ... last] *only the note, in the left margin, is written by S* || 350 accounte] a *corr.* || 351 nor for] *over erasure* || 353 infecting] *the scribe started to write* I *and then erased it* || 357 tutchstone] s *inserted* || 358 waygh] g *over* h || 374 makes] e *corr.* || 377 oaks] o *over* a || 380 Plynny] Pl *over* I || 386 coolde] l *inserted;* spread] *another letter was started but discontinued before the* s || 390 <t>hopes<ts>] *over partially erased* thoughts || 410 roonne] *first* o *over* u || 416 <o>] *erased* || 425 Iealoius] i *inserted;* cannott] tt *over* d || 429 the] *corr.;* hee is speaker] *over erasure* || 430 [t]] *a lump of paste obscures; the rest of the line is written over an erasure, beginning* st; *the words below the line have also been erased, except for* gost is cryor

[44ᵛ–46ʳ] [Southwell drafts, #1] 2 mind] d *over* g || 4 Iobe] *over* hath || 6 from] o *corr.* || 10 cutt] c *over* p; gise] i *over* I || 11 ground] g *over* p || 19 arurs] *first* r *corr.;* weacknis] k *corr.* || 25 holy] h *corr.* || 29 <from] m *corr.* || 32 thar] th *corr.* || 38 our] *partially over and above the* || 39 our] *corr.* || 41–46 but ... oblityy] *written vertically in the left column* || 43 invocate] *first* c *over* g || 44 trenity] y *corr.* || 46 [tha]t] *most of the word is covered by a corner reinforcement* || 47–54 all ... that ... - - -] *written vertically in the right column; all the words in line 54 after the first word,* that, *are trimmed* || 56 but] b *over* o , t *over* r || 59 <---------->] *ink smear deletes the letters* || 71 clay] c *over* re || 74 <yett>] y *over* b || 80 can] c *corr.* || 81 sion] i *corr.;* our] *over* on || 84–86 revelation xiii ... state] *written vertically in the right margin* || 87 <boste>] *corr.* || 95 have] v *corr.;* wlus] *second* u *conjecture, corr.* || 99 pouer] po *corr.* || 102 most] os *over* ig || 103 <-----ser us>] *an ink smear above the line* || 104 god] d *over* e || 111 shoues] *final* s *blotted*

[47ᵛ–51ᵛ] "Thou shalt not commit Adooltery" T Thou ... Adooltery] *the tops of the letters are cut off* || 1 ᵃdulterate] S *added the* a *above* || 3 bodyes] s *corr.* || 5 paynfull] *over erasure* || 6 socyetye] o *blurred* || 8 W] *the scribe apparently forgot to finish the word* W[ith]? || 17 apply] l *corr.* || 27 her] h *corr.* || 30 contemned] t over d || 33 mate] t *over* d || 36 bonde] *over erasure* || 41 carry] *S added* || 44 in] *S wrote* || 49 deede] dee *over erased* wor; woord] *over* deed || 62 parte] p *over* b || 63 sinns] *second* s *inserted* || 65 <bee>] *erased* || 70 le<f>ues] f *erased;* ues *inserted over erased* t-- || 71 ʌ the<a>] *caret inverted* || 73 Cytty] C *over* s || 77 <th> ... <s>] *erased* || 81 hee] *over* doth, *ink smeared* || 84 wedlocke tacke sum uertious] *the tops of the letters are written over three or four deleted and indecipherable words, slightly above the line of text and below the deleted words* Ioyned to a vertuous || 85 tyme] *over* age || 86 The] h *corr.; S added* e || 88 thy] y *corr.* || 92 end] *corr.;* doest] d *corr.;* mate] *corr.; last five words, except* a, *corr.* || 94 state] *corr.* || 104 dvtye] *over* wife || 104–5 wyf ... ofte] *the HS-2 hand; compare the word "wyf" here with that on fol. 72ᵛ, lines 12 and 25* || 106 beautye] *over* wife || 110 lwith] *an* l *was written and not deleted before* with || 114 from] r *corr.* || 119 punishement] s *over* e || 123 the] t *inserted,* he *over* a || 128 lyke] ke *corr.* || 129 loue] u *over* w || 135 hir] r *over* s || 139 cumforts] t *over* f; now] ow *blurred* || 140 <h>] *erased* || 141 stonne] *3 minims to* nn || 144 ʌantes] t *corr.* || 146 <Nor] N *corr.* || 159 whoe] oe *over* se; <s>] *erased* || 160 flesh and] *written over erasure* || 171 slandered] *second* e *inserted;* throgh] *inserted over erasure,* hr *over* by || 179 houde] h *over* l || 187 artire] tire *corr.;* skin] n *over* l || 188 lovinge <s>] lovin *over* harts; <s> *erased* || 190 death doe vs discever] *over erasure,* discever *over* together || 191 withine] *S added* e || 192 make] m *over* b || 197 our] *over* thy || 198 our] *over* t-- || 201 <sdye>] d *over* p || 206 but] *is actually* b<o>t<h>, *with a* u *above the* <o>; <o> *and* <h> *are erased* || 210 deathe] d *and* h *corr.* || 212 doth] h *unfinished* || 214 boorden] *a third minim on the* n *was deleted;* seemeth] *second* e *over* r || 218 connyvencye] *second* c *over* s || 219 <ayre>] e *over* l; heyre] *the HS-2 hand* || 224 byrth] y *over* r || 227 the] *over erased* y-- || 228 sillagismes] *second* l *corr.* || 230 vnlesse] n *corr.* || 231 woold you] y *corr.* || 232 where] *over* ----d; god] g *over* l; he] h *corr.;* barrs] rr *corr.* || 236 whome youre] me youre *over* sesocyty || 237 your] y *over* c || 240 thus] *the HS-2 hand, that of "heyre" in line 219 above* || 243 gy'ue] g *over* t; lords] d *corr.* || 247 and] *over erasure* || 252 yeelds] l *inserted* || 253 begoonne] *first* e *over* o || 264 <thee>] *erased* || 265 as] *inserted* || 267 thy] y *over* e || 268 hygh] g *inserted, over* h || 271 <f------>] *erased* || 273 thou] t *corr.*

[52ʳ–57ʳ] "Thou shalt not steale" *T* Thou ... steale] *the line has been trimmed* || 6 haue a beeinge] *over erasure ending with the deleted* vp || 14 insnare] *S inserted* in || 15 beshur] *S wrote* e *over* ut *and inserted* shur || 19 rackell vepes] *conjecture, meaning rascal weeps; S writes in left margin* || 25 <A wise man> *over erasure of* The god ling || 26 hath] th *over* ue || 30 haue] *over erasure* || 32 <p>] *erased* || 37 Iobe] *two pen strokes above* || 40 craft] c *over* g || 41 <st>yoongg] <st> *erased,* y *over* r, *first* o *inserted* || 44 the] e *over* at || 46 nothinge with] c *and* w *over an ink blot* || 49 52] 2 *over* 1 || 50 dyseased] y *over* e; stomaks] s *over* c || 55 53] 3 *over* 2 || 59 assume] a *over* t || 61–74 <Man hath> a selfe ... rapid - - - -] *written on a rectangle pasted flat onto fol. 53ʳ.* || 62 anexed] *first* e *corr.* || 66 he] e *corr.* || 71 for] f *corr.* || 72 In] I *retained for* f, *S writes* n *over* or *and adds* to || 73–74 this ... - - -] *blurred lines written vertically in right margin by* S || 73 aclsicll] *conjecture for* ecclesiasticall || 75 54] 4 *over* 3; hold] *S wrote* old *over* ave *and added the second* hold || 77 bold] *S added* || 78 gyve] *over erased* take; take] *over erasure* || 79 <so>] *erased* || 87 <t>] *erased* || 88 <s>] *erased* || 90 haulds] *corr.* || 93–94 haue ... reas[on]] *the hand here is also that of fol. 54ᵛ, lines 113–18, but appears nowhere else in the manuscript* || 93 gileful] *a distinct letter "g" is formed by the ornate descender* || 100 ʌmammon] *S wrote an inverted caret, pointing down to* mammon || 107 walloweth in] *over erasure of* hath ------ || 113–18 a prodygall ... corne.>] *see the note above for lines 93–94* || 114 A] *S added* || 121 cutpurse] c *over* r || 124 springs from noe good] *over erasure;* <greate>] *erased, conjecture* || 125 theefe] t *inserted* || 128 them selfes] *first* e *over* i, *second* s *inserted;* to<e>] t *over* d || 130 woolde] *the surface of the paper has peeled off much of the letter* l || 131 wee] *corr.* || 134 ritch] r *corr.* || 139 dye] d *corr.* || 142 mans] *corr.* || 148 yn] y *over* o || 149 valyant] v *over* f, y *corr.* || 155 and] *corr.* || 156 theeves] t *corr.* || 158 are] *the letter* b *was begun before the* a || 160 barrs] *superfluous speck follows* || 164 reame] r *over erased* b || 165 yst] *over erased and* || 167 chaunce] c *corr.* || 169 44] *second* 4 *over* 3 || 175 4<5>5] <5> *over* 4; deseyve] *first* e *corr.* || 179 thys] y *over* e || 181 46] 6 *over* 5 || 182 men] e *over* a || 186 meate] *first* e *over* i || 192 was] *ink blot is before* was, *which is written over erased yet;* heare] *part of a letter (C?) is written over the top of the* h; sleyne] le *corr.*, y *over* e || 199 <48>] *corr.* || 202 gods] g *over* b || 203 that] *another letter was started before the first* t || 205 Admyte] e *over* t || 206 thoroug'h] *part of a letter(?) or an unusual mark is above the* g || 207 <ca>sort] *S inserts* ort, o *over* e || 210 may] y *over* g || 211 51] 1 *over* 0

[57r–58v] [Southwell drafts, #2] 3 altorasion] o *and second* a *corr.* || 4 doo] d *over* g || 10–13 what . . . ball] *S has gone over the words in darker ink* || 12 land] l *over* a || 18 labor] b *corr.* || 24 but] t *corr.* || 25 could] a *corr.* || 26 wherfor] *corr.;* law] w *corr.* || 28 hyer] h *corr.* || 30 fooll] *first* o *corr.* || 33 pan] p *corr.* || 35 theft] *S apparently forgot to add a cross-bar to the* f || 51 this] h *corr.* || 59 esterrs] *first* r *corr.* || 60 if] f *corr.* || 63 epetome] m *corr.* || 66 remayen] *first* e(?) *corr.;* him] *corr.* scies] i *corr.*

[59r] "An Inventorye of the Lady Anne Southwells goods" Possibly in two hands: the title through line 11, in that of John Bowker; lines 12 to the end, of *HS*. Lines 12ff., with more secretary letters, are more cramped and less carefully written; lines 37–43 are even more crowded, perhaps to fit on one page, though the verso is blank. Dashes serving as fillers ending some lines have been dropped.
2 Aprill] *over* Marc || 13 26. Aprill] 6 *corr.*, A *over* M || 14 wth] w *corr.* || 15 scarlett] sc *over* C || 25 suitable] a *corr.* || 37 containeinge] o *corr.*

[60r] "you Gyannts, or Hyennas that doe dwell" Written in brown ink.
1 Gyannts] y *over* i || 7 yeeres] s *inserted* || 12 fable] b *corr., part of a letter visible before* b || 16 Bee] *first* e *corr.* || 20 Epi<taffsms>] <taffs *over* gram || 24 well] e *corr.* || 27–28 *And . . . warre] written with a finer nib

[60v] [The inventory of fol. 59r, continued] 17 12] *over* 2– || 20 sweateinge] *final* e *over* s || 35 toungs] un *lacks a minim*

[61r] "Apparell of my Ladyes" 21 payre] ayre *corr.;* virginmales] *first* i *corr.*, m *over* h || 22 lyne] l *corr.* || 24 grate] a *corr.* || 25 2 brasse] 2 *corr.* || 32 4 Canes] 4 *over* 6

[65r–66r] "A List of my Bookes" Written at three different times, judging from publication dates and stylistic differences: 1) titles numbered 1–34, 2) 35–76 and 3) 77–110. Throughout the second two groups, the abbreviation for "etc." changes: numbers 37, 48, 53, and 72 contain ones made up of an "e," an "x," and a "c"; number 54 has a clear italic "etc," added later. Numbers 82, 87, 89, 92–94, 102, and 104 have an ampersand written with one flourishing pen stroke, followed by a superior "ra'."
10 God's] d *over* l || 22 Cæsars] *final* s *over* e, *which is blurred* || 28 in] i *corr.;* Quarto] u *corr.* || 35 34] 4 *over* 5 || 41 Quarto] rt *corr.* || 46 Crompton's] ro *corr.* || 53 L. Elizabeth] *in margin to the left of no.* 51 || 74 Prest] e *over* i

[66v] "the 3th of ffebruary maister C   Preacher of acton" *T* the 3th . . . acton] *the top of the line has been trimmed* || 14 as] a *corr.*

[67r] "St. Augustine Ca. 8 of his booke. the Citie of god" *T* St. . . . god] *the top of the line has been trimmed* || 7 1th] 1 *over* 9

NOTES

185

[68^{r–v}] "A booke of the nature of foure footted bests" *T* A booke ... Ges[ner]] *the line has been trimmed* || *T*-6 affect] a *over* e || 3 swifft] w *over* h || 5 Hyænna] *first* a *over* e || 16 Pharises] a *over* e || 20 Iuno] o *over* a || 25 and] a *corr.* || 30 Tortiss] T *over* f || 36 Elaphants] E *blurred* || 43 Beuer] *first* e *blurred* || 44 heire] h *over* a*(?)* || 59 against] t *corr.* || 71 sunne] e *over* e || 78 Mayanona] an*(?) corr.* || 85 or] o *corr.*

[69^{r–v}] "Apothegmes" *T* <Epothegmes>] me *corr.* || 25 Sathan] n *over* t || 56 bee] b *over* p || 58 antrapophagie] *first* a *over* o || 63 Pettagogg] a *corr.* || 68 kneele] k *corr.* || 74 ar] *over* is || 80 nor] n *corr.* || 81 <stupifyed] *ink smeared, conjecture;* stupid] d *has extra minim*

[70^{r–v}] "How that the Law of the Gospell is" 4 Philosaphy] a *over* o || 23 nowise] w *over* e || 45 Euangelicall] *first* a *over* e || 48 burning] u *corr.* || 50 creatures] u *over* r || 65 holy] y *over* ie || 65 euangelicall] first a *over*, holye] o *corr.*, y *over* i || 67 euangelicall] *first* a *over* e || 68 felicity] y *over* ie || 68–69 promise] s *corr.* || 80 sleepeth] l *over* p*(?)*

[71^r] [Acton receipts of 1632 and 1633] Thomas Warburton writes the first account; the other two are in the hand of *SR*.

12 <w>halfe] *S corr.* whole *to* <w>halfe

[71^v] [Acton receipts of 1633 and 1634] 2 halph] l *over* r

[72^r] "M^r. Iohnson dyed" 2 Ministe[r]] *the line has been trimmed* || 13 any man In>] *the line through these words is not a crossout, but a blot from the crossout* <and sole heire> *on the opposite folio, line 9;* third] i *over* e || 20 *a heavy line underneath is a blot from the crossout* <sole heire vnto> *in line 19 of the previous page, fol. 71^v*

[72^v] [Acton receipts of 1635 and 1636] The first receipt is in the hand of *SR*; the second and third receipt, of *HS*. The ends of lines 10, 11, 18, and 24 have been trimmed.

10 shillings ... [d]] *ink is smeared over the top of the letters* || 21 deceased] ea *corr.*

[73^r] "To the never dyeing memorye" The paper has three strong vertical creases (which tore and have been mended with strips of paper, on the verso) and two horizontal creases. The lines are written in three columns, with some very cramped lines; an extra *e* appears before most abbreviations of *es*.

14 envious] n *corr.* || 19 it] t *corr.* || 37 discreet] i *over* e || 49 yeare] y *corr.* || 57 Vertuous] V *over* v || 69 Darlinge] D *over* d ||

[73^v] [Fragments] "Angrie / angry" are written in black ink and boldly—in an *X* hand. The upside-down fragments of words are written with a "plumbum," or lead pencil, and the light orange is barely visible; the letters run underneath a strip of paper mending a vertical tear.

1–2 angrie / angry] *written vertically* || 1–7 and ... Lord] *written upside down*

[74^r] "Consecrated to the Memory" The inserted sheet has several horizontal creases and a central vertical one, which has torn, and been mended on the verso.

17 beautie] a *over* u || 26 Octob] O *over* A

Commentary

The commentary offers only brief references for further study. Unless otherwise noted, biblical references are from the *King James* of the bibliography. When the comment is a modernized spelling of the glossed word or phrase, the word begins with a small letter.

[1ʳ] *T*-2 Decemb: 2° 1626°] That is, on the second of December in the year 1626; the ° originated in the Latin ablative ending.

[1ᵃ] The ᵃ following each sonnet's arabic number suggests an abbreviation for the Latin, that is, "prima," "secunda," "tertia," "quarta," and "quinta."

All of the poems titled "sonnet" may be well-known songs or compositions that Southwell, as part of the manuscript culture, made her own with a few changes. In the 1620s and '30s, "the title 'Sonnet' for a lyric poem often denotes, not the traditional stanza form, but that the poem has been set to music" (Mary Hobbs, "Early Seventeenth-Century Verse Miscellanies," *English Manuscript Studies 1100–1700* , eds. Peter Beal and Jeremy Griffiths [London: Basil Blackwell, 1989], 1: 194).

"Sonnet: 1ᵃ" Variations of "Sonnet: 1ᵃ" appear as the first stanza of a lyric in Jones, *Vltimum Vale* (1605, XIV); for his text, see Doughtie, 214; and in Alfonso Ferrabosco, from two manuscripts: 1) Oxford, Christ Church 439, 6:92; and 2) Oxford, Tenbury 1018, fol. 34ᵛ; 6:34ᵛ, in *Ayres*, 1609 (1609, 16), and a text in Doughtie, 298. British Library Additional MS. 24665 also has Jones's melody and text (fols. 22ᵛ–23ʳ). The above information is listed in "Notes and Variants," *English Song 1600–1675: Facsimiles of Twenty-six Manuscripts and an Edition of the Texts*, ed. Elise Bickford Jorgens (New York and London: Garland, 1989), 12:410, recommended by Carolyn C. Kent. For another copy in a commonplace book of 1630, see Folger MS. V.a.339, fol. 192ʳ.

"Sonnett: 2ᵃ" A variation of this appears in Robert Jones, *A Musicall Dreame* (1609, XVII), and a text in Doughtie, 329–30 and variants, 579.

"Sonnett 4ᵃ" This appears in Jones, *A Musicall Dreame* (1609, XV), in Doughtie, 328). "Sonnett 4" is like stanza one in Jones, except for the phrase "sacred-Cristall" (line 4), which replaces "heavenly hallowed."

"Sonnett. 5ᵃ" This sonnet shows the punning and cryptic quality of Southwell's poetry, as illustrated especially by words like "sublime" (with its alchemical and ordinary meaning—the first, in this context, undercutting the second) and "the keper of Romes Capitall" with its meanings: 1. of the stock with which individuals or companies enter

188   COMMENTARY

into business, 2. the Capitoline hill on which stood the temple of Jupiter where the
Sibylline books were kept, and 3. the geese who honked when the Gauls were about
to attack, thus enabling the Romans to save the Capitol. Noted by Pamela Benson, in
an unpublished paper, 1990. For the story of the sacred geese, kept on the Capitol,
who alerted the Roman consul Manlius when Gauls from the Alps threatened the cita-
del of Rome in 390 BC, see *The Aeneid of Virgil*, trans. Rolfe Humphries, ed. Brian
Wilkie, 8. 658–62, and n. 37.
4 bose] Hollow, empty (*OED*).
[2ʳ] [Ralegh, "The Lie"] Lines 31–34, 37–40, and 43–46, says Agnes Latham, are
"peculiar to Lady Anne Southwell" (*The Poems of Sir Walter Ralegh* [London: Constable, 1929], 158). Variations of some of the lines (31–34) and repetitions of other lines
(37–40, within two stanzas) also appear in "Goe soule the bodies guest" of Dalhousie
Manuscript I (*The First and Second Dalhousie Manuscripts Poems and Prose by John
Donne and Others A Facsimile Edition*, ed. Ernest W. Sullivan, II [Columbia: Univ. of
Missouri Press, 1988], 110–11). The possibility of Southwell's contribution is not ruled
out by the appearance of a few lines in the Dalhousie I manuscript. Sullivan explains
that the Dalhousie and Lansdowne 740 manuscripts are closely connected (pp. 8–10).
[3ʳ⁻ᵛ] "To ... Ladye Ridgway" Southwell writes to a friend, Cicely MacWilliams, Lady
Ridgeway, apparently responding to a statement of a preference for prose over poetry.
Cicely MacWilliams, "sometime Maid of Honour to Queen Elizabeth," died in 1627.
Her husband, Thomas Ridgeway, had been created earl of Londonderry in August
1622 (GEC, 8:105–6). Although Southwell's letter has unique elements, it also echoes
well-known ideas from Sidney's "Defense of Poesy."
5–8 It is ... obliuion] For another use of the pearl in relation to poetry, see lines from
"A Chaine of Pearle ... " by Diana Primrose (fl. 1630), *The Paradise of Women:
Writings by Englishwomen of the Renaissance*, ed. Betty Travitsky (New York: Columbia
Univ. Press, 1989), 111–12.
19 Rahabs] Rahab was a harlot whose house was on the wall of Jericho, who harbored
Joshua's spies and let them down on a rope on the other side of the wall. Later, when
Jericho was taken, Rahab and her family were spared and united with the chosen
people (Josh. 2 and 6).
20 Doegs] Doeg (meaning "fearful") was an Edomite, chief of Saul's herdsmen, who,
under questioning, told the truth, which enraged the king so much that he ordered the
killing of the priests, which others refused to do. Doeg finally did, and subsequently
killed even the women, children, and cattle. David, hearing of Doeg's deed, was angry
(1 Sam. 22).
30–33 Some wanton ... opinion] Criticism of Shakespeare's erotic narrative; cf.
Gabriel Harvey's view: "The younger sort takes much delight in Shakespeares Venus,
& Adonis: but his Lucrece, & his tragedie of Hamlet, Prince of Denmark, haue it in
them, to please the wiser sort" (*Gabriel Harvey's Marginalia*, ed. G. C. Moore Smith
[Stratford-upon-Avon: Shakespeare Head Press, 1913], 232, recommended by John
Velz.
35 exorbitant] Diverging from the right path; lawless (*OED*).
36 orbicular forme & motion] An analogy for order and goodness.
38 Micholl] Michal, Saul's daughter and King David's wife, who was rebuked for
mocking the king's religious dancing (2 Sam. 6:16).
40–42 To heare ... art] Criticism of Marlowe's erotic epic, cf. lines 33–35 above. For
discussions of erotic epics by Shakespeare, Marlowe, and others, see the introduction
in Elizabeth Story Donno, *Elizabethan Minor Epics* (London: Routledge, 1963).
43–44 Prophett ... Israell] David.

COMMENTARY   189

56–58 vera . . . o: /] The partially legible note indicates that the letter is a true copy by John, "Do: An:" or "Domini Anno," "In the year of our Lord." The identity of John is unknown. No number is legible, though the letter has to be dated sometime during or before 1627, when Cicely MacWilliams died (GEC, 8:105–6).

[4ʳ] [A letter to Falkland] For Falkland's problems, see *A New History of Ireland*, eds. T. W. Moody, F. X. Martin, F. J. Byrne, vol. 3, "Early Modern Ireland 1534–1691" (Oxford: Clarendon Press, 1976), 238–41. The date under the letter, 1628, is probably a mistake, since the first letter of recall came in April of 1629, according to *A New History*, 240–41. Southwell is returning the kindness shown by the Lord Deputy in his petition of 4 October 1627 to King Charles. Falkland had asked that Captain Sibthorpe, who had served well in the Cadiz expedition and been overlooked for promotion, "be allowed the command of one of the substitute companies sent over" to Ireland (*The Calendar of State Papers Ireland*, ed. Robert Pentland Mahaffy, 1625–32 [London, 1900], 273).

1–2 one word] Southwell criticizes Falkland's use of the word "all."

4–5 watery balls] Eyes; banis'ht Philosopher . . . porto? Bias, who, when urged to escape with his belongings, took nothing, but responded, "omnia mecum porto mea" ("I carry all my belongings with me"), quoted in *Cicero; De Oratore* in 2 vols. Book III together with DE FATO, PARADOXA STOICORUM, DE PARTITIONE ORATORIA, trans. H. Rackham (Cambridge: Harvard Univ. Press, 1942, rep. 1960), "Paradox 1," 11.8–11, 260–61.

6–7 What' . . . still] A statement of Falkland's demotion.

13 Matechyne] An Arabian dance with swords, in which dancers fence and strike at one another, keeping time (Skeat). "A species of this sword dance by some means or other got introduced into England, where it has generally and unaccountably been exhibited by women, whose dexterous feats of tumbling and dancing with swords at fairs, and in the minor theatres, are still remembered by many persons" (Francis Douce, *Illustrations of Shakespeare, and of Ancient Manners: with Dissertations on the Clowns and Fools of Shakespeare*, 2 vols. [London: Longman, 1807], 2:436). For the rarity of this word, see "Other Compositions" in the Introduction.

15 Triumviri] "Nature, chance, and death" (line 13).

18 æquipollent] Of equal weight (*OED*); your perseuerant fauor] probably Falkland's petition for Captain Sibthorpe.

19 plus vltra] L., "Ne plus ultra" ("thus far and no farther") had been the Spanish motto alluding to the Pillars of Hercules, but after Charles V inherited the crown of Aragon and Castile and gained America, he struck out "ne," and adopted "plus ultra." Spain *could* go further. See *Brewer's Dictionary of Phrase and Fable*, 14th ed. (New York: Harper & Row, 1989), 864. Sibthorpe's involvement at Cadiz may have colored Southwell's choice of words.

[5ʳ] [A signed receipt of the 1580s, number 1]

2 Aryan] Aaron; Imogene De Smet suggested this and the other Dutch names in the accounts of the 1580s.

3 ᵍ] Guilder, a gold coin formerly current in England and the Netherlands (a gulden); ˢᵗ] styver, a small coin of the Low Countries, one twentieth of a florin or gulden, or about a penny English (*OED*).

"A Hym to Christ"

2 Prist, Profett, Kinge] For the same phrase, see fol. 18ʳ, line 1 and fol. 26ᵛ, 51.

3 Blest Virgines sonne] For other references to the Virgin Mary, see fols. 25ʳ, 10; and 66ᵛ, 5.

[5ᵛ] "5 predicables"

190 COMMENTARY

For Aristotle's predicables and predicamenta, see "Categoriae," trans. E. M. Edghill, *The Basic Works of Aristotle*, ed. Richard McKeon (New York: Random House, 1941), 7–39.

[6ʳ] [Signed receipts of the 1580s, numbers 2, 3, and 4]
7 Debe hauig] De Bay Howie(?); "De" usually begins a double name.
8 Lymnering] Limner(?), a painter, especially of portraits (*OED*), or possibly a surname here; Iane] Jan.

[6ᵛ] [Signed receipts of the 1580s, numbers 5, 6, 7, 8, and 9]
3 hance] Hans; see also line 22.
9 Serinson] Sorinson.
13 *1588*] The date, closely following the previous account, is puzzling; for the accounts seem to be written consecutively down the page, probably at the same time, even though the ink is slightly darker, beginning with this receipt. Could the writer have switched to the new style of dating or Julian Calendar adopted in parts of the Low Countries? For the problems of dating, see C. R. Cheney, *Handbook of Dates for Students of English History* (London: Royal Historical Society, 1961), 10–11.
15 Ettane Ianne] Ettiene Jan.

[7ʳ] [Psalm 25, to the Earl of Castlehaven]
A translation of Psalm 25. "Writen ... to ye first Earle of Castle hauen" may indicate that the psalm was sent to George Touchet (created Earl 6 September 1616, and died in 20 February 1616/17 [GEC, 3:86]). The earl's daughter Anne, who married Edward Blount of Harleston, Derbyshire, is probably the "A[nne]" of the title (*Collins's Peerage of England*, ed. Sir Egerton Brydges, 9 vols. [London: F. C. and J. Rivington, Otridge and Son, J. Nichols and Co., 1812], 6:554). Although the letters are cropped, the bottom of a *B* is clearly distinguishable and the bottoms of the letters "lunt" are possible; a descending loop suggests the "g" in "daughter," a word for which there is appropriate space before and after the possible "g." The right hand corner has also been torn off, but the space could accommodate the remaining letters "hter." According to Esther Cope, who cites Hastings MSS., Irish Papers, HA. 15939, and HA. 13964, the first earl had a number of reasons for the despondence suggested in the choice of Psalm 25.

If the words are not "A[nne] B[lunt]" and the attribution to the "first" earl is a mistake for the second earl, the notorious Mervyn Touchet, the prayer for the "sins of his youth" may have been sent during the month he was given for repentence before being executed in 1631 for assisting in the rape of his wife and sodomy. See Caroline Bingham, "Seventeenth-Century Attitudes Toward Deviant Sex," *The Journal of Interdisciplinary History*, 1, no. 2 (1971): 447–67 and Bruce Mazlish, "Comment," in the same, 468–72; and note 19 of the Introduction.

The version of Psalm 25 may have been copied from an as yet unidentified translation, for a check of available translations shows that none of them was being copied. See the Coverdale (1535), Great Bible (1539), Geneva (1560), Bishops (1568), and Authorised (1611) in *The Hexaplar Psalter*, ed. William Aldis Wright (Hildesheim & New York: Georg Olms Verlag, 1969, repr. of London: Cambridge Univ. Press, 1911), 53–55; also *The Psalms of Sir Philip Sidney and The Countess of Pembroke*, ed. J. C. A. Rathmell (New York: Doubleday, 1963), 52–54; and those of the popular Sternhold-Hopkins version, *The Whole Book of Psalms, Collected into English Metre, by Thomas Sternhold, John Hopkins, and Others; Conferred with the Hebrew* (Oxford, 1787). Another possible although doubtful source is the translation of the Psalms by Elizabeth Stuart, queen of Bohemia (whom Lady Anne refers to on fol. 22ʳ), in the Heidelberg Library (MSS. 661, 690, and 694, cited in *Kissing the Rod: An Anthology*

COMMENTARY
191

of Seventeenth-Century Women's Verse, eds. Germaine Greer *et al.* [New York: Farrar Straus Giroux, 1988]), 39.

15 dist] The scribe probably meant "didst."

[8ʳ⁻ᵛ] "A Paraphrase vppon Lucius Anneus Seneca"

Seneca, Lucius Annæus (ca. 4 BC–65 AD), Roman Stoic philosopher and poet, tutor of Nero. A successful politician for a time, he was ordered to commit suicide when he fell from the emperor's favor. He wrote some ten closet dramas and many philosophical essays, including *De consolatione, De animi tranquillitate,* and *De clementia* (R & B). Cf. nos. 48 and 66 in the booklist on fols. 65ᵛ and 66ʳ. See also J. H. M. Salmon, "Seneca and Tacitus in Jacobean England," in *The Mental World of the Jacobean Court,* ed. Linda Levy Peck (Cambridge: Cambridge Univ. Press, 1991), 169–88.

34 Soll] The sun or gold, in alchemy (Skeat).

41 Vertue ... Action] Cf. 18ᵛ, 86 (Rev. 20:12).

49 Seas of Gall] Cf. Job 16:13.

[8ᵛ] "Blessed Life" Cf. fol. 47ᵛ, "Thou shalt not commit Adooltery," stanzas 1–4, also condemning the "lazy harts" of the "Sodomytes."

3 gaudes] Trifles (*OED*).

10 Sodom Apples] Dead Sea Fruit, "the vine of Sodom," with "grapes of gall": "their wine is the poison of serpents, the vipers' cruel venom" (Deuter. 32:32); any specious thing (*OED*).

12 Cinque portes] The five senses, although the term literally refers to the five southeastern cities of Dover, Sandwich, Hastings, Romney, and Hythe.

[9ʳ] "Dialogue: / Sonnet." The rhyming "dialouge" has resonances to Sidney's echo poem, no. 31, from "The Old Arcadia," in Ringler.

17 the] thee.

"Sonnet / Beauty, Honor, yeouth, and fortune" The poem, especially lines 11–14, plays with paradoxes centered on that of John 12:24; cf. fol. 43ᵛ, 399–400.

[9ᵛ] "Sonnet: / Like to a lampe wherein the light is dead" Poems using the formula, "Like to a ... ," such as this one and that on fol. 23ʳ, were popular; see, for example, no. 65, Gorges's "Vannetyes and Toyes," probably written in the late 1580s, and "The Lamentation of Richmond," a later poem in "The Olympian Catastrophe"; both are discussed by Helen E. Sandison, *The Poems of Sir Arthur Gorges* (Oxford: Clarendon Press, 1953), 205 and 238–39. M. Crum, discussing Henry King's similar "Sic Vita," says that the pattern for the many seventeenth-century parodies seems to have been "Like to the damask rose," whose author is unknown. King's poem was printed in the 1640 edition of *Poems by Francis Beaumont* with a parody, 'Like a ring without a finger,' as part of a ballad called 'Pretty Comparisons wittily grounded ... To the tune of *Like to the Damask Rose,*' which in turn had been printed as a broadsheet by Francis Coules, Old-Bayly (working 1626–81), reprinted *Roxburghe Ballads,* ed. William Chappell, ii, 1874, 12. A musical setting for the 'rose' is ascribed to Henry Lawes (Crum, 254–55 and 148–49). For examples of commonplace books containing poems with similar patterns, see Folger MSS. V.a.423 (fol. 50ʳ), V.a.345 (fol. 1), and V.a.339 (fol. 224ᵛ). Francis Quarles also wrote one example; see the commentary for the poem honoring Quarles on fol. 17ʳ.

"Sonnett. / O how happy were I dearest"

The poem is unusual among Southwell's compositions in that all of the rhymes are feminine ones. Cf. Maureen Quilligan, "The Sexual Politics of Sidney's and Spenser's Rhyming," *Renaissance Englishwomen in Print: Counterbalancing the Canon,* eds. Anne M. Haselkorn and Betty Travitsky (Amherst: Univ. of Massachusetts Press, 1990), 311–26.

192 COMMENTARY

4 Queene] Punning on the word "queane," an impudent, ill-behaved woman, especially in the sixteenth and seventeenth centuries (*OED*).

[10^r] "ffrayle Loue" A poem in the popular mode, "de contemptu mundi."

17 gawdes] Trifles (*OED*).

23 to ... choke vs] Cf. fol. 31^v, 46–63.

[11^r] "Nature, Mistris off affection" See the similar metrical pattern and discussion in *Sappho: Lyrics in the Original Greek with Translations by Willis Barnstone*, foreword by Andrew R. Burn (New York: New York Univ. Press, 1965), xx; for Sappho's revival in the Renaissance, p. xxii. The rhyming pattern of the short last lines also has echoes of Sidney's translation of the psalms; as in Psalm XIII, Ringler, 285.

3 Wher it hath receiued infection] See the Introduction for the connection between "infection" and homosexuality; for venereal disease, F. G. Emmison, *Elizabethan Life: Morals and the Church Courts* (Chelmsford: Essex County Council, 1973), 31–34.

18 baldness] For the topos questioning the triviality of a full head of hair as a mark of importance, from Synesius, see Rosalie L. Colie, *Paradoxia Epidemica: The Renaissance Tradition of Paradox* (Princeton: Princeton Univ. Press, 1962), 10.

37 yookffelowe] yokefellow, a partner (*OED*).

[12^r–13^r] "Honor thy father and mother" 9–42 Behould ... moornes] Four stanzas describe how the four elements, if "constreyned ... take offence" and act rebelliously: the rock thrown against gravity will "soone" come down (line 24), air confined in a cave will "toyle" (line 26) to come out, and water "pressing" each drop to "hash away" (line 32) acts like a hammer which seems to "chyde / and frett the earth as causer of their stay" (line 34).

21 derogate] Diminish, disparage or impair the force and effect of (*OED*).

32 hash] To slash or hack about, figuratively (*OED*), "frett[ing] the earth."

44–61 Behould ... creature] The three stanzas delineate the standard Scholastic notion of the three souls.

64 Abrams] Whose name was changed to Abraham, "father of many nations" (Gen. 17:5).

69 Achan] Appropriated and hid in his tent a Babylonian garment and a wedge of gold, part of the spoils of Jericho, which had been destined to utter destruction. He was caught and he and his family were stoned (Josh. 7).

70 raboam] Rehoboam, although son of Solomon, had a small mind and was known for his foolish actions; after reigning three years, he lapsed into idolatry (1 Kings 12).

71 Iesabell did Nabaths vynyard hould] Jezebel, the wicked wife of Ahab, who wanted the vineyard of Naboth, so she conspired to have Naboth and his sons stoned and devoured by dogs (1 Kings 21:2–18).

[16^r] "All.maried.men.desire.to.haue good wifes" For the topos of female-superiority, see the Introduction, n. 38; for another example, fol. 26^v. For another "defense" of women, see *The Poems of Aemilia Lanyer: Salve Deus Rex Judæorum*, ed. Susanne Woods (New York: Oxford Univ. Press, 1993), 82–87.

5–8 When ... good] For a pictorial representation, see *The Rohan Book of Hours* Biblioteque Nationale, Paris (M.S. Latin 9471), intro. by M. Meiss, commentary by M. Thomas, trans. by K. W. Carson (New York: George Braziller), 1973, Plate 13.

6 text says ... side] Gen. 1:21–22.

[17^r] "F<w->ayne would I dye" The first initials of the outermost lines (the odd-numbered lines), reading downwards, form the word "FRAVNCIS"; those of the indented lines (the even-numbered lines) form the word "QVARLES." Quarles (1592–1644) moved to Ireland, in 1626, where he acted as secretary to Archbishop Ussher of Armagh. There he wrote *Argalus and Parthenia*, a long romance based on an episode

COMMENTARY

in Sidney's *Arcadia,* according to David Freeman, ed. (Washington: Associated Univ. Presses, 1986), 19. According to a letter Quarles sent from London to Ussher, the writer had left Ireland by 1629. For one of his popular emblem books, see *Divine Fancies* (London, 1632) made up of four hundred epigrams, meditations, and observations. Although the main topic of his work dealt with "the wretchedness of man's earthly existence," he enjoyed great popularity during his lifetime (*DNB,* 16:535–39).

1 Heliconian traine] Helicon, a mountain of Greece anciently sacred to Apollo and the Muses (R & B).

4 maugre] In spite of (*OED*).

[18ʳ–19ʳ] "A Letter to Doctor Adam" A verse epistle to Bernard Adams, born in Middlesex in 1566, admitted scholar of Trinity College at Oxford in 1583 at age 17 and elected to a Fellowship in 1588, which he resigned in 1596. He was made bishop of Limerick in 1603 and died in March 1626. A picture of him still hangs in the dining hall of Trinity College (according to Clare J. Hopkins, Archivist). He was known for having "bestowed much money in repairing Saint Mary's Cathedral of Limerick and in the adorning it with organs and several ornaments" (Anthony A Wood, *Athenæ Oxonienses,* 4 vols. [London, 3rd ed., 1815], 2:869).

1 Adam . . . Kinge] Cf. line 2 in "A Hym to Christ" (fol. 5ʳ); 1–6 Adam . . . vnder] The lines are almost identical to lines 51–56 of fol. 26ᵛ.

17 songe . . . parts] twenty-four measures, the first and last identical parts framing the middle, leading to the "harmony" of line 19; see fol. 26ʳ, line 23 for another use of the phrase. For Renaissance ideas of harmony, see Heninger.

47 Cadmus teeth] Teeth of a slain dragon which, after being sown by Cadmus, produced soldiers.

48 Babells] Gen. 11.

52 chymæra's] A fabled fire-breathing monster (*OED*).

55 Magazine of scrappes] Man's memory, as a storehouse (*OED*).

57 signe at doore] As the Hebrews put signs on their doors (Exod. 12:7).

61 Chimicks] Alchemists'; So'ls] the sun or gold, in alchemy (Skeat).

62 coabations] Mixtures(?); proiection] projection; in alchemy, the casting of the powder of philosopher's stone upon a metal in fusion to effect its transmutation into gold or silver (*OED*).

65–67 threefould . . . life]] The three basic temptations of man and of Christ (Matt. 4), referred to below in lines 69 and 74.

79 Ixions wheele] Ixion, king of the Lapithae, father of Pirithous and (by a cloud formed by Zeus into the shape of Hera) of the centaurs. For boasting of his alleged conquest of Hera, Zeus fastened Ixion to a perpetually turning wheel in Hades (R & B).

80 Tantalized] Tantalus, son of Zeus, father of Pelops and Niobe, king of Mt. Sipylas in Lydia, who, because he revealed the secrets of the gods, was made to stand in Tartarus up to his chin in water under a fruit-tree; when he sought to eat or drink, both the water and the fruit retreated beyond his grasp (R & B).

86 virtue consists in action] Cf. fol. 8ᵛ, 41 (Rev. 20:12).

91 Scala Cæli] Stairs of heaven; cf. Jacob's ladder (Gen. 28:12).

93 three thrones] Of faith, hope and charity, as in lines 95–116.

94 Dis] A name for Pluto (R & B).

113 Elohim] A name for God.

115 Topographick] A description of a particular locality (*OED*).

[19ᵛ–20ᵛ] "An Elegie . . . / to the Countesse of London Derrye" A playful elegy. For Lady Ridgeway, see commentary for fol. 3.

6 Epitome] For other uses of the word by Southwell and John Donne, see commentary for fol. 32ᵛ, lines 5 and 6 and fol. 58ᵛ, line 63.

10 vaute circular] The sky, a "vault circular."

17 hir bosome<s>] From "herba," herbs.

25 <caret>] The word, on a slant in the left margin, was probably written to indicate the insertion of line 26, but crossed out after the addition of the short line pointing more accurately.

28 Madam Tellus] An earth goddess (R & B).

34 the bratts of Opps] Ops, Wife of Saturn, through her cleverness saved her children, Jupiter, Neptune, and Pluto, from their father.

35 Sea of Gall] Job 16:13.

42 Christalline] Heaven, in the Ptolemaic astronomical system, a sphere supposed to exist between the *primum mobile* and the firmament (*OED*); a favorite term for Southwell.

53–58 For . . . baggs] Echoes of Neoplatonism and theories of poetic creativity. Cf. *Plato*, "Ion," 4:277–300.

58 Idea] The Platonic archetype of any class of things (R & B); in letherne baggs] that is, in books (cf. Aeolus's windbags).

63–66 Saynts . . . Trinitye] Criticism against Roman practices that "robb the Trinitye" by praying to saints instead of God.

68 reuerberation] Reflection (*OED*).

71 Landkipp] An obsolete variant of "landscape" (*OED*).

73 bitumeous] Originally, a kind of mineral pitch found in Palestine and Babylon, used as mortar; the same as asphalt (*OED*).

77–82 Poets . . . Asse] Southwell mocks herself as a poet, and possibly, Lady Ridgeway, or, more likely, her Irish ancestors, as followers of Rome.

79 Gods, . . . beates them] Cf. Marsyas, who was flayed for his audacity in challenging Apollo's musical ability.

110 when . . . fleete] Elijah, who did not die but was taken up to heaven in a fiery chariot; Welkin] sky.

116 pismire] Anthill, a name which came from the urinous smell (*DAPW*).

119–20 bell . . . Southwell] The rhyme "bell," "knell" and "Southwell" suggests one pronunciation of her name, although another is suggested by the word "Southey" on fol. 71ʳ, 4. *Debrett's Peerage, Knightage, and Companionage with Her Majesty's Royal Warrant Holders*, ed. P. W. Montague-Smith (Kingston upon Thames: Kelly's Directories, 1966), says, under the Southwell coat of arms, that the pronounciation is "Suthell" (p. 1031).

[21ʳ] "An: Epitaph vppon Cassandra MackWilliams" 1 choakt wᵗʰ gall] Ink was made from "galls (the round excrescences produced by the gall-fly on branches of oak trees) and iron sulphate (usually known as copperas or Roman vitriol), the reaction of the tannic acid in the galls with the iron salt causing a blackish compound to form" (Anthony Petti, *English Literary Hands from Chaucer to Dryden* [London: Arnold, 1977], 7).

4–5 like . . . dead] See fol. 9ᵛ above for other uses of the popular formula.

"Written in commendations of Mʳ Coxe"

See fol. 73ʳ for the elegiac lines on Lady Southwell that Cocks contributed, fol. 65ᵛ for no. 52 of the booklist, and fol. 66ᵛ for scriptural commentary under his name. Roger Cocks (fl. 1635) was the author of *Hebdomada Sacra a Weeke's Deuotion; or Seven Poeticall Meditations upon the Second Chapter of S. Matthew's Gospel* (London, 1630 [*DNB*, 4:657–58]).

COMMENTARY

1–3 Thou ... adorne] The opening lines play on the name "Coxe," suggesting the cock that crows at dawn (line 1); the one that crowed three times while Peter betrayed Christ (line 2, Matt. 26:34), and the figurative one alerting the world to the "blessed'st babe" (line 3).

6 import] Signify (*OED*).

9 A:S:] Southwell plays on her own name, as also on fol. 45ʳ.

10 Rebecca's Twins] Jacob and Esau; Jacob had tricked Esau out of his inheritance (Gen. 27:23).

[21ᵛ] [Henry King, "The Exequy"] Henry King's wife Anne was buried January 5, 1624. Although manuscript copies are frequent, the poem was not printed until 1657 and then anonymously and without King's consent (Crum, 68–72, and commentary with notes, 197–98). The lines here have only a few inconsequential differences from those in Crum.

T writen by] Apparently means "copied by"; Jernegan] for reference to Sir Henry Jernegan's occupation of a house in Acton in 1636, see *The Victoria History of the Counties of England: A History of the County of Middlesex*, ed. T F. T Baker (London: Oxford Univ. Press, 1982), 7:21; and for the death of Mrs. Mary Jernegan of Acton in 1633, see *Abstracts of Probate Acts in the Prerogative Court of Canterbury*, ed. John Matthews and George F. Matthews, vol. 1, 1630–34 (London: Chancery Lane, [1902]), 218.

[22ʳ] "What if I wante the dross of Tagus Strann" 1 Tagus Strann] The longest river of the Iberian penninsula, emptying into the Bay of Lisbon (R & B), wherein gold had been found (Elyot).

5 Hellin] Helen of Troy.

"A letter to ye Duches of Lineox"
Although addressed "to ye Duches of Lineox," the poem centers on Elizabeth, daughter of James I. Ludovic Stuart, Duke of Lennox, was appointed February 1613 to attend Elizabeth to Germany after her marriage to the Prince Palatine with a "train of 22 attendants on himself" (GEC, 7:604–5). Francis Quarles (praised in the poem on fol. 17ʳ), who had been appointed cupbearer to the princess, also went on the expedition (*DNB*, 16:536). Because Southwell writes the next poem about the deceased King of Bohemia and his wife Elizabeth Stuart, she must be the "princes" (line 2) being praised.

3 Not for her tytles] Elizabeth did not become a queen until 1619.

"An Epitaph vpon the king of Bohemia"
The Elector Palatine, Frederick V, was crowned King of Bohemia in 1619; he died in 1632.

4 his wife] Elizabeth Stuart.

"An Epitaph vpon yᵉ king of Swede"
Southwell praises Gustavus Adolphus, who was killed at the battle of Lutzen, 6 November 1632 (Crum, 200); cf. fol. 24ʳ⁻ᵛ.

7 Bellona] Sister of Mars and goddess of war (R & B).

[22ᵛ] "Come forth foule Monster" 27 ecquode] echo.

36 fflagidon] Phlegethon, river of fire in the underworld, flowing into Acheron (R & B).

39 gaue God the ly] That is, challenged God (using the language of the duello) by tempting Eve (line 41).

[23ʳ] "An Epitaph vpon the Countess of / Sommersett" For another reference to the Countess by a contemporary woman, see *The Poems of Lady Mary Wroth*, ed. Josephine Roberts (Baton Rouge: Louisiana State Univ. Press, 1983), 35–36; see also David

196   COMMENTARY

Lindley, "Embarrassing Ben: The Masques for Frances Howard," *English Literary Renaissance* 16 (1986): 346–47, n. 6; and *The Trials of Frances Howard: Fact and Fiction at the Court of King James* (London: Routledge, 1993). For scurrilous short poems about her which appeared in seventeenth-century commonplace books, see those in Folger MS. V.a.162, fols. 33^r and 62^v.

1 To … gone] The line echoes line 1 of King's "The Exequy" (fol. 21^v).

4–17 like … bee] See the commentary for fol. 9^v.

24 liues middwife] For Elizabeth Grymeston's similar discussion of death as a "passing through the veines of life" which a Christian experiences as the "throwes in childe-bed, by which our soule is brought out of a lothsome body into eternall felicitie," see *Miscelanae, Meditations, Memoratives* (1604), 8: D2^v, quoted in Betty Travitsky, ed., *The Paradise of Women: Writings by Englishwomen of the Renaissance* (New York: Columbia Univ. Press, 1989), 55; recommended by Carolyn R. Swift.

33 assise] Session held to administer justice (*OED*).

37 Fenix] Phoenix, an emblem of resurrection; great Hawardes name] for the uncertainty of the family's titles, see GEC, 6:583.

38 Francis] Frances Howard (c.1593–1632) was the second daughter of Thomas Howard, earl of Suffolk and his second wife Katherine Knevet. In January 1606 she was married to Robert Devereux and became the countess of Essex. In October 1613 she obtained an annulment in spite of Overbury's disapproval. She married the favorite, Robert Carr, on 26 December 1613, thereby becoming the countess of Somerset. She and Carr were tried for the murder of Thomas Overbury in May 1616. She pleaded guilty but he did not, according to *Cobbett's Complete Collection of State Trials and Proceedings for High Treason and Other Crimes and Misdemeanors,* ed. Thomas B. Howell, (London: Hansard, 1809), 2:997. Both were found guilty, sentenced to death and imprisoned in the Tower. After being pardoned (1616) and released (1622) she lived in retirement with her husband at Chiswick until her death in 1632 (Beatrice White, *Cast of Ravens: The Strange Case of Sir Thomas Overbury* [London: John Murray, 1965], 190).

[23^v] "Only eight soules, the waued tost Church did keepe" An unfinished poem.

1 eight soules] Referring to those saved after the flood (Gen. 8:18, suggested by Josephine Roberts).

3 Cham] Ham, son of Noah, who, in behaving undutifully, incurred a curse on himself and Canaan (Gen. 9:22–27).

13 Melchon] Milcom, the god Molech (2 Kings 23:13).

14 Esau] See fol. 21^r, lines 10–11.

19 The] They.

20 thakes] A scribal error for "takes"?

22 Skogine] Scoggin, John (fl. 1480), court fool of Edward IV. The anonymous *Jests of Scoggin,* often associated with him, was published in 1565–66 (R & B).

23 Cammell sinnes] A reference to Matt. 19:24, that it is easier for a camel to go through the eye of a needle than for a rich man to enter heaven.

[24$^{r–v}$] [Henry King, "An Elegy upon … Gustavus Adolphus"] Gustavus was killed at the battle of Lutzen, in 1632. See Crum, 77–81 and 200–201, for text and notes.

[25^r] "The more my soule doth shrinke from loue" Each of the three units of verse could stand alone even though they are close together on the upper half of the folio and have no horizontal lines separating them, as the sonnets on fols. 1 and 9$^{r–v}$ do. The three stanzas are also united in an apparent experiment in paradox.

2 Cos: amoris amor] L., "cos," flint, and thus a stimulus: "the cause of love is love." The phrase is alternated with "omnia vincit amor": love conquers all (Vergil, *Eclogues*

COMMENTARY 197

10.69). The colon after "Cos:" is superfluous, as it is also on fols. 1 ("Sonnett:") and 21^r ("An: Epitaph").

[26^r] "Vnless himselfe against himselfe weare bent" A creation poem.

4 Tagus Strann] See fol. 22^r, 1, above; Ophirs gould] Ophir, a country celebrated for its gold and precious stones (1 Kings 9:28, 10:11, 22:48).

10 to . . . rise] The idea is similar to that of fol. 18^v, 86.

21 Docter Featlye] Cf. no. 109 of the booklist (fol. 64^v). The poem was probably written during Lady Anne's years in Acton (1631–1636), for Daniel Featley, a noted disputant, preacher and voluminous writer, was the Rector of Saint Mary's Church in Acton from 1627 to 1643 (*DNB*, 6:1140–44).

30 fiuefoulde trinitye] That is, the five senses.

53–54 Whoe . . . peace] The lines are also on fol. 18^r, 47–48.

53 Cadmus' teeth] See fol. 18^r, 47.

54 Babells] See fol. 18^r, 49.

58 whose . . . roome] The line repeats fol. 18^v, 52.

[26^v] "S^r. giue mee leaue to plead my Grandams cause" This may or may not be a continuation of the poem on fol. 26^r, for both have to do with the creation narrative; it is separated because of the change in focus to "my Grandams cause." The poem on fol. 8^v also begins with the idea that the speaker will "pleade the Cause" of another.

9–19 Our . . . historie] See fol. 16 and, for the topos of female superiority, the Introduction.

26 hermophradite] hermaphrodite. Salmacis, according to Ovid, was a lovely nymph of a fountain in Caria who fell in love with Hermaphroditus when he bathed there. They were united into one person (R & B).

39 Theise . . . iollie] Cf. fol. 10^r, 17.

51–56 Thou . . . vnder] The lines are similar to lines 1–6 on fol. 18^r.

[27^{r-v}] "In this frayle worlde" 4 an honest harted man] A poem from a masculine speaker, probably Henry Sibthorpe, who must have composed it long before Thomas Southwell's death, that is, before "fate" had "all the putt-betweenes remoue[d]" (line 33). For the phrase in line 4, see appendix II (fol. 164^r, stanza 76).

[28^r–29^v] "The ffirst Commandement" The title is a variation of the title on fol. 32^r; the meditation includes material revised from fols. 33^r and 42^v–43^r.

12 momentanye] An obsolete form of "momentary" (*OED*).

20–36 that . . . aright] Cf. fol. 42^v, 346–64.

20 carieers] Career, the short gallop of a horse at full speed, or a charge (at a tournament or in battle); obsolete; and Fr. "carrière," applied specifically to the course or trajectory of the sun or a star through the heavens (*OED*). See also Shakespeare's *Much Ado about Nothing*, II.iii.242 and V.i.135.

24 with wth] The scribe probably forgot to delete one.

26 aconite] Poisonous plants.

49–54 With . . . brest] These lines, with slight variations, are the only ones on fol. 142^v of British Library MS. Lansdowne 740, where they are not part of either meditation.

90 noe Iod or tittle] Matt. 5:18.

110–114 Then . . . mee] Cf. fol. 32^v, lines 95–99.

116–121 Loue . . . contemne] The lines are a corrected version of lines 43–48 on fol. 33^r.

[30^v] "An abstract of The liues of the Romaine Empourers" See no. 21 in the booklist, "Suetonius, of the 12 Cæsars" (fol. 65^r).

9 Ptolamie] King of Egypt who ruled in 51 BC with his sister Cleopatra (R & B).

15 Brutus ... sonn] According to Suetonius, Caesar loved Servilia, the mother of Marcus Brutus, "beyond all others." When Brutus rushed at Caesar, the latter said in Greek, "You too, my child?" (*Suetonius,* trans. by J. C. Rolfe, 2 vols. (London: Heinemann, 1935, 1:69 and 111). Later writers took the word "child" to mean physical offspring. Plutarch, for example, says that Brutus, "who was born in that time when her [Servilia's] passion was in full blaze, was his own son" (*Plutarch's Lives,* trans. Bernadette Perrin, 11 vols. [London: Heinemann, 1943], 6:135).

[31ʳ–32ᵛ] "Who euer sawe himself but in a myrrour" 4 impostures] Abscesses or boils (cf. *Hamlet* IV.iv.127).

42 Sallomon] Solomon, son of David and third king of Israel, known for his wisdom (1 Kings 7:48–51).

41 for ... doth] An unfinished thought.

57 onely ... thee] Cf. fol. 10ʳ, 23.

64 they] The "servants" of the three stanzas above.

65 owe] own.

[32ᵛ–33ᵛ] "I am thy god" The complete title is a variation of the title on fol. 28ʳ: "The ffirst Commandement. / Thou shalt haue noe other gods before mee."

5–6 thou ... all] Cf. John Donne: "the heart of man, / Is an epitome of God's great book / Of creatures" ("Eclogue, 1613," line 51).

18 war the robe of a trancelusantraye] Translations of the deuterocanonical Sirach speak of wearing wisdom's yoke like a "robe of glory" (6:31), which seems to be the sense here. The *OED* gives an example of "transluce" in "Let joy transluce thy Beauties blandishment."

43–48 Loue ... conteme] Cf. fol. 29ᵛ, lines 116–21.

78 opprest by Laban, ... by his brother, hatid] Jacob was forced to work for his father-in-law Laban for many years in order to gain Rachel; his brother Esau hated Jacob because he had deceptively gained his father's inheritance (Gen. 27–31).

93–94 schoole, ... foole] Southwell uses the rhyme again on fols. 35ʳ, 82–83 and 37ʳ, 119–20; she had also used it earlier (fols. 9ʳ, 3–4 and 20ᵛ, 115–16). For another opinion on the rhyme, see Shakespeare's *Much Ado about Nothing,* V.ii.39.

[34ʳ–35ʳ] "Thou shalt not make to thy self / any graven Image" For influences, see Isa. 45:15–24.

5 Horeb] The mount of God in Sinai, sometimes equated with Mount Sinai, where the law was given to Moses (Exod. 3:1 and 19:20).

15 Ball] Baal, a supreme male divinity, considered responsible for the fruitfulness of the earth, honored in licentiousness (1 Kings 16 & 18).

24 Sall to Pall] Saul of Tarsus, who persecuted Christians until his conversion (Acts 7, 8, and 9). After Acts 13:9, he is called only Paul (*West.*).

32 pas uis of our ⟨natur⟩] The past vice of our nature: original sin.

35 Dannyell ... de⟨nn⟩] Dan. 6:16.

36 afflyctions stoue] The fiery furnace in which Shadrach, Meshach, and Abednego were tried by Nebuchadnezzar and miraculously delivered (Dan. 3).

45 Edomits] Edomites, 10,000 descendants of Esau, who had invaded Judah, and were killed; Amazyah] who slew them (2 Kings 14:7, *West.*).

65 treeis] Tress(?), applied to the rays of the sun; cf. fol. 32ᵛ, 18.

67 alyes] Allies.

78–79 the foole ... noe god] Ps. 14:1.

82–83 schoole ... foole] Cf. fols. 33ᵛ, 93–94 and 37ʳ, 119–20.

COMMENTARY

199

[35ʳ–37ʳ] "Thou shalt not take the / name of god in vayne" This meditation is enlarged in Precept 3 (fols. 142–55), appendix II.

34 Sophissems and eulings] A specious but fallacious argument, used either to deceive or mislead, or employed as a means of ingenuity in reasoning (*OED*); eulings] that which easily takes hold (*OED*), that is, deceptively appealing rhetoric.

55–56 Hee . . . poore] James 2:1–7.

75 errant] Errand, or commission (*OED*).

79 stet] Conjecture. Although the *OED* gives 1755 as the first use of this, Southwell uses it here above a stanza that had been crossed out, just as "stet." is used in Precept 4 (appendix II), next to stanzas 92 and 95. Below stanza 90 is the sentence, "These verses & those that follow though crossed out ar fitt to stand."

80 care hath ravens fed] Job 38:41.

89 generall asize] The last judgement.

119–20 scoole . . . foole] Cf. fols. 33ᵛ, 93–94 and 35ʳ, 82–83.

[37ʳ–44ʳ] "Thou shalt keepe holy the / saboth daye" This meditation is enlarged in Precept 4 (British Library Lansdowne MS. 740, fols. 156 67), appendix II. Because lines 327–44 here refer to James I, the poem must have been written before or during 1625, when the king died. The lines referring to James are not in British Library Lansdowne MS. 740.

4 valence] A border of drapery hanging around the canopy of a bed (*OED*).

62 goosell] To spend time foolishly (*OED*).

69–70 thy . . . simpathy] Eph. 5:23–25.

79–80 Iorny . . . Ierusalem] That is, a short journey going down into a valley and up the other side.

83 lo] Conjecture; as in Rev. 14:1?

89 X] An emphasis on a painful topic or simply a reminder to correct "mush" to "much"?

92 argent feeld] The white color which represents silver in coats of arms (*OED*).

104 Elysha] The prophet chosen to succeed Elijah (1 Kings 19:16–19).

105 him . . . his] The child's.

107 Absolon] Absalom, the rebellious son of David, who was caught by the branches of an oak tree while riding and subsequently slain by Joab (2 Sam. 18:14).

116 Horebs] Horeb's, see fol. 34ʳ, 5.

121 unglings] Younglings.

123 face, . . . grapes] For such paintings by the Italian Arcimboldo, see Andre Pieyre de Mandiargues, *Arcimboldo the Marvelous*, conception by Yasha David, ed. Patricia Egan, trans. I. Mark Paris (New York: Abrams, 1978).

133 dalida] Delilah, who tricked Samson into telling her the secret of his strength and then betrayed him to the Philistines (Judg. 16).

174 hath] Hate; homisite] Homicide.

175 advocate] Lawyer; Iarr] Jarr, a state of discord (*OED*).

179 chancery] The court of the Lord Chancellor of England; until 1873, the highest judicature next to the House of Lords (*OED*).

182 maude] Obsolete past tense of "made" (*OED*).

183 Iosephs] Joseph, the eleventh of Jacob's twelve sons, was his father's favorite so his jealous brothers tried unsuccessfully to kill him (Gen. 37, *West.*).

191–92 helmet of salvation / brestplate of fayth] Isa. 59:17.

193 David] Meaning "beloved," second king of Israel, father of Solomon and author of the Psalms.

195–206 And . . . dead] The lines echo the sense of triumphant glory in John's Book of Revelation; apocalyptic images recur, such as the "holy lambe," "kingly bordered throne," "seven seald booke," "glorius Iasper stone," "prophet into deathfull terror strooke," and "this lambe, this lyon."

218 dis] Dis, a name for Pluto (R & B).

223 diuedoppers] A small diving waterfowl, a term applied ludicrously to a person (*OED*).

226 commande the mountaynes] Mark 11:23.

227 soonn stande senternell] Sun (Josh. 10:12–13).

228 thy . . . sittyes] A reference to the trumpets that blew before the walls of Jericho fell (Josh. 6:20).

231 reth∧<an>atitian] Obsolete form of "mathematician" (*OED*).

232 [mount]] See textual notes for this and 234.

233 [ ]tions] [His ac]tions?

245–46 those that . . . men] Mark 1:17.

259 goulden number] Cf. Pythagorean number theory (Heninger, 71–145).

265 droom] Drum.

267 Syon] The hill on which was situated the old city of Jerusalem (Deuter. 4:48); symbolically, Jerusalem, as a holy city.

271 congleutenates] "To ioyne togyther, as it were glewyd" (Elyot).

280 scala celi<e>] L., stairs to heaven.

281 Dorion] The Dorian mode, an ancient Greek one in music, prevailingly solemn and simple (*OED*).

283 double dyopasanse] Diapason. In medieval music theory, a diapason is the interval of an octave; it may include all the tones, or be a part sounding such a consonance or concord (*OED*); see also Heninger, 95–100.

286 axell tree of destynye] Poetically, the pole of heaven (*OED*). See *The Revels Plays Tamburlaine the Great Christopher Marlowe*, ed. J. S. Cunningham (Baltimore: Johns Hopkins Univ. Press, 1981), IV.ii.50, *I Tamburlaine* with a note, p. 181, listing other uses in *II Tamburlaine* (I.i.90) and *Doctor Faustus* (vi.38–41). Shakespeare uses the phrase once in *Troilus and Cressida* (I.iii.66).

311 congruitye] Agreement, as in Latin constructions (*OED* and Elyot).

314 moods] The form of a verb which indicates whether it is a fact, command, possibility, or wish; tropes] figures of speech.

327–344 Witnesse . . . escape] A tribute to James I, whose *Demonologye* (Edinburgh, 1598) Southwell mentions in Precept 3, stanza 82. See James's books, on a variety of topics, in the *STC*.

348 career] Course (*OED*); see fol. 28ʳ, 20, above.

354 aquinet] Aconite.

358 Salomon] Solomon, son of David, and third king of Israel (1 Kings).

366 Varro] A learned Roman scholar (116–ca. 27 BC), of whose more than 70 works on almost every branch of knowledge only *De lingua Latina* and *De re rustica* survive (R & B).

367 paze] Pase, an obsolete form of "pace," to take a paseo or walk (*OED*).

380 Plynny] Caius Plinius Secundus (23–79) Roman naturalist who also followed a high career in war and politics. His *Historia naturalis*, in thirty-seven books, is encyclopedic in its treatment of geography, medicine, and art. Although often wildly inaccurate in discussing geology and botany, it enjoyed great popularity for centuries (R & B).

383 brothers] Moses and Aaron, outsmarting Pharaoh (Exod. 7, 8, 17:12).

385 smale wand] Small wand, the "rod" of Exod. 7:9–20.

COMMENTARY

201

399–400 grayne ... take] John 12:24.

408 waxen plewmes ... soon] Female Icarus.

414 Debora] Deborah, a Hebrew prophetess and judge who sang triumphantly when Barak overcame the tyrant Jabin (*West.*, Judg. 4–5).

415 Nabals wife] Abigail, who saved her foolish husband and all his men from David's wrath and later became David's wife (1 Sam.:25).

417 Iehell] Jael, Heber's wife, who killed Sisera by putting a spike through his temples as he lay asleep (Judg. 4:17–22); Iudas] probably a scribal error for "Iudiths." See the Introduction for the comparison of this stanza with its parallel in Lansdowne MS. 740, fol. 158ᵛ, stanza 24.

424 Gydeons bande] The band was reduced to three hundred at God's direction, according to the way they lapped water (Judg. 7).

429–30 speaker ... burges ... cryor] Positions in Parliament; a burgess was a representative of a borough, corporate town or university in the English Parliament (*OED*).

[44ᵛ–46ʳ] [Southwell drafts, #1] See the Introduction for the problem of Southwell's handwriting and the change in editorial method.

7 why ... boundes] Punning, through a literalized metaphor.

10 sofisticke] Sophistic; in the sense of sophistry.

16 toplis heauen] Topless heaven; cf. Marlowe, "the topless towers of Ilium," in *Doctor Faustus*, ed. J. D. Jump (Cambridge: Harvard Univ. Press, 1962), scene xviii, line 100, p. 92.

24 a worme A:s I am] Ps. 22:6.

27 the beast's foull marke] Rev. 16:2.

38 our ... awaye] Rev. 2:5.

46 oblityy [apostasy?] See Precept 4, stanza 17: "The first day voyd & emptye doth present / Adams apostasye, voyd of all grace."

53 grieatling bomp [pomp] so roman [Roman] preate] That is, pomp of the high and mighty, so Roman in its style, prate.

58 a brocon contrite harte] Ps. 51:17.

62 couet] This might also be "sow" since *c* is sometimes used for *s* and *u* for *w*.

63 [justices]] That is, his five wounds which made redemption possible.

64 tomes] Books, but in the revised line, "like Thomas's doubt"?

65 raeor] Another attempt at a word to express a ray of blinding light?

68 working ... trembling] Phil. 2:12.

69 polings] The Last Judgment.

70 <that ... untorlude] The faith-and-works controversy.

80 sin of berth] Original sin.

81 proud puisant sion[Sion]] Or Zion, the southwestern hill of Jerusalem, surrounded on all sides except the north by deep valleys. (Cf. Rev. 14:1: "And I looked, and lo, a Lamb stood on the mount Sion, and with him an hundred forty and four thousand, having his Father's name written in their foreheads.")

89 [Ishmael]] Gen. 16:16.

90 [Esau]] Gen. 27:41.

93 [Thyatira]] Rev. 1:11. *S* may have been writing the source included, i.e., Rev. 2:4, from her memory.

97 [Cyrus's]] A king of Persia (Isa. 44–45)?

102–103 for ... blasfemies] Rev. 13:1–6.

108 Ioane] Pope Joan; *S* mentions the woman who, according to popular legend, disguised herself, got herself elected pope and ruled efficiently, fooling everyone. She herself grew restless, however, became pregnant, and gave birth in the middle of a

202   COMMENTARY

liturgical procession. See Giovanni Boccaccio, *Concerning Famous Women,* trans. G. A. Guarino (New Brunswick: Rutgers Univ. Press, 1963), 231–34.

109 elias] Elias, or Elijah, who could "cumplayne" because he did not die for his faith but was taken into heaven in a fiery chariot (2 Kings 2:11).

[47ᵛ–51ᵛ] "Thou shalt not commit Adooltery" For influences on Southwell's thinking about mutuality in marriage and the possibility of divorce when the woman is wronged, note that "Caluins Institutions" is no. 1 of the booklist; and no. 2 is "Caluins Sermons vpon Iob." See also Jane Dempsey Douglass, "Christian Freedom: What Calvin Learned at the School of Women," *Church History* 53 (1984): 155–73; and *Women, Freedom and Calvin* (Philadelphia: Westminster Press, 1985).

2 noysome] Noisome, harmful (*OED*).

11 Etnean] Aetna, the highest volcano in Europe and largest mountain in Sicily (R & B).

14 Hermophradite] An effeminate man or virile woman; a catamite (*OED*). See fol. 26ᵛ, 25–28, for a different context. For a discussion of the hermaphrodite, and especially as a derogatory concept, see Carla Freccero, "The Other and the Same: the Image of the Hermaphrodite in Rabelais," *Rewriting the Renaissance: The Discourses of Sexual Difference in Early Modern Europe,* eds. Margaret W. Ferguson, Maureen Quilligan, and Nancy J. Vickers (Chicago: Univ. of Chicago Press, 1986), 145–58.

19–24 The Sodomytes ... land] See the drafts on homosexual pursuits as those of a world upside-down (fol. 57ʳ, lines 18–23).

25 X] The "X" above "grandome Eve in paradyse" may suggest a cross-reference to the argument for her "Grandams cause" on fol. 26ᵛ.

48 well] we'll.

51 he ... swoord] Rev. 13:10.

104–5 wyf ... lyfe] See "Characteristics of Her Writing" in the Introduction.

125–26 but ... moorne] The story from the deuterocanonical Book of Tobit of how Tobias escapes death, although he is marrying a widow whose previous seven husbands had been killed by Asmodeus, the evil spirit, on their wedding day (*West.*, 51).

162 Elkenah] Elkanah, father of Samuel and husband of Hannah and Peninnah. Hannah, unable to bear children, was harassed by Penninah, but Elkanah comforted her, saying, "Am I not better to thee than ten sons?" Finally, after special vows to the Lord, she bore Samuel (1 Sam. 1).

164 her churlish fathers] Laban, Rachel's "churlish" father, refused to let Jacob leave (Gen. 29–31).

168 Elie] Eli, the high priest who thought that Hannah was drunk as he watched her pray for a son (1 Sam. 1:13).

176 Putyfar] Potiphar, officer of the guard and husband of the woman who tried to seduce Joseph, and on failing, persuaded her husband to imprison the "Iust Ioseph" (line 178) on a false charge (Gen. 39).

186–202 for thy ... crownes] The lines that a husband "cryes."

187 as ... ies] The correction reads: "as is the optike artire to the ies."

203 batalia] Arrangement of troops for action (*OED*).

213–14 soe ... sweete] Matt. 11:28–30.

228 barbara] A term, through its three "a"s, designating the first word of the first figure of syllogisms, "a" indicating a universal proposition. A syllogism in "barbara" is one in which the major and the minor premises, and the conclusion, are affirmatives: thus, all animals are mortal; all men are animals; therefore all men are mortal; selarent] celarent. By its vowels, the word represents the "eae" form, with its negative, affirmative and negative propositions. "Barbara" and "celarent" are words for logical forms,

COMMENTARY

203

found in Aristotle, "De Interpretatione," trans. E. M. Edghill, *The Basic Works of Aristotle,* ed. Richard McKeon (New York: Random House, 1941), 38–61, and taught as mnemonic devices by medieval logicians. The vowels indicate the mood (that is, affirmative, negative, partial affirmative and partial negative) in the traditional order: major premise, minor premise, conclusion. "Barbara" and "celarent" are the first two words of nonsense lines in Latin, taught as a mnemonic device which enumerated the nineteen valid moods of the four figures of syllogisms. See Sr. Miriam Joseph Raugh, *Everyday Logic* (South Bend: McClave, 1948, rev. 3rd ed.), 147–75.

[52^r–57^r] "Thou shalt not steale" 7–24 for your . . . back] Lines against wars, inspired by "ambytious covetous desyre."

12 Achabs prophets] False prophets who tricked Ahab (1 Kings 22:6) into going to war, where he was slain.

13 pouder] The [gun]powder policies by which "kinggs" (line 1) set fire to "fey'ldes of corne" (line 9).

19 rackell vepes] A conjecture, meaning "rascal weeps."

27 soonne of David] Solomon.

28 all was vanytye] Ecclesiastes.

29 rewle] Rule.

31 Nabuchadneser] Nebuchadnezzar, who was known for his military conquests and buildings, both palaces and temples, but went mad (Dan. 4, *West.*).

33 Dyves] The rich man who refused Lazarus's request and was punished (Luke 16:19–25).

34 Symon] A sorcerer who tried to buy the privilege of conferring the Holy Spirit, but was rebuked by Peter (Acts 8:9 and 18).

38 Saule . . . afflycted] King of Israel, yet troubled by an evil spirit (1 Sam. 16:14).

39 Absolon] Absalom, David's son, who was slain by Joab after his hair was caught in a branch (2 Sam. 15 and 18).

41 Roboams soonne] Abijah, son of Jeroboam, who failed to recover from a childhood illness, in spite of his mother's pleading for him (1 Kings 14).

42 Samson] Whose arms were tied by Delilah, but without weakening him (Judg. 16:8–9).

47 Achans theft] Achan appropriated and hid in his tent a Babylonian garment and gold, part of the spoils of Jericho. He was caught and he and his family were stoned (Josh. 7, *West.*).

50 fleame or gale] phlegm or gall.

52 kytes] Birds living on carrion.

81 strencke] strength.

107–12 <Hee . . . wronggs] The Dives and Lazarus story (Luke 16:19–31).

114 best] beast.

130 brakes] Tree-stumps or broken branches; a clump of bushes, brushwood, or briers, a thicket (*OED*).

139 seles] sells.

147 moodd] mud.

151–52 <To. . . love] Without charity, all else is nothing (1 Cor. 13).

187 if a sparrow] Matt. 10:29.

191–92 the foe . . . sleyne] Absalom, who rebelled against David, had long hair, which was caught in the branches of an oak; as Absalom hung, he was slain by Joab (2 Sam. 18:14).

204   COMMENTARY

216 lyturgy] Punning on "lethargy," coming from the "store of treasure" which may "dull thee" (line 215) and on "liturgy" as a service from which "want must pull" one.

[57ʳ–58ᵛ] [Southwell drafts, #2] The lines in Southwell's hand continue the meditation against stealing, but they soon speak about other topics. See the Introduction for discussion of Southwell's writing and the editorial method used in transcribing the folios.

13 tim*es* carryi\<n\>ng ball] A reference to early pocket watches, which were spherical. See Cedric Jagger, *The Artistry of the English Watch* (Rutland, Vermont: Charles E. Tuttle, 1988), 11–12.

18–23 it [that] ... lands] A discussion of homosexual pursuits. See the revised phrasing connecting the idea with "Sodomytes" (fol. 47, lines 19–24).

22–23 Beca*use* ... lands] Cf. broadsheets of the world upside-down.

27 toplis sci*es*] topless skies; cf. fol. 45ʳ, 15, and Marlowe's line.

42 coude] Or, "couth," that is, "known" (*OED*). Lines 42–46 allude to Platonic knowledge, as recollection. Cf. *Plato*, "Meno," 3:1–56. Lines 47–60 speculate on the doctrines of Averroism, that is, that man's soul is material.

48 each ... corrupsion] That is, dissolution into not-being. Popular Aristotelianism.

50 what ... eruption] What cannot "touch," that is, that which is not material cannot decay. Speculation on the doctrines of Averroism, that is, that man's soul is material.

59 [Esthers]] The Book of Esther relates how Esther, a Jewish maiden, dwelling in Susa, the Persian capital, became queen of Ahasuerus, or Xerxes (485–65 BC), and was instrumental in rescuing her compatriots from the destruction prepared for them by Haman, the king's favorite.

63 his ... epetome] That is, Christ's body epitomizes the world; cf. fol. 19ᵛ, line 6, and fol. 32ᵛ, 5 and 6, and Donne, "Eclogue, 1613," line 51, and "The Canonization," line 43.

64 all undon] That is, from being Divinity only, "standing thar," should "all co*n*troll," that is, through redemption.

66 \<for age\>] The rhetoric of a conclusion to prayer: "for all ages."

[59ʳ] "An Inventorye of the Lady Anne Southwells goods" 10 mattock] An agricultural tool, used for loosening hard ground, grubbing up trees, and similar tasks (*OED*).

25 Cappan] "Kappie," a coal-scuttle bonnet, from "cap," a piece of iron that covers the end of an axle tree (*DAPW*).

26 vallance] A border of drapery hanging around the canopy of a bed (*OED*).

29 els] An ell is a former English unit of cloth equal to forty-five inches (*OED*).

30 holland] A linen fabric, originally called Holland cloth, from the province of Holland in the Netherlands (*OED*).

32 bed tester] A canopy over a bed or the framework for it (*OED*).

36 bolster] A long stuffed pillow or cushion (*OED*).

37 busking] From "busk," attire, dress, decoration, and hence a decorative tapestry (*OED*); fl' ells] "Fl'" may refer to a Flemish ell, that is, 27 inches (*DAPW*); see also Arnold, under "Bayes"), or a Florentine ell, a long ell, a particular kind of cloth (*OED*).

39 close stoole] A stool holding a chamber pot (*OED*).

42 say Curtaine] A delicate serge or woolen cloth (*DAPW*).

[60ʳ] "you Gyannts, or Hyennas that doe dwell" An elegy for a "Captaine" (line 4) who died at twenty-five (line 7); possibly Southwell's younger brother, Christopher, who was killed at Ostend. The long siege of Ostend came to an end on 17 September 1604 (*A Jacobean Journal*, ed. G. B. Harrison, [London: Routledge, 1941], 159).

1 Hyennas] Cf. the mini-beastiary on hyenas (fol. 68ʳ, 1–6).

21 one] on.

COMMENTARY

205

[60ᵛ] [The inventory of fol. 59ʳ, continued] A continuation of the fol. 59ʳ inventory, where the last date is April 26.

Note the trunks of books in lines 9 and 14 and the booklist on fols. 64ᵛ–66ʳ.

13 Rundlett] A cask of varying capacity; Aquavite] any form in which ardent spirits have been drunk, as brandy, whiskey (*OED*).

17 diaper] Linen fabric woven with small simple designs, chequer or diamond pattern (Arnold).

21 whitsonday] The Feast of Pentecost.

38 Truckle bedds] Trundle beds, that is, a low bed on small wheels or castors, pushed beneath a 'high' or 'standing' bed when not in use (*OED*).

[61ʳ] "Apparell of my Ladyes" 1 Kersye] A kind of coarse narrow cloth, woven from long wool and usually ribbed (*OED*).

3 watchet] A light blue color, cloth or garment (*OED*).

4 doublet] A square bodice or jerkin. See Arnold, fig. 229.

5 Calamintha] Calamanco, a woolen stuff of Flanders, glossy, and garments of this material; stomachers] an ornamental covering for the chest, often covered with jewels (*OED*).

7 swatchett] Related to "swatch"(?) a sample piece of fabric; huffles] Because the bowl of the *h* is written over, could the word be a scribal error for "ruftes" or "ruffles," for the wrists (Arnold)?

12 bodyes] Bodice, a term applying to both the stiffened inner garment and the upper part of a woman's gown fitted close to the body (Arnold).

13 Kirtle] Usually worn with an overgown, as the backs were often made with different materials and not intended to be seen (*OED*).

14 pantafles] Pantofles, an indoor slipper or loose shoe, especially the high-heeled cork-soled chopins (Skeat).

17 beuers] That is, beaver hats (*DAPW*). Cf. "of the Beauer," fol. 68ʳ.

21 virginmales] Virginal, an oblong spinet, but set in a box or case without legs (*OED*); Iack] Jack, a drinking measure; half-pint (Skeat).

22 skymmer] Used in skimming milk or cheese-making (*OED*).

23 buckinge tubb] For steeping or boiling clothes in lye (*OED*).

24 pondringe tubb] Pondering tub, for weighing (Skeat); peele] peel, a flat, long-headed shovel, generally of wood, used for taking bread and pies in and out of a brick oven (*OED*).

28 trenchers] Knives (*OED*).

30 flock bedd] A material consisting of the coarse tufts and refuse of wool or cotton (*OED*).

32 fowleinge peeces] A light gun for shooting wild fowl; firkins] small casks for liquids (*OED*).

34 halbard] A combination spear and battle-axe, consisting of a sharp-edged blade ending in a point, a spear head, mounted on a handle 5 to 7 feet; heryet] heriot, armor (*OED*).

[65ʳ–66ʳ] "A List of my Bookes" See Sr. Jean Cavanaugh (Introduction, n. 34), for information about the titles, taken from the *STC* of 1926, which offers useful information about titles and numbers of reprints. For a study of other Renaissance libraries, see Francis Wormald, and C. E. Wright, eds., *The English Library before 1700: Studies in Its History* (London: Athlone Press, 1958); and Sears Jayne, *Library Catalogues of the English Renaissance* (Berkeley, 1956). Cf. the three "Truncks of bookes" moved from Clerkenwell to Acton (fol. 60ᵛ, 9 and 14).

53 L. Elizabeth] Written in the margin, left of #51. This may refer to Southwell's

206   COMMENTARY

mother, Lady E. Harris; to her daughter, Lady E. Dowdall; to Sir Thomas's relative at Elizabeth's court, Lady E. Southwell; or to another.

56 Palionis] Probably a scribal error for "Talionis."

[66ᵛ] "the 3th of ffebruary maister C   Preacher of acton" *T* C] Probably "Coxe." See the Introduction for his role at Acton.

4–5 Rachell wept] Jer. 31:15.

[67ʳ] "St. Augustine Ca. 8 of his booke. the Citie of god" *T* St. Augustine] Living from 354 to 430, he was Bishop of Hippo, a father of the church, a powerful antagonist of the Donatist, Pelagian, and Manichean heresies; he influenced the whole body of medieval dogma, and his *Confessions* and *The City of God* have remained literary classics of Christianity (R & B). For verification of the "8" in the title, see "St. Augustin's 'City of God'" in *A Select Library of the Nicene and Post-Nicene Fathers of the Christian Church*, ed. Philip Schaff, 1st ser., 2:5.

[68ʳ⁻ᵛ] "A booke of the nature of foure footed bests" See *The Historie of Fovre-Footed Beastes*, collected out of all the Volumes of Conradvs Gesner . . . by Edward Topsell (London, 1607) and *The History of Serpents* (London, 1608). For excerpts, woodcuts, and discussions of selections from the two works, see Malcolm Smith, *Topsell's Histories of Beasts* (Chicago: Nelson-Hall, 1981).

T-2 C[onradvs] Ges[ner] The top of the line has been trimmed.

11 Lamia] A fabulous monster supposed to have the body of a woman, and to prey upon human beings and suck the blood of children. Also, a witch (*OED*).

15 Aristottle] See his *The History of Animals, On the Parts of Animals,* and *On the Generation of Animals, The Basic Works of Aristotle,* ed. Richard McKeon (New York: Random House, 1941), 633–88.

17 Poet] Aristotle.

23 exemptile] Removable (*OED*).

44 makes . . . hat] Cf. fol. 61ʳ, 17.

45 Castoreum] A secretion from the beaver, a creamy, orange brown substance, with a strong penetrating odor; a medicine used as a stimulant and antispasmodic (*OED*).

49 epolepticall] Of the nature of epilepsy, a disease of the nervous system; parolepticall] related to psycholepsy, a condition characterized by sudden changes of mood tending toward depression (*OED*).

59 Camelion the] Camelion. They.

64 bucking time] Mating time for animals (*OED*).

78 Poets] Aristotle's.

[69ʳ⁻ᵛ] "Apothegmes" 3 Bushop Kinge] For King's poems, see fols. 21ᵛ and 24ʳ⁻ᵛ.

23 ‹Tambarlin] Tamerlane (?1333–1405), Mongol conqueror of most of southern and western Asia; the protagonist of Marlowe's two plays (1590) (R & B).

29 exolation] Exolution, the action of setting free 'animal spirits.' (*OED*).

37 Spainricks] This and most of the terms in no. 14 have to do with alchemy and related schools of philosophy.

44 Doggmaticks] Philosophers proceeding upon *a priori* principles accepted as true, instead of being founded upon experience or induction (*OED*).

69 Custorium] Cf. Castoreum; cf. fol. 68ʳ, 49, above.

[70ʳ⁻ᵛ] "How that the Law of the Gospell is" 23 letted] Hindered (Skeat).

[71ʳ] [Acton receipts of 1632 and 1633] 4 Souththey] The spelling suggests the "Suthell" pronunciation, as prescribed under the Southwell coat of arms in *Debrett's Peerage*, in contrast to lines where the "well" of Southwell is rimed with "bell" and "knell" (fol. 20ᵛ, 119–20).

14 Michelmas daye] The feast of St. Michael the Archangel, Sept. 29 (*OED*).

COMMENTARY 207

[72^r] "M^r. Iohnson dyed" For Robert Johnson, see the Introduction.

    13 <any man In>] See the textual notes.

[72^v] [Acton receipts of 1635 and 1636] 23 o^r lady,_∧ ^{day}] The Feast of the Annunciation to the Virgin Mary, March 25.

[73^r] "To the never dyeing memorye" 49 climactericall] Applied to the 'grand climacteric,' or sixty-third year of life, a point at which a person was supposed to be especially liable to change in health or fortune (*OED*).

[74^r] "Consecrated to the Memory" 26 Climatericall] As on fol. 73^r, l. 49.

First-Line Index of Poems

All deletions have been omitted, superscript letters normalized, and end punctuation dropped. Following the first line of each poem is the folio on which the poem appears, an abbreviated title if one is included or, in brackets, a suggestion of the poem's content. Brackets also include information not in the folios: an author other than Anne Southwell, a well-known title, the songbooks in which the text has been set to music, and another book in which the poem appears. See Peter Beal, *Index of English Literary Manuscripts* (London: Mansell; New York: Bowker, 1980–) for other manuscript copies of poems by Ralegh and King.

"Accept thou Shrine of my dead Sainte" . . . . 21v [King, "The Exequy"]
"Adam first preist, first Prophet and first Kinge" 18r, "Letter to Doctor Adam"
"All maried men desire to haue good wifes" 16r
"Alpha Omega, Oh thow first and Last" . . . . 5r, "A Hym to Christ"
"Anger proceedes from a surcharged Gaule" . . . . 8v, "Anger"
"Anger what art thow? Hast thow treuth to tell" . . 9r, "Dialouge: / Sonnet."

"Beauty, Honor, yeouth, and fortune" . . . . 9r, "Sonnet"

"Come forth foule Monster, at truthes barr to stand" 22v

"Fayne would I dye whil'st thy braue muse doth liue" . . . . 17r, [F. Quarles]
"ffarewell fond World, the onely Schoole of Error" . . . . 1r, Sonnet 3
"ffly from the world, o fly, thow poore distrest" . . . . 1r, Sonnet 1
   [Robert Jones,*Vltimum Vale*, XIIII, 1605, in *Lyrics*, p. 214; Alfonso
   Ferrabosco, *Ayres*, XVI, 1609, in *Lyrics*, p. 298; British Library Additional
   MS 2445, "Giles Earl's Songbook," in Jorgens, Vol. XII, p. 410; and
   Folger MS V.a.339, fol. 192r.]
"ffrayle Loue is like faire flowrie fields" 10r
"Fortie twoe yeares; before oure sauiours birth" . . . 30v, "Romane Empourers"

FIRST LINES OF POEMS

209

"God doth with doggs adulterate weights exempte" . . . . 47v, "Adooltery"
"god tooke thee oute of claye, and gaue thee lyfe." . . 32v, "I am thy god . . ."
"Goe sole the bodies guest" . . . . 2r [Ralegh, "The Lie"]

"Harken you potentates and mighty kinggs" . . . . 52r, "Thou shalt not steale"
"Here lyes a king, and gods anoynted" . . . . . 22r, "An Epitaph . . . Bohemia"

"If in the flesh where thow indrench'd do'st ly" . . . . 1r, Sonnet 4
    [Jones, *Vltimum Vale*, 1609, XV, in *Lyrics*, p. 328]
"If to be borne the Image of the Lord" . . . . 12r, "Honor thy father"
"In six dayes god made this admyred balle" . . . . 37r, "Thou . . . saboth daye"
"In this frayle worlde, where soules in earth are cladd" 27r
"In this our hartes corruption is most exprest" . . . . 35r "Thou . . . name"
"It is an easy taske to pleade the Cause" . . . . 8r, "Seneca"

"Like a cold fatall sweat which vshers death" . . . 24r, [King, "G. Adolphus"]
"Like to a lampe wherein the light is dead" . . . . 9v, "Sonnet"

"Maliciouse fate enuyinge humaine glorie" . . . . 22r, "Epitaph . . . Swede"

"Nature, Mistris off affection" 11r
"Noe man may see the face of god and liue" . . 34r, "Thou . . . graven Image"
"Now let my pen bee choakt with gall" . . . . 21r, ". . . Mackwilli*a*ms"

"O how happy were I dearest" . . . . 9v, "Sonnett"
"Only eight soules, the waued tost Church did keepe" 23v

"Raise vp thy ffacultyes my Soule ti's time" . . 28r, "Thou . . . noe other gods"
"Seest thow a man that's vassaliz'd to pleasure" . . . . 8v, "Blessed Life"
"Shall I sublyme my Soule to frame a letter" . . . . 1r, Sonnet 5
"Since thou fayre soule, art warbleinge to a spheare" . . . . 19v, "Elegy"
"Sr. giue mee leaue to plead my Grandams cause" 26v

"The more my soule doth shrinke from loue,
    ye more, loue doth inflame her" 25r
"Thou faythfull Harrold of the morne" . . . . 21r, "Mr. Coxe . . . booke"
"To tell the shrine that its faire saint is gone" . . . . 23r, ". . . Sommersett"
"To thee my soule I raysc" . . . . 7r [Psalm 25, to . . . Castlehaven]

"Vnless himselfe against himselfe weare bent" 26r

"Vouchsafe this fauor; as to tell me how" . . . . 22r, "Duches of Lineox"

"What if I wante the dross of Tagus Strann" 22r
"When I sitt reading all alone that secret booke" . . . . 1r, Sonnet 2
    [Jones, *Vltimum Vale*, 1609, XVII, in *Lyrics*, p. 329.]
"Who euer sawe himself but in a myrrour" 31r

"you Gyannts, or Hyennas that doe dwell" 60r

Renaissance English Text Society

Officers and Council

President, Arthur F. Kinney, University of Massachusetts at Amherst
Vice-President, A. R. Braunmuller, University of California, Los Angeles
Secretary, Carolyn Kent, New York, N.Y.
Treasurer, Mario A. Di Cesare, University of North Carolina, Asheville
Past President, W. Speed Hill, Lehman College, City University of N.Y.

Thomas Faulkner, University of Washington
Roy Flannagan, Ohio University
David Freeman, Memorial University, Newfoundland
Suzanne Gossett, Loyola University of Chicago
Elizabeth Hageman, University of New Hampshire
David Scott Kastan, Columbia University
John King, Ohio State University
Arthur F. Marotti, Wayne State University
Steven May, Georgetown College
Janel Mueller, University of Chicago
Sr. Anne O'Donnell, Catholic University of America
G. W. Pigman III, California Institute of Technology
Lois Potter, University of Delaware
George Walton Williams, Duke University

International Advisory Council

Dominic Baker-Smith, University of Amsterdam
K. J. Höltgen, University of Erlangen-Nürenberg
M. T. Jones-Davies, University of Paris-Sorbonne
David Norbrook, Magdalen College, Oxford
Sergio Rossi, University of Milan
Germaine Warkentin, Victoria University in the University of Toronto

RENAISSANCE ENGLISH TEXT SOCIETY

211

Editorial Committee for *The Southwell-Sibthorpe Commonplace Book*
    Arthur Kinney, Chair
    Carolyn Kent
    Josephine A. Roberts
    Laetitia Yeandle

The Renaissance English Text Society was established to publish literary texts, chiefly nondramatic, of the period 1475–1660. Dues are $25.00 per annum ($15.00, graduate students; life membership is available at $500.00). Members receive the text published for each year of membership. The Society sponsors panels at such annual meetings as those of the Modern Language Association, the Renaissance Society of America, and the conference at Kalamazoo. General inquiries should be addressed to the president, Arthur Kinney, Department of English, University of Massachusetts, Amherst, Mass. 01002, USA. To join, write to M. Di Cesare, Department of Literature and Language, University of North Carolina, Asheville, NC 28804.

Copies of volumes X–XII may be purchased from Associated University Presses, 440 Forsgate Drive, Cranbury, NJ 08512. Members may order copies of earlier volumes still in print or of later volumes from XIII, at special member prices, from the Treasurer.

FIRST SERIES

VOL. I. *Merie Tales of the Mad Men of Gotam* by A. B., edited by Stanley J. Kahrl, and *The History of Tom Thumbe,* by R. I., edited by Curt F. Buhler, 1965. (o.p.)

VOL. II. Thomas Watson's Latin *Amyntas,* edited by Walter F. Staton, Jr., and Abraham Fraunce's translation *The Lamentations of Amyntas,* edited by Franklin M. Dickey, 1967.

SECOND SERIES

VOL. III. *The dyaloge called Funus,* A Translation of Erasmus's Colloquy (1534), and *A very pleasaunt & fruitful Diologe called The Epicure,* Gerrard's Translation of Erasmus's Colloquy (1545), edited by Robert R. Allen, 1969.

VOL. IV. *Leicester's Ghost* by Thomas Rogers, edited by Franklin B. Williams, Jr., 1972.

THIRD SERIES

VOLS. V–VI. *A Collection of Emblemes, Ancient and Moderne,* by George Wither, with an introduction by Rosemary Freeman and bibliographical notes by Charles S. Hensley, 1975. (o.p.)

212 RENAISSANCE ENGLISH TEXT SOCIETY

FOURTH SERIES

VOLS. VII–VIII. *Tom a' Lincolne* by R. I., edited by Richard S. M. Hirsch, 1978.

FIFTH SERIES

VOL. IX. *Metrical Visions* by George Cavendish, edited by A. S. G. Edwards, 1980.

SIXTH SERIES

VOL. X. *Two Early Renaissance Bird Poems,* edited by Malcolm Andrew, 1984.

VOL. XI. *Argalus and Parthenia* by Francis Quarles, edited by David Freeman, 1986.

VOL. XII. Cicero's *De Officiis,* trans. Nicholas Grimald, edited by Gerald O'Gorman, 1987.

VOL. XIII. *The Silkewormes and their Flies* by Thomas Moffet (1599), edited with introduction and commentary by Victor Houliston, 1988.

SEVENTH SERIES

VOL. XIV. John Bale, *The Vocacyon of Johan Bale,* edited by Peter Happé and John N. King, 1989.

VOL. XV. *The Nondramatic Works of John Ford,* edited by L. E. Stock, Gilles D. Monsarrat, Judith M. Kennedy, and Dennis Danielson, with the assistance of Marta Straznicky, 1990.

Special Publication. *New Ways of Looking at Old Texts: Papers of the Renaissance English Text Society, 1985–1991,* edited by W. Speed Hill, 1993. (Sent *gratis* to all 1991 members.)

VOL. XVI. *George Herbert, The Temple: A Diplomatic Edition of the Bodleian Manuscript (Tanner 307),* edited by Mario A. Di Cesare, 1991.

VOL. XVII. *Lady Mary Wroth, The First Part of the Countess of Montgomery's Urania,* edited by Josephine Roberts. 1992.

VOL. XVIII. *Richard Beacon, Solon His Follie,* edited by Clare Carroll and Vincent Carey. 1993.

VOL. XIX. *An Collins, Divine Songs and Meditacions,* edited by Sidney Gottlieb. 1994.

VOL. XX. *The Southwell-Sibthorpe Commonplace Book: Folger MS V.b.198,* edited by Sr. Jean Klene. 1995.